Adam LeBor is an author and journalist with more than twenty-five years' experience, who brings alive the human story behind his tenacious investigations. He is the author of eight critically acclaimed books including *Hitler's Secret Bankers*, *Complicity with Evil: The United Nations in the Age of Modern Genocide* and a biography of Serbian leader Slobodan Milosevic. He lives in Budapest.

Visit his website at www.adamlebor.com.

By Adam LeBor

NON FICTION

A Heart Turned East:
Among the Muslims of Europe and America

Hitler's Secret Bankers:
How Switzerland Profited from Nazi Genocide

Surviving Hitler:
Choice, Corruption and Compromise in the Third Reich
(*with Roger Boyes*)

Milosevic: A Biography

City of Oranges:
Arabs and Jews in Jaffa

Complicity with Evil:
The United Nations in the Age of Modern Genocide

The Believers:
How America Fell for Bernard Madoff's $65 Billion
Investment Scam

FICTION

The Budapest Protocol

THE
BELIEVERS

How America Fell for Bernard Madoff's
$65 Billion Investment Scam

ADAM LEBOR

PHOENIX

A PHOENIX PAPERBACK

First published in Great Britain in 2009
by Weidenfeld & Nicolson
This paperback edition published in 2010
by Phoenix,
an imprint of Orion Books Ltd,
Orion House, 5 Upper St Martin's Lane,
London WC2H 9EA

An Hachette UK company

10 9 8 7 6 5 4 3 2 1

A CIP catalogue record for this book
is available from the British Library.

ISBN 978-0-7538-2743-7

Typeset by Input Data Services Ltd, Bridgwater, Somerset

Printed and bound in the UK by
CPI Mackays, Chatham ME5 8TD

The Orion Publishing Group's policy is to use papers that
are natural, renewable and recyclable products and made from wood
grown in sustainable forests. The logging and manufacturing
processes are expected to conform to the environmental
regulations of the country of origin.

www.orionbooks.co.uk

For Bob and Peter Green,
the best of New York

Contents

Acknowledgements

My thanks first of all to my editors at Weidenfeld & Nicolson and my agent for their faith in and enthusiasm for *The Believers*. Alan Samson and Bea Hemming deftly combined steady encouragement with gentle pressure when needed. Laura Longrigg was always inspiring and her valuable advice helped polish the book. It was also a pleasure to work with Martin Soames and I learned much from his legal diligence. Tarda Davison-Aitkins' careful copy-editing rendered the manuscript clean and readable.

I am blessed with numerous friends in New York, many of whom helped with *The Believers*, especially Ernest Beck, Joshua Freeman and Shari Spiegel who made numerous telephone calls and sent emails on my behalf as did Chris Condon in Boston. The irrepressible Peter Green was, as ever, a mine of information, leads and contacts. Bob Green cordially hosted me for several weeks, opened numerous doors across Manhattan and introduced to me to the insightful David Stone. Dan Friedman of the *Forward* newspaper and Ben Cohen of the American Jewish Committee were deft guides to New York Jewish communal organisations. Jack Schwartz added valuable historical and literary depth and nuance. Dan

Smith helped decipher charities' tax returns. Rabbi David Gelfand, of Temple Israel, brought a vital theological perspective. Steve Fishman of *New York* magazine and Clive Irving and Deborah Dunn of *Condé Nast Traveler* shared numerous useful leads.

My friend Jeff Weintraub led to me to Mark Gerson, who shared his insight into the world of high finance and who with his wife Erica was a generous Shabbat host. Ed Nicoll was an invaluable guide through the canyons of Wall Street. In Palm Beach I am especially grateful to Saul Irving, who showed me around the island, Anthony Jacobs, who generously recounted his own involvement with Bernard Madoff, and Richard Rampell for his local insight. I am grateful to all those who consented to be interviewed, whether on the record or on a background basis, and to those who helped facilitate these interviews, especially Seth Faison.

The day after Bernard Madoff's arrest on 11 December 2008 editors around the world dispatched teams of reporters to cover one of the biggest stories of the twenty-first century. This one, as they say in newsrooms, 'had legs'. While most of this book is based on my own first-hand reporting and interviewing, I am happy to acknowledge the fine work of my many colleagues in unearthing the details of the Madoff fraud and its aftermath. The *New York Times*, *The Times*, the *Wall Street Journal*, the *Financial Times*, Bloomberg and *Vanity Fair* in particular have all done excellent work. One of the best things about being a journalist is the camaraderie, and many reporters were generous in sharing their knowledge and expertise, none more so than James Bandler and Nicholas Varchaver of *Fortune* magazine, who, together with Doris Burke, wrote one of the earliest and most incisive accounts of Bernard Madoff's rise and fall. I have also drawn on the interview transcripts of *Frontline: The Madoff Affair*, an excellent documentary produced by PBS in Boston. The programme can be viewed in full on the web at http://www.pbs.org/wgbh/pages/frontline/madoff/. James Bone and Christine Seib, correspondents for *The Times* in New York, were always welcoming and extremely helpful. Richard Beeston, the foreign editor of *The Times*, was supportive of a correspondent who corresponded very little while this project was under way. Many thanks to Cathy Galvin of the *Sunday Times* magazine for her encouragement of this and other book projects over the years. Thanks also to Zack Roth of talkingpointsmemo.com, Janet Lorin of Bloomberg, Angela Montefinise of the *New York Post*, Michael Weiss of tabletmag.com, Alan Furst, Thomas Escritt, Keith Dovkants, Sam Loewenberg, Bea Klokan and Nick Thorpe.

Special thanks to Justin Leighton, for his encouragement and friendship over the last twenty years, off and on the road, and for his faith in this book. Thanks most of all, of course, to my wife Kati and our children, for their love and support.

'Why, sometimes I've believed as many as six impossible things before breakfast.'

The Red Queen in *Through the Looking Glass, and What Alice Found There*, by Lewis Carroll.

Prologue

The simplest way to understand how Bernard Madoff persuaded thousands of investors to pour billions of dollars into his investment scam is to think of it as a cult. The cult of Madoff followed all the necessary rules. It was founded and run by a godlike figure whose decisions could never be questioned or challenged. Its devotees believed themselves to be part of an elect group, with access to a secret credo denied the rest of the world. It used coercion against unruly members and even had its own initiation ceremony. The godlike figure was Bernard Madoff, who charmed, bullied, and terrorised his subordinates, and devotees. The secret knowledge was his arcane investment strategy, couched in pseudo-scientific terms that could never be properly understood but which members believed would provide them with eternal wealth. The coercion was Madoff's demand for confidentiality, and unquestioning loyalty. Those asking too many questions were threatened with expulsion and the closure of their accounts, with being cast out of the elect, into the financial wilderness. The initiation ceremony required that would-be investors be repeatedly rejected and told the investment fund was closed. Eventually Madoff would 'reluctantly' make space and the grateful initiates rushed to hand over their life savings.

The cult of Madoff was astonishingly successful. Bernard Madoff was a financial criminal genius who ran the largest and most enduring fraud in modern history. His elaborately engineered scam, investigators believe, lasted for decades. It reached from Wall Street and across America, to Europe and further East. Each month thousands of personal clients, many of whom were sophisticated investors in their own right, received detailed accounts of stock trades that had never taken place, and account balances that did not exist, none of which they questioned. His institutional investors included numerous well-respected banks, and finance companies. Madoff not only duped the Securities and Exchange Commission (SEC), which regulates the American financial industry, he frequently sat on finance industry committees. He helped create the US's secondary stock exchange, after the New York Stock Exchange, the NASDAQ (National Association of Securities Dealers Automated Quotations) in 1971, and served as its chairman. He also ran one of the largest and most successful share trading firms in the US – a separate operation to his investment fraud.

Respected by his peers, worshipped by his clients, Madoff became very wealthy. He and his wife Ruth owned a duplex apartment on the Upper East Side of Manhattan valued at $7 million with monthly maintenance charges of $6,500, a holiday home in Palm Beach, Florida, valued at $11 million, another in Montauk, Long Island, New York, worth close to $7 million, and an apartment in Cap d'Antibes, in the south of France, valued at $1 million. He had a half interest in an aircraft worth $12 million. He owned four boats including a 27-metre Leopard yacht called *Bull* moored in France worth

$7 million; a fishing boat in Palm Beach, also called *Bull*, worth $2.2 million, and *Sitting Bull* in Montauk, worth $320,000. Madoff owned furniture and household goods in his four homes worth $8 million, including a $39,000 Steinway piano and silverware valued at $65,000 in his New York apartment. Madoff's financial holdings included $17 million in cash and $45 million worth of securities. Much of this was paid for by his fraud, and almost of all it, apart from $2.5 million granted to his wife Ruth, was seized by the US government in June 2009.[1]

Madoff was a master manipulator who, among his many victims, specifically focused on his fellow American Jews in what the SEC defines as an 'Affinity Fraud'. This type of fraud targets the members of a specific religious or ethnic group, abusing the trust and acceptance of insiders to defraud other members. Masterminds of affinity frauds, wrote the SEC, 'often enlist respected religious or community leaders from within the group to spread the word about the scheme by convincing those people that a fraudulent investment is legitimate and worthwhile. Many times those leaders become unwitting victims of a fraudster's ruse. These scams exploit the trust and friendship that exist in groups of people who have something in common.'[2] This is precisely how Madoff operated. He developed a sophisticated network of contacts across Jewish communal institutions including charities, schools, universities, synagogues and country clubs, and stole their money. He even defrauded Elie Wiesel, the Nobel laureate and Holocaust survivor. Some investors may have suspected that Madoff was stretching legality to its limits, as no other financial institution provided such steady returns regardless of how the stock market performed, but as long as the money kept flowing in – or appeared to – few probed further. Any doubters were seduced by what one Wall Street investment banker calls 'the gentle perfume of the illicit'.

There was, it seems, almost no human limit to Madoff's avarice. One summer his son Andy got into trouble while swimming off Long Island. He was rescued by a young man whose father was a plumber. Madoff rewarded the family by inviting the plumber to invest his life savings of $100,000. That too vanished. In fact Madoff seemed to take a perverse relish in his human connection with his victims. In spring 2009 Simon Levy,[3] a Jewish man in his seventies, sat slumped in a chair, dressed in a crumpled tracksuit as the movers packed up his spacious flat on one of the most expensive streets on Manhattan's Upper East Side. He could barely speak more than a few words at a time. Levy had known Madoff for forty years. He and his wife had dined three or four times a year with Madoff and his wife. Levy invested everything with the man he thought was his friend. Many in New York now refer to Madoff as a financial terrorist. Comparisons are frequently made with September 11, not in terms of lives lost, but in the shock to New York's collective psyche. This may be over-dramatising, but the damage Madoff has wreaked is incalculable and will last for generations. Two of his victims have committed suicide. Life savings and inheritances have vanished. Charities and foundations have evaporated. Businesses have collapsed. Homes have been sold, much loved possessions auctioned off. Elderly people hoping for a comfortable retirement now live in desperation, fear, and uncertainty.

Madoff's investment fund was a sophisticated Ponzi scheme. Ponzi schemes are a type of pyramid fraud, run on the 'rob Peter to pay Paul' principle. They do not generate any revenue but rely on a steady stream of new investors whose cash pays the profits promised to earlier investors. Eventually, when the scheme's obligations exceed its assets, it collapses. Charles Ponzi, an Italian immigrant to the United States, lived in Boston in 1920 and promised investors a return of 40 per cent in ninety days, compared to 2 per cent a year in bank savings accounts. He planned to take advantage of exchange rate differences by buying inter-national postal coupons in countries with weak currencies, such as Italy, which would be redeemed in the United States for a profit. Ponzi mania swept through New England and thousands rushed to invest. In one three-hour period he took in $1 million.[4] When the scheme collapsed an investigation revealed that Ponzi had purchased a total of $30 worth of coupons.

Madoff's genius was to reverse the Ponzi's usual psy-chological appeal. Instead of spectacular, short-term returns, he gave long-term, modest, but still above average rewards, usually paying out around 10 or 12 per cent a year. A privileged few clients allegedly received higher rates. Hedge funds and high-tech stocks soared and plummeted, but Madoff's fund kept steadily rolling along, and when investors asked to withdraw some of their monies, they merely had to fill in a simple form. The dollars arrived, without fail, a few days later. Madoff did not tout for business. Instead he turned potential customers away, according to the June 2009 SEC lawsuit against Cohmad Securities Corporation, one of his principal feeder funds, much of which he co-owned with his longtime friend Maurice 'Sonny' Cohn. 'Madoff played hard-to-get, shunning one-on-one meetings with most individual investors and arbitrarily refusing prospective investors for what appeared to be whimsical or snobbish reasons. By creating an air of prestige and exclusivity, many of BLMIS' [Bernard L. Madoff Investment Securities LLC] victims felt privileged to be allowed to invest with Madoff and BLMIS and many prospective investors angled for ways to get in.'[5]

Even with the stock market boom of the 1990s, many on Wall Street wondered how Madoff did it. It was virtually unheard of for an investment fund to pay out the same above average return each year for so many years. The SEC was warned repeatedly, specifically, and in great detail, about Madoff but failed to close down his fraud. Madoff's Ponzi scheme collapsed on the morning of 11 December 2008, when he was arrested by the Federal Bureau of Investigation (FBI). The sub-prime mortgage crisis had already brought down two of Wall Street's biggest investment banks, Bear Sterns and Lehman Brothers, threatening the US's very solvency. US financial regulators and world leaders were frantically trying to prevent a global economic meltdown. Madoff's institutional investors were demanding withdrawals of billions of dollars – but the dollars no longer existed.

The Madoff fraud raises numerous questions, some of them deeply unsettling. Why did Madoff continue to run a criminal enterprise for so many years when he was already a multi-millionaire and a pillar of the New York financial establishment? How could he get away with it for so long? How could a prominent Jew do this to his own people, to charities and Holocaust survivors? Did he work alone, and if not, who was helping him? What were the regulatory authorities doing? There is a powerful argument that had the credit crunch not happened, and had various institutional investors not demanded their money back, that Madoff's Ponzi scheme would still be running, and investors like Simon Levy would have remained blissfully unaware that their Madoff statements were fiction and that their savings had long ceased to exist.

Over the following pages I will trace the history of the Madoff family, from Eastern Europe to Manhattan, detail Madoff's rise, and explain his modus operandi, both legitimate and criminal. I will open up the world where he operated: from the salons of Manhattan, to the country clubs and golf courses of Long Island and Palm Beach. Their power structure, communal psychology, and the tribal codes of Madoff's biggest investors will be peeled back and examined. I will detail the network of relationships across which hundreds of millions of dollars flow, and show how Madoff exploited them. And I will answer the most puzzling question of all: why did so many people give him not just a proportion of their savings, but, like Simon Levy, almost *all* of them?

For con-men credibility is everything. Madoff was certainly credible. He was one of the 'Masters of the Universe', the financial titans immortalised in Tom Wolfe's zeitgeist novel of 1980s New York, *The Bonfire of the Vanities*. His firm, BLMIS, was headquartered over three floors of the Lipstick Building, an iconic landmark building in mid-town Manhattan at 885 Third Avenue, New York. Madoff was well known across Wall Street and at the SEC's offices in Washington, DC, for decades. With his wavy, patrician silver hair, tailored suits, and avuncular manner, he looked like a favourite elderly relative, and indeed was known to his investors as 'Uncle Bernie'. They dubbed him the 'Jewish T-bill', named after US Treasury Bills, the safest investment. 'He was really very likeable, he was self-deprecating and not imperious,' recalls Ed Nicoll, a New York financier who has known Madoff for more than twenty years. 'It was a strange combination of being humble but also regal.' For many, it was a seductive mix. When I asked Simon Levy why he had broken the golden rule of investment – diversify – and had placed most of his assets with Madoff, he answered: 'Because I had known him for forty years . . . There are a lot of people who do illegal transactions, but he would have been the least likely one we thought of.'

Yet unlike many of his Wall Street peers, Madoff generally avoided the limelight and the glamorous parties of Manhattan society. He gave to charity – a requirement for anyone networking in the American Jewish world – but discreetly. Bernard and Ruth Madoff usually ate dinner at Primola, an expensive but unremarkable local Italian restaurant near their home. Before his arrest there were few mentions of Madoff in the media, apart from sporadic mentions in the financial trade press. Bernard Madoff was certainly wary of inquisitive journalists poking into his business methods. A rare profile, published in *Barron's* magazine in 2001, was headlined: 'Don't Ask, Don't Tell'. The author asked how Madoff's fund produced such high returns, and what was his investment strategy. Madoff stonewalled.[6]

Madoff did tell a little more at a discussion at the Philoctetes Center in October 2007 when he appeared on a panel discussing 'The Future of the Stock Market'. The Philoctetes Center for the Multidisciplinary Study of the Imagination, to give it its full name, is a well-meaning arts and culture centre on Manhattan's Upper East Side, an affluent upper-middle-class area with a substantial Jewish population. Philoctetes sponsors free events such as art-house films, exhibitions, and intellectual discussions. It aims, as its website explains, to 'promote an integrated, interdisciplinary approach to the understanding of creativity and the imaginative process'. Its directors are Edward Nersessian and Francis Levy. Nersessian is a clinical professor of psychiatry and psychoanalyst, whose numerous papers include 'Cat as a fetish: Reflections on female sexuality'. Levy is a writer and self-confessed 'compulsive fitness addict' who works out for several hours seven days a week, and has a third-degree black belt in karate.

This may seem unlikely company for Madoff but he could not really refuse. Madoff had been close friends with Francis Levy's father, Norman F. Levy, who died in 2005 at the age of ninety-three. Levy was one of several older Jewish businessmen that Madoff successfully courted. Levy was a very rich man indeed, who had made his fortune in real estate, specifically the skyscrapers of mid-town Manhattan, the busiest commercial district in the United States. Levy had offices one floor below Madoff in the Lipstick Building. Like many successful American Jewish businessmen, Levy senior was a generous and dedicated philanthropist. The Betty and Norman F. Levy Foundation reported assets in 2007 of $244.4 million.[7] Its funds were invested with Bernie Madoff, whom Norman F. Levy described as 'honourable'. Levy and Madoff supported many of the same charities, such as Yeshiva University, a Jewish university in Manhattan, the Lincoln Center Theater, and the Gift of Life, a south Florida charity that matched leukaemia victims with potential bone marrow donors.

The panel moderator was Justin Fox, of *Time* magazine, and other speakers included Professor Ailsa Roell, of Columbia University, an expert in international financial regulation, Muriel Siebert, the first woman to own a seat on the New York Stock Exchange, and Josh Stampfli, head of the automated market-making group at BLMIS, which was part of the trading arm. The discussion, which was filmed by the Center and can be viewed on the Internet,[8] was a relaxed but informative affair. The panel, all of whom were experts in their field, ranged widely over the history of Wall Street, the changes in trading, the intricacies of trading strategies, the effects of computers and automation, and the regulations that govern the market. Madoff wore his customary grey suit and light blue shirt, his lack of a tie his only concession to it being the weekend. He looked bored at the start, sitting back in his chair, but soon came alive when it was his turn to speak. He sounded wise and well informed, backed up by his younger colleague Stampfli.

With hindsight, of course, many of the comments that Saturday afternoon seem eerily prescient. Madoff's firm, said Fox, was 'one of those really important parts of our financial system that doesn't show up in the headlines'. Madoff himself opined that 'Today, basically the big money on Wall Street is made by taking risks'. He complained about the regulatory burdens imposed by the SEC. 'The cost of regulation has dramatically increased ... when I go down to Washington and meet with the SEC and complain to them that the industry is either over-regulated or the burdens are too great, they all start to roll their eyes, just like all of our children do whenever we talk about the good old days.' He joked about the advantages of automation in trading: 'So we determined that the best thing for us to do was basically to take the human being out of the equation ... and turning it over to a computer to make your decision – I guess you could also program the computer to violate the regulations but we haven't gotten there yet.' The audience laughed enthusiastically.

But no matter how much the market is computerised, there will always be a human factor. Perhaps Stampfli said it best. He was discussing the effect of emotions, specifically greed and fear, on how people buy and sell, and the importance of the herd instinct in shaping the market. 'Greed is a slower, more gradual process, where everyone kind of gets pointed in the same direction. Then, at some point, valuations reach their limit; everybody's bought that can buy; as much margin has been taken out that can be taken out. You run out of people that can continue to support the trend.' And then, he explained: 'All of a sudden, everybody in the herd needs to turn around and run for the exit and the door simply isn't large enough for everybody to get through.'

1

Yekkes vs. *shtarkers*

*'My grandparents ran a Turkish bath in the area that
served as a focal point for many new immigrants of
different nationalities who nonetheless shared common
aspirations.'*

Peter Madoff, brother of Bernie, and trustee of the Lower East
Side Tenement museum, in 2005.[1]

The story of Bernard Madoff's fraud begins a century
ago in a rancorous divide between rich and poor American
Jews. David and Rose Madoff, his paternal grandparents,
arrived in the United States in 1905 from Warsaw at the
age of twenty-three. Around this time Benjamin and Gussie
Muntner, his maternal grandparents, came from Galicia, the
north-eastern province of the Austro-Hungarian empire.
Both couples were part of the biggest wave of Jewish emi-
gration in history, four hopeful newcomers among the two
and a half million who between 1881 and 1923 fled pogroms,
oppression, wars, and revolutions for a new life in America.[2]
Neither the Madoffs nor the Muntners were rich, and life
was tough for the new arrivals. They were far from home

1

and family. The culture shock was immense. They had to learn a new language. Communications with the old country were slow and difficult. But they had made it to America, *Der Goldene Medinah*, The Golden Country as it was known in Yiddish, the language of the Eastern European Jews. American Jewish greetings cards a century ago showed well-dressed, prosperous immigrants beckoning their relatives across the sea from Russia. There was some anti-Semitism, to be sure, but no Czars, no Cossacks, and no pogroms. In the back streets of Warsaw and a remote province of the Austro-Hungarian empire the images must have seemed like a mirage. But the American dream was real.

David and Rose Madoff settled in Scranton, northeast Pennsylvania. Scranton was a pleasant, bustling city of about 100,000, with fine stone buildings and a railway station. It was home to many new immigrants from Eastern Europe, who often worked in the city's two main industries: coal mining and textiles. David Madoff was a tailor. By 1920 he and Rose had four children, Abraham, Ralph, Berthel, and Rachel. Some time in the 1920s the family moved to the Bronx in New York City, a tough working-class area just north of Manhattan. The 1920 census records that the Muntners lived at the other end of New York City, in Brooklyn. Benjamin Muntner was trained as a plumber but worked in a store. Gussie, his wife, was illiterate. They had three daughters: Dinah, Fannie, and Sylvia, who was the youngest.

There have been Jews in America since the seventeenth century. Several dozen Sephardic families, Jews of Spanish and Portuguese descent fleeing the Inquisition, arrived with the first Puritan settlers. By the time of the American Revolution in 1776 the community numbered about 10,000. A century later, after a substantial wave of immigration from Germany and Austria, America was home to 250,000 Jews. Many of the German Jews, known as *Yekkes*, were sophisticated urban professionals: bankers, lawyers, and businessmen. They soon prospered. The most important one hundred or so German families were enormously influential and helped turn New York into an international financial centre. They included the Lehmans, founders of Lehman Brothers bank; the Astors, who made a fortune in fur trading, real estate, and opium; the Goldmans, who founded Goldman Sachs; the Guggenheims, and other banking families such as the Kahns, Lewisohns, Schiffs, and Warburgs.

The *Yekkes* were horrified at the waves of Jews pouring in from Eastern Europe. The new arrivals like the Madoffs and the Muntners threatened everything the *Yekkes* had constructed: their cosy, faux haute-German bourgeois lifestyles built on wealth, status, and assimilation. Most of all, they reminded the *Yekkes* that no matter how financially successful they were, they too were still outsiders. The WASP elite, the White Anglo-Saxon Protestants, whose lineage reached back to seventeenth-century Britain and Holland, looked down on all the Jews, including the *Yekkes*. The *Yekkes* traced their roots back to eighteenth-century Bavaria, and sneered at the new arrivals from Poland and Russia. This bitter divide, between the *Yekkes* and the East European Jews, is of much more than historical interest. It is a crucial element of the Madoff story. It shaped his generation's psyche and left a sour legacy of resentment that still rankles today.

The German Jews feared – correctly as it transpired – that the immigrants would foster anti-Semitism. Some were Communists, Anarchists, or Zionists. They spoke a bastard dialect with a thick accent. They were noisy and rough-mannered. They came from primitive *shtetls*, Jewish villages in the backwaters of Eastern Europe, with no running water or electricity. The German Jews labelled them *Ostjuden*, Eastern Jews, or even 'Kikes', a derogatory term which probably derives from the habit of Jews who were illiterate in English signing documents with a circle, rather than a cross. (*Kikel* is Yiddish for circle.) 'To be sure, many of the German Jews perceived the Eastern European immigrants as uncouth, destitute, uncivilised and therefore threatening to their own position in American society. There was nothing novel in their fears; middle-class members of minority groups who are themselves of precarious status typically hold the lower-class members of their group in contempt,' notes the historian Chaim I. Waxman.[3]

The richest *Yekkes* lived in luxury in townhouses or sprawling apartments. Most settled in the prime real estate of Manhattan's Upper East Side between East Sixtieth and Eightieth Streets, from Fifth Avenue, where they had sweeping views of Central Park, to the grand residences of Park Avenue. When banker Jacob Schiff's entourage and family travelled by train to California, they needed five private carriages. Felix Warburg, another banker, had a squash court in his town and country house, and owned four Stradivarius violins. Adolf Lewisohn, yet another wealthy New York banker, employed thirty gardeners on his estate in Westchester. The families enjoyed lives of Teutonic, bourgeois precision. 'It was a world of quietly ticking clocks, of the throb of private elevators, of slippered servants' feet, of fires laid behind paper fans, of sofas covered in silver satin ... of heavily encrusted calling cards and invitations to teas, coming out parties and weddings, but all within the group,' writes the historian Stephen Birmingham in *Our Crowd*.[4]

Birmingham's book, which was first published in 1967, quickly became a bestseller. The phrase 'Our Crowd' entered common parlance in Manhattan, the New York equivalent of PLU (People Like Us), as in 'they are very our crowd' or they would like to be 'our crowd'. The book touched something in Manhattan's zeitgeist and turned into something more profound, argues Marie Brenner, a writer for *Vanity Fair* magazine. *Our Crowd* 'became a template for achievement that was discussed in many Jewish homes across America'.[5] And while the *Yekke* dynasties employed legions of uniformed staff to service their palatial homes and complicated travel arrangements, one key value was sacrosanct: no showiness. Neither the bankers nor their wives wore ostentatious clothes or flashy jewellery. Bernard and Ruth Madoff had been married for eight years when *Our Crowd* was published. They would certainly have heard of it, and Ruth may have read it. In later years, as the Madoffs advanced in Upper East Side society, they took certainly took the *Yekkes*' tenets to heart: both were elegant, understated dressers whose jewellery was tasteful and discreet.

The newly arrived Eastern European Jews were not part of Our Crowd. They mostly lived on the Lower East Side. Though only a few miles from the Upper East Side, it may as well have been another planet. The Lower East Side was a giant *shtetl*, transplanted to the back streets of Manhattan. Crowded with tenement slums, sweatshop factories, backroom bars, and bordellos, it was run by *shtarkers*, tough guys who knew how to look after themselves. A *shtarker* is not necessarily a criminal, but all the criminals were *shtarkers*. The gangs controlled everything, taking protection money from stallholders and shopkeepers when they weren't stealing their stock. Wide-eyed 'Greenhorns', or newcomers, were liable to be stripped of everything by agile street kids picking their pockets, or by con-men. The grimy streets and alleys were in a constant state of ferment.

The *Yekkes* and the Eastern European Jews even prayed differently. The *Yekkes* worshipped at Temple Emanu-El, then the largest synagogue in America, on East Forty-third Street and Fifth Avenue. Emanu-El was a Reform synagogue, where Jewish laws were adjusted for the modern age. The services were calm, composed, and orderly, as befitted its self-regarding and distinguished congregation. The Eastern European Jews worshipped in *shtibls*, tiny one-room syn-agogues in cramped tenements, rocking themselves into trances, like in the old country. Partly out of charity and partly out of self-interest, the German Jews organised a support network to speed the integration of the new arrivals. But the East European Jews did not want the *Yekkes*' charity, so they set up their welfare organisations.

The second- and third-generation American Jews have long moved out of the Lower East Side, to the Upper East and West Side of Manhattan, the suburbs, or Long Island. But they still treasure their family roots in its back streets and alleys. They take great pride in their *shtarker* grandparents, who slaved for long hours in a new country, in tough con-ditions, hustling to make a living and provide for their fam-ilies. They have neither forgotten nor forgiven the *Yekkes*' disdain for their Yiddish-speaking ancestors. Madoff cer-tainly never did. In later years he specifically targeted the Jewish elite of the Upper East Side, channelling their wealth into his Ponzi scheme. 'There was a kind of resentment, a rivalry, a wish for one-upmanship in Madoff,' speculates Daphne Merkin, a New York writer who has extensively chronicled the world of moneyed New York, and whose brother Ezra was one of Madoff's most important business associates. 'The people he dealt with were generally more established than he was. He was an Eastern European Jew among West European Jews, some of whom were *Yekkes*. Under that cool, friendly exterior of nice "Uncle Bernie", I imagine there was contempt.'

The Jewish immigrants to America brought immeasurable human capital to their new, young homeland. Their descendants have contributed to every aspect of American society: they are doctors and lawyers, social workers and artists, writers and politicians. They have founded universities and hospitals, industries and business empires. For many American Jews, the United States really was the *Goldene Medinah*, but woven in with the multitude of success stories is another, darker history: of Jewish gangsters and criminals of which Bernard Madoff is now the most notorious. For all his uniqueness Madoff is part of a dark continuum. The difference is that he used computers instead of baseball bats.

The Jewish gangsters thrived on the Lower East Side. There, poverty, squalor, a culturally dislocated population, and a corrupt and inefficient police force proved a fertile breeding ground for crime. In this respect, the Jewish immigrants were no different to their Irish, Italian, and other Eastern European peers. In a strange way, the Jewish criminals signified the success of the Jews' assimilation. They were a sign of normality. Years later, David Ben-Gurion, the first prime minister of Israel, said that when Israel had prostitutes and criminals it would be a normal state like any other. What fascinates, both then and now, is the contradiction between Jewish religious ethics, which gave much of the world its moral code, and the lives of men like Bernard Madoff and his criminal predecessors, who identified themselves as Jews, and who lived in a Jewish world.

In the early years of the twentieth century two gangs continually fought for control of the Lower East Side's brothels, card games, drug smuggling, and protection rackets. The Jewish gang was led by Max Eastman, the Italian one by Paul Kelly. Eastman was born in Brooklyn but moved to the Lower East Side in search of adventure. He was a thug and a pimp, with a battered face and body that bore the scars of numerous street brawls. A former bouncer, he carried a club on which he carved a notch each time he wielded it. Paul Kelly, whose real name was Paolo Vacarelli, was a professional boxer. He used his prize money to open several brothels. Both gangs worked with Tammany Hall, the home of the corrupt Democratic Party machine. They assaulted voters, blocked polling booths and stuffed ballots to get the desired results. The police, paid off, did nothing. The Kelly gang controlled the area west of the Bowery, while Eastman's mob had the east. Eastman was arrested, sent to prison, served with valour in World War I, and was eventually murdered in 1920. Kelly became a union racketeer, and died of natural causes, in the mid-1930s.

Within a few years the street kids who started out picking pockets and turning over handcarts on the Lower East Side were running far more sophisticated operations: protection rackets, bootlegging operations, and trafficking in women and drugs. They organised labour strikes, and violently broke them up when required. By the 1920s the bosses still needed *shtarkers*, of course, but the *shtarkers* were no longer the bosses. The businessmen had arrived. Arnold Rothstein was an early predecessor of Bernard Madoff. He too was a criminal genius who understood that crime run professionally and competently, like a real corporation, offered enormous opportunities for wealth. Like Madoff, Rothstein was known among his contemporaries by his nicknames: 'The Brain', 'The Big Bankroll', and 'The Man Uptown'.

Unusually for a gangster, Rothstein grew up in a town house on the Upper East Side. His father, Abraham, was a wealthy man who owned a shop and cotton-processing plant. He was a part of the city's establishment, friends with Governor Al Smith, and Judge Louis Brandeis, the first Jew to be appointed to the Supreme Court. When Rothstein married a non-Jewish girl, his father, as tradition demanded, declared his son dead, and said *Kaddish*, the mourning prayers. F. Scott Fitzgerald based the character Meyer Wolfsheim, a Jewish gangster, on Rothstein in *The Great Gatsby*. Rothstein was a bootlegger, rather than a con-man, but in many ways he was Bernard Madoff's intellectual godfather. 'He understood the truths of early century capitalism (hypocrisy, exclusion, greed) and came to dominate them,' writes Rich Cohen in his study of American Jewish gangsters, *Tough Jews*.[6]

Rothstein fixed the 1919 Baseball World Series, so that the favourites, the Chicago White Sox, threw the game, thus turning an enormous profit on bets. Like Madoff, Rothstein thought globally. Instead of running a few caseloads of whisky in from Canada across Lake Michigan, Rothstein brought across a whole shipload of whisky from England. The ship waited just outside American waters, off the coast of Montauk, Long Island. Rothstein bought a fleet of speedboats to ferry hundreds of cases ashore to be distributed across New York. Like Madoff, Rothstein was an elegant dresser, who wore understated, tailored suits, hats, and well-shined shoes. He taught the gangster Lucky Luciano and many others how to dress. Rothstein honed the 1930s menswear style that is now a hallmark of that era, immortalised and glamorised by Hollywood. Rothstein's use of Montauk is a resonant footnote. That stretch of the shore was then deserted and undeveloped, but is now an expensive strip of beach-front land. Among the houses along the waterfront is a large mansion by the sea formerly owned by Bernard Madoff.

Max Eastman used his fists, Arnold Rothstein his accountants. Meyer Lansky, history's most notorious Jewish gangster, built on and further honed Rothstein's methods. By the late 1930s Lansky had built a sophisticated illegal gambling empire that stretched from New York to Florida and Cuba. Lansky, who was immortalised as Hyman Roth in *The Godfather*, was also a financial genius and set up numerous sophisticated schemes to evade taxes and launder money. Together with his friend and colleague Bugsy Siegel, he built The Flamingo hotel in Las Vegas, which launched the desert city as a gambling and pleasure capital, and acquired substantial real estate in Miami. Like Madoff, Lansky made extensive use of the global banking system, in his case funnelling money through Swiss banks. In 1969 an extensive investigation into the links between organised crime and Swiss banks by the *New York Times* reported that Lansky even had his own money manager in Switzerland: 'He lives in Lausanne when he is not busy in Geneva, Zurich or Toronto conferring with members of the Lansky apparatus, making investments for a commission and picking up cash deposits for the Swiss credit bank and other institutions.'[7]

Lansky fled to Israel, where he hoped to spend his retirement, but under severe pressure from the United States government he was extradited back home, even though as a Jew he was entitled to Israeli citizenship. Lansky was eventually judged unfit to stand trial. Lansky was supposedly worth $300 million but he died in comparative poverty, in 1983 in Miami at the age of eighty-one. And just as investigators are now searching records across the world in an attempt to trace the billions of dollars that flowed through Madoff's Ponzi scheme, much of Lansky's fortune was never located, if it ever existed.

Communal leaders, Rabbis, and the Yiddish press condemned the Jewish gangsters as thugs and killers. They were violent and brutal. They stole from and terrorised their own people. They brought shame and anti-Semitism down on the community. But some Jews took a quiet, private pride in the criminal *shtarkers*. Lansky's gang attacked and broke up Nazi meetings. His business empire was flourishing and expanding across America. The Jewish criminals were part of the Lower East Side's history. In America, unlike the old country, the Jews stood up for themselves. The Italians, the Irish, and the Jews ran New York. The Italians and the Irish each had their mafias. Why should the Jews be any different?

In the early 1930s Ralph Madoff met and married Sylvia Muntner. They had a daughter, Sondra, and a son, Bernard, followed in April 1938. Peter, their youngest son, was born seven years later. Bernard Madoff spent much of his boyhood on the Lower East Side, playing in the same streets and back alleys where the Jewish gangsters operated. Benjamin and Gussie Muntner, his maternal grandparents, and two of his aunts, managed a Turkish bath in the Bowery, the heart of the area. There Benjamin's skills as plumber came in very useful. Madoff loved to visit his grandparents and ran around the *shvitz*, as it was known. A *shvitz* was a place to get clean – especially when the tenements lacked baths or showers – but was more than that. It was a social centre, especially popular with the *shtarkers*. Here sensitive business could be discussed, turf wars negotiated into lines of demarcation, and enemies meet on neutral territories. That world, of *shtarkers*, and *shvitzes*, is gone now. There are no more turf wars between Jewish and Italian gangs. The Lower East Side, like almost all of Manhattan, has been gentrified. The Bowery's backroom bars and brothels are now chic cafés and nightclubs. The time they spent both with their grandparents and at the Bowery made a great impression on Bernie Madoff and his younger brother, Peter. Peter Madoff served as a trustee of the Lower East Side Tenement Museum, at 97 Orchard Street. The Museum recreates the building as it was a century ago and recounts the life stories of immigrants to Manhattan. He paid for a Washington lobbying firm to work for federal funding for the museum.

Bernard Madoff ordered no rivals to be hit, or their legs to be broken. Instead he would use his reputation and technology to take international fraud to a level of complexity of which even Meyer Lansky could only have dreamed.

2
Happy days

Assets: Cash on hand $200. Liabilities: None.

Bernard Madoff's 1959 application to the Securities and Exchange Commission to register as a broker-dealer.[1]

It took a generation or so, but as the Jews of the Lower East Side prospered, they slowly moved out to the suburbs. By the early 1950s Ralph and Sylvia Madoff had settled in Laurelton, a middle-class area of Queens, an outer borough of New York City. Laurelton was just beyond the end of the subway but was linked to Manhattan by the Long Island Rail Road. America's post-war economic boom had ushered in the golden years of suburbia. Eisenhower, one of America's most popular presidents, sat in the White House. America was strong and confident, sure that it would win the Cold War and the space race with the Soviets. Cheap mortgages for returning members of the military had rapidly accelerated the spread of the city, and new townships of quiet, tree-lined streets evolved. A 5 per cent down payment of $800 would pay for a deposit on a family house. Consumer goods that were once expensive luxuries such as fridges, washing machines, and vacuum cleaners were now taken for granted. It was an extraordinary jump in social mobility. The children of immigrants who had slaved in sweatshops and lived in cramped, unhealthy tenements, enjoyed spacious, airy homes, with separate bedrooms for their children, and a garden. They went on cruises, travelled on aeroplanes, and drove enormous cars with confident, curved fins and spoilers. The Madoffs lived in a brick house with three bedrooms with a separate garage on Two Hundred and Twenty-eighth Street.

Laurelton was quiet, safe and family orientated with a friendly, village atmosphere. It had its own synagogue and Jewish community centre, a Chinese restaurant, and ice-cream parlour, where families met on the weekends. Those were innocent days, recalls a friend of the Madoffs who grew up with them in Laurelton.[2] 'Laurelton was extremely comfortable, even though it was just within the border of New York City. It was like growing up in an upstate rural town. It was very quiet and safe. All the children went to the same neighbourhood elementary school. We went in the morning, came home for lunch, and then went back. It was a little town, very safe, a magical place to live.' Vera Gitten, who went to primary school with Madoff, remembered how as a younger boy he was boisterous and enjoyed attention. Together with his best friend, Madoff wrote, rehearsed, and performed a musical comedy at Laurelton's elementary school, at the age of ten or eleven. Wrapped in their parents' bed sheets, Madoff and his friend played desert sheikhs.[3] The audience laughed uproariously.

As Madoff grew from a boy into a teenager his parents began to think about which high school he should attend. These years, from the age of fourteen to eighteen, would likely determine his future. Laurelton was in the catchment area of Andrew Jackson High School, named after the seventh president of the United States. But Andrew Jackson did not have a very good academic reputation. There were private schools in the area though they were too expensive. Far Rockaway High School, on the Long Island peninsula, was the best option. It was a public school but had an excellent academic record, strong swimming and football teams, and was easily reached by train. Although Far Rockaway was out of Laurelton's catchment area there was a way around this: Jewish students simply had to say that they wanted to study Hebrew. Andrew Jackson did not have a Hebrew department; Far Rockaway did.

Madoff was accepted and was happy to start high school. Far Rockaway felt like a home from home. Like Laurelton, Far Rockaway was overwhelmingly Jewish and middle class. There were four grades, each with 300 to 350 pupils. About half of each grade were known as 'honour' students, of above average intelligence and achievements. The teachers were excellent. Like many New York public schools in the 1950s Far Rockaway had inadvertently benefited from the pre-war Depression. With the economy collapsing there were few career opportunities for bright young graduates, so a disproportionate number became teachers, recalls Arthur Traiger, who taught English at Far Rockaway during the 1950s when Madoff studied there. 'Everyone on the faculty was a star, very well trained, and bright, dedicated people. The school had a superb reputation, we sent kids to Harvard, Yale, Princeton, the top schools, our best students were able to get there without too much trouble. We had a heavy-weighted honour group. That came from the Jewish population. They were very eager for their children to do well in school, they had a good reputation for studying hard.'

Far Rockaway's alumni include two Nobel laureates in physics, Richard Feynman and Burton Richter; one in medicine, Baruch Blumberg, a congressman, William F. Brunner, and Carl Icahn, the billionaire financier who is one of the richest men in the world. Madoff, who is certainly Far Rockaway's most notorious graduate, did not shine intellectually and was not an honour student, says Arthur Traiger. 'I did not know him or his parents. He was never one of my students and probably the reason for that is that I was teaching the brightest groups at the time.' Apart from swimming on the school team and qualifying as a lifeguard, Madoff's other noteworthy activity was being appointed 'locker guard', ensuring that the teenagers did not get too unruly while they changed for the pool, and showered and dressed afterwards. While Madoff was a good swimmer he was not quite good enough to compete individually and only swam in team relay races.[4]

He was, however, good at spotting opportunities for making money. Almost all the houses in Laurelton had a garden, but who had time and energy to walk around with a watering-can to keep the lawn green? Nobody. The answer, Madoff realised, was to install garden sprinkler systems. This was the birth of the age of consumerism, when Americans wanted – and expected – appliances that saved time and made their lives easier. What applied to the kitchen and the laundry would also do for the garden. All they had to do was turn on the tap and the water would flow. Nothing too spectacular, just a steady stream that kept the gardens green and beautiful. Everybody wanted to feel that troublesome, complicated matters were taken care of, that everything was under control so they could tick a box on their to-do list and get on with more interesting pastimes. It was a useful lesson, and one he would remember in the future. Madoff's sprinkler business was extremely successful and earned him several thousand dollars.

Friends and neighbours admired the young man with the entrepreneurial spirit. So did his girlfriend, Ruth Alpern. Madoff was besotted with Ruth. He picked her up from home every morning and they took the train to school together. She was slim, blonde, clever, and popular. They had started dating around the time that Madoff was sixteen and Ruth was coming up to her fourteenth birthday. Ruth had been voted 'Josie College', a 1950s school honour, by her classmates, who predicted great things for her. 'Ruth was serious about Bernie all through high school. She was cute, smart and popular,' remembers the Madoffs' childhood friend. 'She was very well liked. I was a year older than she was and she also friendly with all my friends. That year age difference is a big deal when you are fourteen years old but it didn't matter with Ruth. She wasn't boisterous or attention-seeking, she was quiet, a good athlete and accepting.'

This was the era immortalised in the American comedy series *Happy Days*, which starred Henry Winkler as 'The Fonz', the leather-jacketed cool guy dispensing advice to the high school students. It was a more innocent age of jukeboxes and soda fountains, bobby-sox and decorous dates at the 'Itch', the local cinema, or the drive-in hamburger restaurant. 'I was a Laurelton girl,' wrote Sondra Madoff on a Laurelton reunion website. 'Laurelton was a terrific place to grow up in . . . I can certainly relate to Sue's memories of the train, the

"Itch", the Chinese restaurant and my own special favourite
... Raab's ice cream parlour.'[5]

These were indeed happy days for the teenage sweethearts.
Madoff was bursting with ideas, but Ruth had a cooler head.
She was very good with numbers and came from a more
intellectual background. 'Bernie's traded up,' the local gossips
whispered. But the young couple complimented each other
in looks as well as temperament. Madoff too was good-
looking, with regular, even features. Dressed in a slim-fitting
tuxedo, with his hair slicked back, he looked like a film
star. 'The girls thought he was cute and desirable,' says the
childhood friend. Madoff knew when and how to hustle. He
smiled a lot, but there was determination behind the grin.
'Bernie was hard-working and ambitious,' recalls Joe
Kavanau, who has known Madoff since his late teens. 'Bernie
was a good guy, we had a very easy relationship. He was my
friend.'

John Maccabee also thought Bernie Madoff was his friend,
but learned an early lesson about trusting him. In the summer
of 1956, just after Madoff graduated from Far Rockaway,
Maccabee was swimming with him and another boy called
Mike off the coast of Neponsit, in Queens. Madoff and Mike
suggested they all swim out to a sandbar, beyond the waves.
The sea looked inviting that hot summer's day, the waves
high but manageable as they slowly crested and broke onto
the sloping, golden sand. John hesitated over Madoff's challenge, for he had never ventured out that far before. The
Atlantic currents were powerful and even the strongest
swimmer could get into trouble. But John had faith in Bernie
and Mike. Bernie swam on the school team, specialising in
the butterfly, and was also a lifeguard. Mike was about to

marry John's sister. If John couldn't trust them, whom could he trust? The three boys set out into the water. John began swimming with energy and speed, but soon began to falter in the powerful waves. The two older boys pulled ahead. John saw Madoff staring at him on each stroke, as his head cleared the water and he turned to breathe. Madoff may have realised that John was in trouble but did not stop, slow or even offer to help him. The swim back to the shore was even harder. This time Madoff had some advice for the younger boy: swim slower and take longer strokes. John was dizzy and exhausted when he finally stumbled onto the sands. 'Trust yourself,' Madoff said, in his nasal New York accent. It was more prophetic advice than he knew.[6]

Bernie and Ruth were a popular couple, but his parents sometimes seemed formidable rather than friendly. They were polite enough when Bernie's friends visited but were not the most welcoming of hosts, especially by the standards of 1950s suburbia, when doors were rarely locked. Ralph, his father, was tall and well-built, and seemed to be 'a tough guy, not someone to mess with', remembers one person who met him several times. Sylvia, Bernie's mother, was tall and slender, with dark hair. Ruth's parents, Saul and Sara Alpern, were a different kind of people, recalls Ruth's friend. They were warmer, and more intellectual. Saul was a Certified Public Accountant, and Sara, unusually for middle-class Jewish women of that era, trained as a part-time social worker, the friend recalls. 'They were both quiet types of people and somewhat intellectual. Most mothers then were not college-educated, and were just high-school graduates. She seemed to be more intellectual than other parents.'

Ralph Madoff, it seems, was a something of a *shtarker*. He

may have been aloof because he had problems with the tax authorities. Together with three associates, he owed a tax debt of $13,245.28, equal to $100,000 in today's money, according to an investigation by *Fortune* magazine.[7] The taxes were assessed in 1956, the same year that Bernie and John Maccabee were swimming off the coast of Neponsit in the summer. It seems that Ralph and the other debtors could not pay the tax bill, and the authorities placed a charge on the family home, making it collateral against the bill. The charge was not removed until 1965, when the house was sold.

After graduating from high school Madoff enrolled at the University of Alabama in Tuscaloosa. Alabama was an odd choice for a Jewish boy from New York, recalls Arthur Traiger. Far Rockaway graduates usually tried for a place at the Ivy League schools of Harvard, Yale, and Princeton, if they were intelligent enough and could afford them, or headed northwest to universities in Michigan or New Hampshire, or stayed in New York. 'It was very unusual for kids at Far Rockaway to go to Alabama. I really don't why he would go there. I knew all the kids and they very rarely went down south.' Down south, though, had one advantage, especially for students with average grades: its universities were much easier to get into, and they welcomed students from out of state.

At Alabama Madoff joined a Jewish fraternity, Sigma Alpha Mu. Fraternities provide an instant peer group, a place to live, social life, and a support network. Fraternity life was made famous in the American college film *Animal House*, with its non-stop parties, beer, and girls. The film was of course an exaggeration, but for most young men going to

college is a great adventure. Not for Madoff though. He was
not happy at Tuscaloosa. He was a long way from New York.
Not just physically – it was a drive of just over 1,000 miles
(1,600 km) – but culturally. Alabama in the 1950s was a
bastion of segregation and was deeply conservative. New
York too was divided by race and ethnicity, and black people
were a rare enough site in Laurelton. But black women were
not arrested in Manhattan for refusing to give up their seats
for white men, as Rosa Parks was in Montgomery, Alabama,
in 1955.

Most of all, Madoff missed Ruth. He was used to seeing
her every day, and now he was lucky if she visited every
couple of weeks. He plodded along but found it hard to settle
or make any lasting friendships. Perhaps he knew he would
not stay long. When Allen Salkin, a journalist at the *New
York Times*, tracked down the other members of Sigma Alpha
Mu most could barely remember Madoff.[8] His college life
was apparently quite unremarkable. 'He wasn't an outstanding athlete or outstanding with girls. I just don't remember anything outstanding about him. Nice enough, not a
particularly good student as I recall,' said Malcolm Lindy.
Even his roommate, Martin Schrager, struggled to remember
much. 'There was nothing nefarious about the guy. When
I heard years later that he was who he was, I was astonished.
He never seemed like the kind of guy who could move
millions on Wall Street.' Ruth, however, was another matter.
'The main thing I remember is that we had a big dance and
he invited a girl all the way from New York. She was a
looker,' recalls Jay Salkin, Allen Salkin's father.

Madoff left Alabama and transferred to Hofstra College
on Long Island. Hofstra was just ten miles from Laurelton

and he commuted. Hofstra now is a university and well regarded, but in the late 1950s it was a mediocre institution. 'Bright kids did not go to Hofstra then,' says Arthur Traiger. Nevertheless, Madoff was much happier at Hofstra than in Alabama and in later years became a trustee of his alma mater. He was near Ruth and could build up his brokerage business. They married at Laurelton Jewish Center in November 1959. It was an elegant affair, a sit-down dinner with dancing for about one hundred people, and very enjoyable, recalls Ruth's friend. 'In those days there was nothing very distinctive about weddings, they were all much the same, apart from one or two individual touches. But Ruth looked lovely. She always cared about her appearance.'

Madoff graduated from Hofstra in 1960 and enrolled at Brooklyn Law School, together with Joe Kavanau. The two young men often travelled to college together. Classes lasted from 9 a.m. to noon, and were mostly lectures in halls that seated 125 students. The halls were divided alphabetically, from A to L and M to Z, so Madoff and Kavanau sat separately. By now Madoff had started his stock trading business. After six months he reported a single stock position: $300 worth of shares of a company called Electronic Capital.[9] Law seemed less and less appealing, especially spending hours in the not very glamorous confines of Brooklyn Law School. 'It was probably as unmemorable as any school could be,' recalls Joe Kavanau. Madoff did not return to law school after his first year. He knew he was not going to be a lawyer. He was working hard building up his business which was starting to make money.

Bernie and Ruth Madoff moved into their first home, a small apartment in the Bayside area of Queens, paying rent of $87 a month. Joe Kavanau stayed on a second year at law school, and the two couples remained close friends after he married his girlfriend Jane. They enjoyed the lives of typical American young marrieds, going out in the evenings or taking skiing trips to upstate New York, Kavanau recalls. 'We went out to dinner, we went to their apartment. Occasionally they would come to us, but mostly we went to theirs. Bernie did not like to drive and I did not mind it.' The two men would go and play golf, while their wives went shopping. Madoff was comfortable with Kavanau, but he could still be shy, or even socially gauche around people he didn't know – particularly if they came from a more intellectual background or were better off. He sometimes became tongue-tied or jumbled his words, but he was determined to polish his social skills. The real business in America – as everywhere else – was done with handshakes, and introductions, through friends of friends, at dinners, drinks, charity receptions, on the golf course, and especially at country clubs, where middle-class Jewish families spent their recreational time playing tennis, swimming, or just relaxing in the fresh air.

Madoff began to build the network of contacts that would lead him eventually to most coveted prizes of all: the business, religious, and philanthropic leaders of the Jewish establishment. Whatever wrongs the patronising Upper East Side Jews had once done to the Bowery's *shtarkers* would eventually be avenged on an almost Biblical scale.

3
Early adopters

'After college I married Bernie Madoff, FRHS class of 1955. Bernie and I worked together in the investment business he founded in 1960.'

Ruth Madoff writing in an update for the fiftieth reunion of Far Rockaway High School.[1]

Carl Shapiro was impressed with the young Bernie Madoff. Shapiro knew how tough it was to build up a business from nothing, and Madoff had grit, drive, and determination. Shapiro was a fashion magnate who had founded the Kay Windsor women's clothes company, one of the largest female fashion companies in the United States. He first met Madoff in 1960, through a mutual friend, and was probably the first of numerous extremely rich Jewish entrepreneurs that Madoff would ensnare over the following decades. 'He was twenty-two years old, a smart young guy. A friend asked me to meet him, maybe throw him a little business. I had plenty of irons in the fire, so I declined. But my friend insisted,' Shapiro said.[2]

Shapiro was born in 1913 and was twenty-five years older

than Madoff. He lived in Boston, with his wife, Ruth. They had three daughters, but no son. As well as running Kay Windsor, Shapiro also traded stock and shares. In the days before computers this was a painstaking process. Wall Street in the early 1960s was a far more sedate place than today. Hours were shorter, lunches were longer, and business much slower. There were no computers or electronic trading. Madoff promised to complete Shapiro's trades in record time. Shapiro decided to take a chance. 'In those days it took three weeks to complete a sale. But this kid said he can do it in three days. And he did.' Shapiro then wrote Madoff the largest cheque he had ever seen: for $100,000. It is unclear precisely when Madoff set up as an investment manager, but Shapiro seems to have been one of his first clients. Shapiro trusted Madoff to invest his money as he saw fit, and paid him a regular annual return. 'He did very well with it, and that was the beginning,' Shapiro recalled. The end would come forty-eight years later, when Shapiro reportedly lost about $400 million of his personal wealth,[3] and his charitable foundation up to $200 million.[4]

Madoff was rapidly turning his initial $200 investment in his trading operation into a substantial stake. By the end of 1961 he was reporting assets under management of $16,140 to the SEC. This was an impressive amount of money for someone just of out college. The word was spreading across Queens about the smart young trader. The parents of John Maccabee, whom Madoff had not helped when he and John swam out to sea together, were also early investors. Madoff showed them his bank statements, and explained how he had invested all the $5,000 that he saved from working as a lifeguard and installing sprinkler systems. They were impressed. 'They demanded quarterly returns and for years the golden-yellow Madoff cheques arrived on time and usually for the correct amount,' Maccabee recalled. Maccabee's mother had studied book-keeping and carefully scrutinised every statement, looking for discrepancies. If she found one she called Madoff's secretary, and demanded to speak to him, telling him that he was, for example, $17 out. Madoff would offer to make up the missing amount in the next quarter. Maccabee's mother was having none of it. She required a cheque immediately for the missing amount. 'You're killing me,' said Madoff, laughing. 'On the contrary, Bernie,' she replied, 'I pray daily for your health.'[5]

Madoff dreamed of a job on Wall Street but he knew his best chance of getting there was by working for himself. Wall Street is a street in Manhattan which runs through the historic heart of the financial district but the term means more than a stretch of buildings and pavements. Wall Street is shorthand for the American financial establishment, which did not look kindly on young hustlers from Laurelton, Queens. Wall Street then was a cosy cartel, divided up between the great Jewish banking families and their WASP counterparts. The great German Jewish dynasties, the Lehmans, the Kuhns, the Loebs, and the Warburgs were almost as powerful and intertwined in the 1960s as when Madoff's grandparents arrived at the turn of the century. The WASP establishment was rooted in Connecticut rather than Berlin and Frankfurt, but was just as exclusive. J.P. Morgan, the most powerful American banker in history, built his bank into the world's first billion-dollar corporation – in 1901. The WASPS often disdained the Jews as parvenus. The Jews in turned mocked the WASPs as the 'white shoe brigade'. These were graduates of the Ivy League universities such as Yale and Harvard, who were not smart enough to get jobs with the major corporations, and who wore white buckskin loafers to work.

Neither group traded in over the counter (OTC) shares. These are shares in small companies that were not traded on a stock exchange, but by dealers and brokers on the telephone.

Madoff set himself up as a wholesaler in OTC shares. He did not deal directly with clients who wanted to buy or sell stocks. He was a middleman, who bought from and sold to brokers who were acting for their clients. Madoff made the trades, while Ruth did the book-keeping. He worked out of Alpern and Heller, her father's accounting firm on Forty-second Street in mid-town Manhattan. Madoff appropriated part of a desk and installed his own telephone line, but his sales pitches and deal-making were disrupting the accountants' work. Sherman Heller, Saul Alpern's partner, demanded that Madoff get his own office and so he moved out.[6] It was probably time, as Madoff's business was now established enough to warrant his own office, with his name on the door: Bernard L. Madoff Investment Securities.

Around this time Madoff's mother Sylvia ran into trouble with the authorities. Like her son, Sylvia Madoff was trading in stocks and shares. Gibraltar Securities, a broker-dealer, was registered at the Madoff home on Two Hundred and Twenty-eighth Street in Laurelton. A registered address was a requirement for such firms. In August 1963, the SEC began proceedings against forty-eight broker-dealers, including Sylvia Madoff, on charges of failing to file reports of their financial conditions with the possibility of revoking their licences. The following year the SEC dropped the proceedings against several of the forty-eight firms, including Gibraltar Securities. The SEC and the troublesome firms probably worked out a deal: stay out of business and there will not be any penalties, speculated *Fortune* magazine.[7] It was also curious that Gibraltar Securities was headed by Sylvia Madoff rather than her husband. The stock exchange and financial services industries were still dominated by men in the early 1960s. Ralph Madoff may have opened Gibraltar Securities in his wife's name because of his own troubles with the federal tax authorities and his tax debt of $13,245.28. Either way, there were two potential lessons for Bernard Madoff to learn from Gibraltar Securities: there was money to be made on the stock exchange, and rules could be bent, perhaps even broken, with no personal legal consequences.

OTC stocks were sometimes traded in a grey area. In many respects the whole OTC market was a free-for-all. As there was no centralised information exchange, the dealers could make up prices and charge whatever they could get away with. Stock prices were listed on information sheets that were circulated through the market, known as the Pink Sheets, listing the dealers who were willing to trade and the prices they were quoting. But the Pink Sheets were a day old, and were mostly used as a telephone directory. As *Fortune* notes: 'This was not the staid institutionalised world of the New York Stock Exchange. Since they did not trade on a cen-tralised exchange and there was no technology to provide up-to-date prices, over the counter dealers could – and did – take all sorts of liberties with their quotes.'[8] Not surprisingly, the over the counter market was often referred to as the 'under the counter market'.

Madoff recalled those early days with nostalgia when he

spoke at the Philoctetes panel discussion in New York in October 2007. 'In those days, over the counter stocks were traded always over the telephone with no automation. So you would call a broker; the broker would call up over the telephone any number of dealers like myself, and there were hundreds of dealers around the country that were making these markets. It was an arduous process of saying, "Okay, where can I buy 100 shares of Intel or 100 shares of Apple," which of course didn't exist at that time, nor did Intel. We would negotiate over the telephone.'[9] Madoff was also a 'market-maker' in OTC stocks, the OTC equivalent of a specialist dealer on a stock exchange. If a client wanted to buy 500 shares in a certain company, he would call his stockbroker and instruct him to make the purchase. The stockbroker would execute the order by going to a market-maker such as BLMIS, which had the contacts to get the best price. The market-makers offered the stockbroker the shares at a quoted price. They then bought the stock them-selves before selling it on to the stockbroker, thus providing liquidity for brokers who lacked sufficient funds.

By the late 1960s BLMIS was booming. In 1967 Madoff reported assets under management of $127,517 to the SEC. Two years later that had leapt to $555,157. The word was spreading through Jewish suburbia about Madoff's business. But only a select few knew that as well as running a successful trading operation, Madoff had another business. He was an investment adviser, offering high and steady returns to those lucky enough to be invited in through his father-in-law.

Michael Bienes had never really wanted to become an accountant, but as a child of the Depression he knew he needed a profession. And if he had any doubts, his mother drummed the lesson into him. She herself was a book-keeper and knew how the world worked: 'You gotta make a living and accountants always make a living,' she told him. Bienes graduated from New York University in 1958. He worked for two accounting firms and liked neither before joining the Internal Revenue Service (IRS) as a field agent. That was much more interesting than sitting in an office poring over company books. Bienes was a natural and was soon promoted to instructor, then supervisor. The problem with working for the IRS, however, was that he would never be rich. No matter how high he rose, government service could never compete with the private sector. So one day Bienes went to see his supervisor. 'I remember saying, "Charlie, you want the American flag behind your desk. I want the Cadillac in front of my door. I have to go." And I did.'

But where to get that job that would pay for the Cadillac? Unknown to Bienes, in December 1967 Saul Alpern placed a death notice in the *New York Times* obituary page. His partner, Sherman Heller, who had thrown Madoff out for disrupting the office with his sales calls, had died suddenly of a heart attack in his late forties. The notice said: 'Saul Alpern, partner, and members of the firm of Alpern and Heller record with sorrow the passing of an esteemed colleague and friend and extend their heartfelt sympathy to the bereaved family.' Heller's death was not only shocking news, it also left Alpern bereft of a tax expert. Which Bienes was. A mutual acquaintance of both men recommended to Bienes that he apply to Alpern for a job, saying that it could lead to a partnership. The word 'partnership' had a magical connotation for him, Bienes recalled. 'I was an only child and

I always felt that someone who could talk about their partner, I envied them. I wanted to have a partner so I went for the interview.'

Saul Alpern was then in his mid-sixties. He introduced Bienes to another one of his partners, Frank Avellino. Avellino had worked for Alpern and Heller for a decade, and joined the firm in the late 1950s straight from college. He was shorter than Bienes and wore glasses, but here was the brother Bienes had always longed for. 'I took one look at Frank and, believe it or not, I fell in love, as only one man could fall for another. I said, "This is the guy I want to be with". It was not a good deal. I gave up a lot of fringe benefits. I put in a lot more hours. But Frank and I bonded together ... We were partners before we were partners,' Bienes recalled in an interview with the Public Broadcasting Service (PBS).[10] Bienes started work for Saul Alpern in 1968. Soon afterwards Saul Alpern asked him if he wanted to invest with Bernie Madoff. His son-in-law paid 20 per cent a year, he assured Bienes. Alpern was channelling numerous relatives, friends, and his own clients through to Bernie, Bienes says. 'He was doing it for the cronies, for the clients, Saul's clients, Saul's friends, Saul's family.' Bienes declined, then.

Not only were Wall Street and the New York Stock Exchange more sedate than today's frenzied bear-pits, they were far less regulated. Just like the City of London, Wall Street was controlled by self-perpetuating cliques. The Jews and the WASPs lived parallel lives and mingled only when business demanded, but both groups were deeply conservative and resisted government attempts to make the financial industry transparent and accountable. Insider trading, the use of non-public proprietary information for personal profit, was considered by many to be a perk of the job. For example, if a broker's client wanted to buy a million shares in General Motors, that would be sufficiently large to make General Motors' share price move upwards. Such an investment indicated to the market that the company was strong, economically sound. So before the stockbroker placed the order for his client, he would make his own purchase of General Motors shares, and turn a profit on their increase in value. This is also known as 'front-running'. If a broker heard from a contact at the country club or on the golf course, for example, that a bank was about to make a major investment in a company, he would buy up as many shares as he could afford, sharing that knowledge with a chosen few, knowing that the share price would soon rise, and he could turn a profit by selling his holdings. He would then, in turn, when he came across similarly profitable nuggets of information, return the favour.

In later years Madoff sought investors in the salons of the Upper East Side and the country clubs of Palm Beach, Florida, home to some of the richest people in the United States. In the 1960s Saul and Sara Alpern worked a less illustrious circuit for their son-in-law: the holiday-makers in the Catskill Mountains, to the north of New York City. This was known as the 'Borscht belt', after the beetroot soup that was a favourite with Eastern European Jews. The 'Borscht belt' was affordable and within easy reach of Manhattan, offering *haimishe* (home-style) food, a Jewish atmosphere, comedians, variety shows, and plenty of famil-iar faces. The Borscht belt was a small, cosy world of mutual friends and relatives, where everybody knew one another, a kind of idyllic *shtetl*, transported from Eastern Europe to the freedom and security of America. There was an old joke about the dinners at Catskill hotels: one guest says to another: 'The food here is terrible.' The second replies: 'Yes, I know – and such small portions.' In that *haimishe* world, of shared culture, religion, and ethics, an introduction and a firm handshake were all that was needed to ensure mutual trust. For two decades Saul and Sara Alpern were regular guests at the Sunny Oaks hotel, Woodridge, which was owned by Ted and Cynthia Arenson. Sunny Oaks was not a luxurious place, but its rickety wooden bungalows were comfortable and clean. The Alperns lived near the Arensons in Brooklyn and had become friends. They spent each summer there. Ted Arenson's son, David, worked as a waiter at the hotel while he was at college. 'They were easy guests. They never complained and although they took one of the best rooms in the house, they weren't fancy people,' he wrote on his blog, CLL Diary. 'He [Alpern] knew people on Wall Street, certainly through Madoff and his circle, and was instrumental in spreading the word at the hotel when good business opportunities came along.'

When Alpern spoke about business, people listened. The other Jewish guests were intelligent professionals; they were teachers, lawyers or they worked in the fashion business. But for many, finance still had a hint of alchemy. Wall Street was opaque, an insider's racket and everyone knew it operated through contacts and networks. Here was a well-known, respected Certified Public Accountant (CPA), with a successful practice in mid-town Manhattan. If Alpern recommended to his friends that they invest with his son-in-law – his own family, after all – there was simply no reason not to trust him. So Ted and Cynthia Arenson, and later David, who used to serve Saul Alpern his dinner, all invested with Madoff's fund. The Arensons opened their account with $50,000. Many others followed. 'Way back when, our little hotel turned out to be fertile ground for investors for Bernie. Almost everybody in the family had a Madoff account. Accounts radiated out through the guest population, through our distant relatives and the distant relatives of guests,' wrote David Arenson. 'Madoff was synonymous with [the word] bank in our circle. It was like Kleenex for tissue or Xerox for photocopy. I'll put the money in Madoff. I'll take it out of Madoff. Gifts, trips, cars, down payments on houses, all came from Madoff.'[11] Nobody ever questioned Madoff's legitimacy.

Perhaps if the investors had seen the paperwork, they might have. Saul Alpern ran his son-in-law's investment fund out of a green plastic loose-leaf book, according to Michael Bienes. 'He had these blank sheets printed up and Nanette, the secretary, would type them in, and he would do the pencil work. You got a transaction, and then the next transaction, you got the cheque from the previous transaction.' Initially Madoff had set up several investment accounts from Alpern's clients but the amounts were too small to justify the paperwork and record keeping. Madoff told his father-in-law that he could not deal with them. Instead an account was opened called A&A, which stood for Alpern and Avellino. Frank Avellino, whom Bienes idolised as the brother he never had, was now Alpern's partner.[12]

The innocuous-sounding A&A account was a crucial development in Madoff's investment business. It was an early feeder fund, meaning an investment operation that channelled money straight to Madoff. Over the years the feeder funds would feed billions of dollars into his Ponzi scheme, and the feeder funds would eventually help destroy it.

4
Getting rich in Roslyn

*'So we came up with the concept of developing a screen-
based trading mechanism where prices would appear
on a computer screen. That was the start of NASDAQ.'*

Bernard Madoff's (disputed) account of how he and his brother
Peter invented automated stock trading in 1971.[1]

As Madoff's business empire expanded, he and his
wife began to drift apart from Joe and Jane Kavanau. The
Kavanaus moved to Rye Brook, a city north of Manhattan
in New York State. The Madoffs moved to Roslyn Estates, a
charming up-market village in Nassau County, on the north
shore of Long Island. The Madoffs lived in a spacious ranch-
style house, with a large garden. They had two children,
Mark, born in 1964, and Andrew, who was two years
younger. The two families kept in touch by telephone, but as
they put down roots in their new homes, they met less and
less frequently. 'It just happened, they lived where they lived,
we lived where we lived. Their kids and our kids became
friendly with local kids, we were never not friends, we just
didn't see each other, it was too far,' recalls Joe Kavanau.

Also, perhaps, because the Madoffs were moving up in the world. They were making new friends, whom Madoff hoped to turn into clients. Roslyn was full of potential clients for his investment fund. Homes on this part of Long Island were much sought after. It was hard to believe that such a beautiful rural idyll, of verdant countryside, abundant trees, and tranquil ponds, was just half an hour from Penn Station in midtown Manhattan on the Long Island Rail Road. The Roslyn area, especially nearby Roslyn Village, is rich in history and culture. Two districts are protected historical monuments, including rows of beautifully preserved houses on Main Street that pre-date the American Civil War. Roslyn Harbor houses the Nassau County Museum of Art, with a notable collection of modern art. Roslyn's Jewish community centre is one of the most impressive in New York State. 'Roslyn was an upper-class, predominantly Jewish neighbourhood. Most of the fathers were doctors, lawyers or businessmen, and were pretty successful,' recalls a childhood friend of Mark and Andrew Madoff.[2] Unlike Ralph and Sylvia Madoff, Bernard and Ruth were always friendly and welcoming to their children's friends. 'Bernie and Ruth were always pleasant and hospitable. They were a very close family. I don't ever remember Andy or Mark going to a summer sleep-away camp, which was unusual.'

The Roslyn area was a close-knit circle, where social, business, and children's friendships all interlinked. Barely 1,000 people lived on Roslyn Estates. Fred Wilpon, a wealthy real estate broker, lived nearby and later bought the New York Mets. His son Jeff went to Roslyn High School with Mark Madoff. Wilpon was one of numerous prosperous residents of Roslyn to invest with Madoff. Most belonged to one of Long Island's country clubs. The country club is a peculiarly American social phenomenon, and played a crucial role in keeping the money flowing into Madoff's fund. Country clubs are nonresidential luxury resorts, a cross between the gentlemen's salons of Whitehall, and a five-star sports resort, where members spend their weekends or holidays and entertain guests. The clubs usually have a swimming pool, golf course, tennis courts, a spa, and an excellent restaurant. The more luxurious the facilities, the higher the joining fee and the annual membership fee. Some country clubs charge $100,000 to sign up, and another $25,000 a year to use the facilities. The names, such as Long Meadows or Fresh Meadow, are signifiers, suggesting a bucolic retreat where everyday cares will melt away.

But country clubs are about much more than exercise and fresh air. They are about power, discrimination, and status. They have shaped American society, and did so in a way that opened a myriad of doors to Madoff. 'The country club has had a profound effect on the development of American society and one of the most dynamic part of the American social scene in the twentieth century, the suburbs,' says historian John Steele Gordon.[3] And because country clubs are rooted in mimicry they are also a symbol of insecurity. The first clubs were opened in the nineteenth century by old established families in New York and Boston, who were descended from the early Protestant settlers. Unlike their British counterparts, the American aristocracy, such as it was, had no historic country estates to retire to at the weekend. They were an urban elite who made their fortunes in business, commerce, and manufacturing. So they built their own faux rural idylls, where they could spend their weekends playing cricket, golf, socialising, gossiping, and matchmaking their sons and daughters.

Initially, Jews were allowed to join these clubs. But just as the German Jews had feared, the massive wave of Jewish immigration at the end of the nineteenth century triggered a growing anti-Semitism. Jesse Seligman, a banker, was a member of the Union League Club in New York. But the club turned down his son for membership, because he was a Jew. Seligman resigned although the club refused to accept it – arguing that although Jews who were already members could stay, there was no room for more, even relatives. Because private clubs could legally decide whom they wanted to allow to join, the WASPs' clubs could, and did, discriminate against Jews, blacks, and Hispanics. At one club near Washington, DC, black Americans were not allowed to join, but black foreign diplomats were welcome.

Anti-Semitism flourished among sections of American society both before and after World War II. Henry Ford's book *The International Jew*, a four-volume work first published in the 1920s, was based on the notorious forgery, *The Protocols of the Elders of Zion*, which purported to outline an international Jewish conspiracy to control the world. Ford, the owner of the Ford Motor Company, was an extremely powerful and influential industrialist, and his book was widely read. Hitler kept a picture of Ford by his desk. Numerous American universities ran a quota system to keep out Jewish students, especially those from immigrant families from New York, including several Ivy League colleges, which lasted until the 1950s. There was widespread discrimination against Jews at resort hotels also. In 1953 the Anti-Defamation League (ADL), a Jewish campaigning organisation based in New York, found seventy-three of eighty-eight hotels and apartments in Fort Lauderdale, Florida, displaying anti-Semitic signs such as 'Restricted Clientele' and 'Gentiles Only'. The ADL repeatedly tried to book rooms at numerous hotels across the state using Jewish-sounding and non-Jewish names. There were no rooms available for the Jewish names but plenty for their Christian equivalents.[4]

As American society grew and became more complex, different subgroups built their own clubs. The Mount Prospect Country Club, near Chicago, was popular with gangsters. Jewish Hollywood moguls joined the discreet and super-luxurious Hillcrest, in Los Angeles. The social complexities and hypocrisies of the growing country club scene provided inspiration for artists and writers. The composer Scott Joplin wrote 'The Country Club Rag' in 1909, while Henry James was fascinated by the clubs' finely delineated social gradations. They inspired Groucho Marx to make his famous quip that he wouldn't join any club willing to have him as a member, although he did join Hillcrest. The story goes that one club said he could enter, even though he was Jewish, but could not use the swimming pool. Marx replied: 'My daughter's only half Jewish – can she go in up to her knees?' Perhaps the most resonant literary work set in this world is *The Embezzler*, by Louis Auchincloss, who was a scion of the Manhattan WASP establishment. The novel recounts the life of Guy Prime, a gilded youth born into the elite of Manhattan society. The tale unfolds during the Depression. When the economy crumbles, Prime embezzles a fortune from a charitable foundation for which he is responsible, in an attempt to keep his business empire afloat.

His crimes are eventually uncovered and he spends the rest of his life exiled to Panama, waiting to die.

The WASPs mimicked the British aristocracy, whose country lifestyle they admired but could never be part of. The Jews mimicked the WASPs, whose country lifestyle they admired, but could never be part of. And so the cycle continued, as each new wave of newly prosperous immigrants built their own clubs. By the early 1960s there were 3,300 country clubs spread across the United States, with 1.7 million members. Madoff was a member of three such clubs: Fresh Meadow, a predominantly Jewish country club that was a short drive from his home in Roslyn; the Atlantic Golf Club; and the most sought-after Jewish country club of all: Palm Beach. Fresh Meadow has a superb golf course, which drew attention across America when it opened in 1923, with its Colonial-style club house, swimming pool, and bar. For Madoff the country clubs were a more honed version of the Sunny Oaks hotel in the Catskills. Saul Alpern, Madoff's father-in-law, was able to work the guests at Sunny Oaks because of their shared religious and cultural background, exploiting the closely knit social circle. But anybody could stay at Sunny Oaks. It was a hotel, open to the general public. Country clubs offered much greater opportunities for Madoff. Firstly, the members were usually well off and successful, if not millionaires, so they had plenty of disposable income and savings to invest. More subtly, membership certified the passing of numerous tests of suitability, not just in terms of economic status, but also shared social and cultural mores. Each knew the other had been preselected.

This deliberate targeting of social and ethnic peers, known as 'Affinity Fraud', has a long and ignoble pedigree. Decades before Madoff swung his first club on the Fresh Meadow golf course, Richard Whitney was working the salons and clubs of Manhattan's WASP elite, during the 1930s. Whitney, like Madoff, had perfect credentials to dazzle his socially similar victims. Whitney's ancestors arrived in America from England in the seventeenth century, which placed him at the very peak of WASP social standing. He was educated at Harvard, where he joined its most exclusive club, the Porcellian. He was the chief broker for J.P. Morgan, the world's most powerful investment bank, and during the early 1930s served as president of the New York Stock Exchange (NYSE). He was a fixture on the New York social scene and was appointed treasurer of the New York Yacht Club. Like Madoff, Whitney was well dressed, with carefully barbered grey hair. When after the crash of 1929 Congress called for more regulation, Whitney argued strongly against it, on the grounds that stockbrokers were gentlemen and did not need to be regulated. Whitney lost his battle with Congress and in 1934 the Securities and Exchange Commission (SEC) was founded.

Whitney retired as president of the NYSE the following year. He was a poor businessman and lost a fortune backing an apple-flavoured alcoholic drink. He borrowed from friends and relatives, and then began helping himself to various funds of which he was a trustee, including the NYSE pension fund. In 1938 the SEC asked the NYSE for details of member firms' accounts. NYSE officials discovered that Whitney had been falsifying his books. As *Newsweek* magazine records, Whitney pleaded with Charles Gay, the new president of the NYSE, not to turn him in, saying, 'After all, for millions of people I am the NYSE.'[5] Gay refused and

Whitney was sent to Sing Sing prison in New York for five to ten years. A crowd of thousands turned out at Grand Central Station to see him led away in handcuffs to the train that would deliver him to prison. Whitney served less than four years in prison and later became a farmer and businessman.

Club membership then was not a safeguard from fraudsters but precisely the opposite. The false sense of security membership bestowed made it a hazard. Members dropped their guard in the clubhouse bar. Nor did it satisfy the secret insecurity that still gnawed inside some successful Jews: to show that they had made it, and were respected by their peers. This 'status anxiety' and the hunger of peer acclaim were crucial in bringing investors to Madoff, argues the American Jewish writer Ron Rosenbaum. 'This is a scandal that hinges on a false connection between country club membership and "respectability." Bernie seems to have preyed on those Jews who worship the false idol of WASP respectability. The sham gentility of country club life.' Independent-minded Jews such as Rosenbaum's father, who laughed at what he saw as Jewish attempts to mimic the WASPs, were ostracised. 'There were two sides to the family I grew up in. One, my mother's side, the country-club side (some of them, anyway) made clear – in ways subtle and overt – that they looked down on my father, because he couldn't afford – actually, better, wasn't interested in – joining country clubs, much less seeing them as symbols of status and, yes, respectability.'[6]

And for many members, the pseudo-bourgeois pleasures of the country clubs to which Madoff belonged brought no peace, only a kind of torment. On the golf course, in the changing room, and the bar after a game, they whispered among themselves about an incredible investment opportunity.

It beat the markets year after year. But infuriatingly, there was no application process. It was all done by word of mouth. How to get to Bernie Madoff? No matter how well the doctors, lawyers, and real estate brokers had done, it seemed there was always something better, just out of reach.

Not for Michael Bienes. Bernard Madoff lay naked next to him on a massage table at the New York Athletic Club. The two men had just gone swimming together. But this was a more complex invitation than a chance to exercise. Bienes had been working for Saul Alpern for a couple of years and Madoff wanted to get his measure. There was no talk of business, just pleasant social chitchat, he recalls. 'We didn't discuss anything really. I think he wanted to get the feel of me, you know, and bring me into his orbit.'[7] Madoff was certainly a shrewd manipulator of the human psyche. Numerous interviews with those who knew him confirm that he could instinctively sense the emotional needs of whomever he was talking to. He knew whether they craved social acceptance, financial security, or high profits. He knew when to keep a distance and when to draw his prey in closer. He knew when to impress with his business skills, as he had done with Carl Shapiro, and when to be cool, and aloof. He could use his charm and charisma to take control of a room. He could also terrorise anyone nearby. Bienes was easy to manipulate.

Bienes, the boy born in the Depression, was suitably impressed by the athletics club and its facilities. The only child who longed for a brother relished the curious intimacy of being naked with someone he greatly admired. Bienes was no fool, however. He had graduated from college and worked very hard to pass his CPA exams. Alpern and Heller was now

Alpern and Avellino, and Bienes too had hopes of becoming a partner. Still there was something about Bernie Madoff that made him go soft inside: a mix of awe, adoration, and a powerful longing to be accepted. 'He had an aura about him ... a confidence, the way he was set up, the way he looked, the way he spoke.' Madoff's self-possession and charm were not only impressive in themselves, but drew in those around him. 'The self-confidence – he just evoked confidence in you, that he knew that he was in control and if he was around, everything was fine ... He wore the best shirts and always French cuffs. Beautiful. He had a body that was right, that was set up perfectly.'

The social and economic upheavals that shook America during the 1970s were good for Madoff. They opened cracks in the old order, shook out the creaking, conservative establishments and brought new opportunities. The American economy was battered by oil shocks, inflation eventually hit double figures, and economic growth slowed. The Vietnam War and the Watergate scandal left America psychically drained and disillusioned. The hippie revolution had outraged the older generation and energised their children. This was the 'me decade', the phrase coined by the writer Tom Wolfe. 'The new alchemical dream is: changing one's personality – remaking, remodeling, elevating, and polishing one's very self ... and observing, studying, and doting on it. (Me!)'[8] Old certainties evaporated, institutions crumpled. The ripples that began on Haight Street, San Francisco, the epicentre of the sex and drugs revolution, overturning the old order, eventually hit Wall Street. The gentleman banker, with leisurely work hours, long lunches, and a secure portfolio of long-held family clients, was about to become extinct.

These were the end days for the old Wall Street dynasties, both WASP and Jewish. The historic institutions that could not adapt to the brash new age would soon die, merge, or fade into history.

Madoff planned his attack on the financial establishment from his new headquarters at one of the most prestigious addresses in the financial district: on Wall Street itself. There BLMIS leased a whole floor with a trading room, and offices. The revolution in Wall Street would be not sexual, but digital. Encouraged by his brother Peter, Madoff had grasped the potential of computers to automate and accelerate trading. The faster, and easier, it was to trade, the more money there would be to make. Peter Madoff was seven years younger than his brother and had joined BLMIS in 1965 while he was still a student. He graduated from Fordham Law School in 1970 and started work full time for his brother's trading operation. Peter was married to Marion, another Laurelton girl, whom he had met at Queens College. Peter Madoff was quieter and more intellectual than Bernard. Bernard Madoff knew computers would shape the future of Wall Street, but he never became expert in the technicalities of how that would happen. That was Peter's department. 'Bernie and his brother were very close. Initially when you met one, you met the other. Bernie made the same impression on me that he made on a lot of people. He was very self-confident and very polished,' says Ed Nicoll, whose company Waterhouse Securities used BLMIS to execute share orders in the 1980s. 'Peter was very technologically savvy for his time. I had the sense that it was Peter who drove the computerisation of the Madoff business.'

NASDAQ helped make Madoff's first serious fortune.

NASDAQ, based in New York, stands for the National Association of Securities Dealers Automated Quotations. Launched in 1971, it was a computerised share price information system for the National Association of Securities Dealers (NASD). Buying and selling shares was no longer a tedious process of checking the Pink Sheets and telephoning brokers. The computer screens showed the stocks, together with their 'bids', the offered buying price, and the 'asks', the offered selling price. The actual deal still had to be done over the telephone, but this was many times faster than the previous system. Eventually, the whole process became fully automated. From the moment of NASDAQ's inception Madoff was deeply involved in the organisation. Back in 1960 Carl Shapiro had been impressed that Madoff could make trades in three days. Even in its most primitive incarnation, NASDAQ revolutionised both the speed and volume of stock trading. Information was now freely available in real-time. The potential was enormous.

Diana Henriques of the *New York Times*, who has covered the SEC for decades, argues that Madoff is one of a dozen or so people who could legitimately claim to be one of the fathers of NASDAQ. 'He worked assiduously for the notion of an automated stock exchange and in his capacity as chairman of the NASD helped NASDAQ get born.'[9] The launch of NASDAQ and the advent of computers revolutionised Wall Street. They also heralded a power shift, away from the White Shoe firms, and the establishment, towards mavericks like BLMIS. The New York Stock Exchange grandees looked askance, but Madoff argued persuasively that automated trading was in everybody's interest. It speeded up transactions and facilitated multiple-order flows. It reduced paperwork, and therefore labour costs, so was much cheaper for everyone. Automated trading benefited not just retail customers, but also big institutions, such as pension funds which handled government money. It was a win-win situation, Madoff claimed, and should be widely adopted.

In later years Madoff claimed that he and Peter invented the concept of screen-based trading. Madoff told the Philoctetes panel: 'In about 1971, computers were showing up and being used. So we saw – meaning my brother and myself – that there was an opportunity to bring automation into the over the counter marketplace and create some visibility and transparency in the marketplace. So we came up with the concept of developing a screen-based trading mechanism where prices would appear on a computer screen. That was the start of NASDAQ.'[10] Madoff claimed that BLMIS, and four other firms, including Merrill Lynch and Goldman Sachs, approached the NASD with a proposal to build a screen-based trading system which became NASDAQ.

But Madoff's claims that he helped launch NASDAQ are disputed. Charles Justice, the former chief technology officer of NASDAQ, said that Bernard Madoff was not 'involved in the founding of NASDAQ at all' and that he played no role in the design of its technology.[11]

Either way, Bernard Madoff was not quite as smart and street-sharp as he believed. He too could be a believer. Like the future victims of his Ponzi scheme, Madoff was also seduced by the allure of money, glamour, and a plausible manner – especially when the rich and famous were elbowing one another out of the way to invest. Madoff fell victim to one of the great American con-men of the 1960s, Jack Dick.

Like Richard Whitney, Dick used his network of connections in American society to first win his victims' trust and then defraud them. Unlike Madoff, Dick was a showman, who revelled in media attention. He lived in Dunnellen Hall, a twenty-eight-room Jacobean mansion, with a view of Long Island Sound. His electricity bill alone topped $1,400 every month. His Black Watch Farms which sold investments in Angus bulls paid for some of his lavish lifestyle. Madoff committed to investing $85,000 with Dick and made initial payments totalling around $28,000.[12]

Gay Talese, of the *New York Times*, chronicled an auction at Black Watch Farms in 1964. The star of the show was a 1,900 lb Scottish bull called Escort of Manorhill. The animal itself was not for sale, but Dick was auctioning off the rights to one-third of its sperm, as such a fine creature would doubtless sire many more of similar stature. This was a very different social circle to the Jewish establishment that Madoff would later plunder, but there was still the same sense of being on the inside track to a bargain denied to lesser mortals. Talese wrote: 'It was a rich crowd here today. They were tweedy and continental; they were cattlemen from Argentina and squires from Scotland and England and Canada.' The buyers included Senator Albert Gore Sr and even a representative from former [US] President Eisenhower's farm. After much excitement the auctioneer got the final bid up to $187,500, the highest price ever paid for part of a bull in America, future emissions of sperm included.[13]

In September 1971 Dick was arrested and charged with stealing $840,000 by forging documents to get a loan. Dick's fraud started in August 1967, according to the Manhattan District Attorney's office. A New York taxi driver had invested in Black Watch Farms in promissory notes. (A written promise to pay a specified amount of money to another on demand or at a given time in the future.) Dick took the notes to a money-lending corporation on Seventh Avenue, using the notes as collateral. As taxi drivers were not usually very wealthy, Dick falsified the taxi driver's financial statements, making him seem much richer than he was, and received a loan of $40,000. Dick was known, according to the District Attorney's office, as 'a tycoon and art collector'. He approached an affiliate of the money lender on Seventh Avenue, asking for a loan of $800,000 to buy art. He pledged 2,500 shares as collateral, although the shares were not his and had been sent to him accidentally by his broker. Dick got the $800,000 and spent it on paintings of eighteenth-century hunting and sporting scenes, which looked suitably imposing on his mansion walls. But in 1969 the stock market began to fall, the 2,500 shares lost their value and the money lenders demanded more collateral.

Dick solved this, temporarily at least, the same way that Madoff later did: he forged statements. Dick falsified eleven invoices from three well-known art galleries in New York, and ascribed 'astronomical values' to his paintings. The money lenders kept pressing, and Dick eventually gave them the paintings. As the *New York Times* reported: 'When the company tried to sell the canvases it discovered they were relatively worthless.'[14] So was Madoff's $28,000 stake in Black Watch Farms, as the company went bust. That was not the end of the story. A firm called West End Livestock acquired its remaining assets and sued Madoff, along with other investors who had written promissory notes, for the remainder of their investments, in Madoff's case around $58,000. The case was eventually settled although it is not known how much more Madoff paid.[15]

Dick was arrested in September 1971 and released on $2,500 bail. He was never brought to trial and died three years later of a heart attack while being driven home by his chauffeur. Dick's scam has several similarities with Madoff's Ponzi scheme. Both men used complicated paper trails. Madoff sent investors fake statements every month of balances that did not exist and trades that had not taken place. Dick falsified documents to certify that assets were worth many times their true value. Both men tried frantically to salvage their schemes when they began to collapse and both were brought down in part by a declining stock market. As a defrauded client, Madoff must have read the article in the 1971 *Wall Street Journal* on Dick. Even after Dick was arrested, his charisma endured. One victim eulogised the fraudster with praise that could also apply to Madoff: 'He's one of the most brilliant persons I ever met. If he has any flaw, one critic says, it's confidence in his own judgment that is so excessive it borders on a belief in his own infallibility.'[16]

Bernard Madoff lost thousands of dollars. He may have learned something from Dick's criminal methodology, but it appears the most important lesson passed him by. Like Dick, he would eventually be brought down by an external slump.

5
The first millions

'The tougher we were, the more money came in.'

Michael Bienes, on the feeder fund he and Frank Avellino ran for Madoff.

Saul Alpern retired from full-time work, took the green folder, the record of Madoff's investment fund, with him to Florida, lay back and enjoyed the sunshine. Managing the fund was enough to keep him busy. Alpern worked out the payments, sent the information to his secretary Nanette, and she dealt with the clients' paperwork, according to Michael Bienes.[1] Alpern and Avellino became Avellino and Bienes, when Bienes was made a partner. The firm's main business was still accounting, but Madoff's investment fund just kept growing and growing. By the end of the 1970s, running Madoff's fund composed more than one-third of the firm's business and still the cheques kept pouring in. They were deposited at the end of each week in a bank account. Each quarter Madoff's fund sent a cheque to Avellino and Bienes. They paid out interest to clients who wanted their dividend, or let them roll it over.

The monies were very welcome, but the increasingly detailed account calculations were not, especially in the pre-digital age. They decided on a simple solution: each client would receive a set rate of interest, which was determined by the amount of their investment. For example $200,000 would get 17 per cent, raised to 18 per cent for friends. Smaller amounts got 16 or 15 per cent. Every quarter clients received a statement. They could roll over the interest or withdraw it, as they wished. Bienes recalls: 'People could see it, understand it, and we could account for it so easily.' These fixed interest rates may have been simple to administer but were extremely risky for Avellino and Bienes. Accountants, like lawyers, are required by law to be personally responsible for their actions. If everything went wrong, they would be personally liable for any debts. But they had faith in Madoff. 'We always stood behind it. That's how much we believed in Bernie,' says Bienes.

So did the customers who were begging to sign up. There was no advertising and no marketing, except Bernie's appearances on the country club circuit. Even then he did not obviously tout for business. The very fact of his presence was a kind of walking advertisement, triggering whispered asides and subtle nods in his direction. The usual heavy sales approach adopted by fund managers was reversed at Avellino and Bienes into a stonewall technique. The secretarial staff were trained to turn away enquiries from anyone who telephoned the office. The secretaries thanked the caller for their enquiry, and hung up. The only way through was by personal recommendation from another client.

Despite their importance to him, Madoff kept Bienes and Avellino at a distance. The same technique that worked so well on his customers worked on his accountants. The less social contact they had, the more they wanted. The three men always met at Madoff's office in Wall Street. Madoff offered neither coffee nor water. When Madoff invited Avellino and Bienes to the bar mitzvah of one of his sons, both men swooned. A bar mitzvah takes place when a Jewish boy turns thirteen and marks the passage from boyhood to adulthood. It is an intensely proud, emotional moment for the family, and usually only close friends and relatives are invited to the synagogue ceremony and party. Madoff was now a wealthy man. Yet Madoff, perhaps under Ruth's influence, was not ostentatious. The synagogue ceremony was followed by a buffet lunch. There was none of the showy one-upmanship that sometimes marked Jewish family events. 'I was very impressed because he did not go over the top,' recalls Bienes. 'He was a wealthy guy, you know, but he did it in a moderate way.' Bienes and Avellino met Madoff in the middle of the dance floor. They thanked him for inviting them. Madoff replied: 'Hey, come on, we're family, aren't we.' Bienes was hooked for life.[2]

The stonewalling, combined with the steady, above average returns, only made would-be clients even more determined to be allowed to join the fund. Word of mouth, the sense that investors were in on a secret, to be shared only with a select few, was the best marketing. By 1983, according to Bienes, the firm had dropped its accounting clients and was working full time for Madoff's fund. Asked by PBS whether he thought it was all too easy, Bienes replied that he and his wife realised that 'God wanted us to have this and be a conduit for good causes and that's why we began to giving to charity in the amounts that we did.' He saw no indications of wrongdoing and the firm received records of Madoff's share transactions, Bienes said. (At the time of writing, July 2009, it was not clear precisely when Madoff's investment fund became a Ponzi scheme. In March 2009 Madoff confessed in court that the fraud, to the best of his recollections, began in the early 1990s. Investigators believe it commenced 'at least as early as the 1980s'. Bienes has not been charged with any wrongdoing.) [3]

During the 1970s and 1980s Bernard Madoff sat on several NASD committees, and was chairman of the District 12 committee, representing the New York area. 'Bernie's strategy was to get actively involved in all aspects of the industry,' says a member of several NASD committees at the time. 'He had a much bigger presence than the size of his firm would naturally warrant. By being visible he would boost his business. They never said no. They volunteered for everything. It was a very smart move.'[4] So was joining the Cincinnati Stock Exchange (CSE), where Peter later sat on the board. The CSE was a route to attack the NYSE. The Intermarket Trading System (ITS), which linked all the US stock exchanges, had been introduced in 1978. Madoff was desperate to get a connection. If he could plug into the ITS, he could see how NYSE brokers were trading. Which is why the NYSE blocked every attempt by NASDAQ to join the ITS. By 1981 Cincinnati was operating as an all electronic stock exchange, connected to the ITS. Madoff was in.

The NYSE grandees looked even more askance as Madoff wined and dined political contacts in Washington, DC, and at the SEC. NASDAQ traders, who were very much the second tier of Wall Street, did not usually take such a high public profile and lobby regulators and policy-makers, says Diana Henriques of the *New York Times*. But Madoff pressed the case for automation, and it worked. 'Madoff began to see and talk about its advantages to the overall system, how it would improve America's competitive advantage in the great financial marketplace that the world was becoming. And regulators heard that message and respected his opinion. He got drawn into the forums and the conferences and the public hearings where this issue got aired. And that added to his public stature, which was unusual for a guy on the trading side of the Wall Street world.'

Automated trading opened a whole new world of possibilities, Madoff realised. Most NYSE brokers charged a fee for trading stocks. This was how they made their money. Madoff did not charge a fee. He paid one. Brokerage houses that placed an order for BLMIS to execute their order received a cent or so per share on each order. This practice, known as 'payment for order flow', caused fury at the NYSE, whose veteran brokers regarded it as little more than a bribe. They regarded Madoff as a parvenu, an arriviste from NASDAQ who with grubby backhanders was overturning the correct way of doing business. Madoff could not care less what the White Shoe brigade thought. He was only interested in making money. And he was: by 1982, BLMIS reported net capital of $5.5 million.

One day in March 1984 a friend of Elaine Squillari told her that a brokerage firm on Wall Street was looking for a receptionist. Squillari was thirty-four, a single mother of two lived in Brooklyn and was working part time in a bank. Was she interested in the job, the friend asked? Yes, was the answer. Squillari dressed conservatively in a black skirt, tweed blazer, and business shoes, and took the subway into Manhattan, slightly nervous. Squillari had heard of Madoff, and knew his reputation as a smart Wall Street operator. BLMIS then occupied a floor and a half at 110 Wall Street, employing about forty people. Madoff's secretary Barbara greeted Squillari, warning her that her boss was 'very particular and very conservative and the phone is his lifeline', before she walked Squillari into Madoff's large corner office.

'He was in his mid-forties, with long, wavy, European cut hair. His shirtsleeves were rolled up and he was on the phone. He motioned for me to sit down,' Squillari recalled in *Vanity Fair*.[5] 'Through open sliding doors, I could see the trading room, all sleek and modern, in shades of grey and black.' Madoff apologised for keeping her waiting. 'My firm is built on reputation and I like the way you sounded on the phone. How someone sounds on the phone is very important to me, because it's the first impression people get.' Madoff looked her up and down. He liked what he saw. 'Appearances are very important and the way you are dressed is perfect.' After fifteen minutes Madoff offered Squillari the job. He was especially impressed that the bank she worked for had taken her back after she had had her two children. She asked if she could think about it and get back to him. Madoff replied: 'I have something to do but I will be back in ten minutes. You can give me your answer then.' Squillari's answer was yes. After she accepted, Peter Madoff came into Madoff's office. Bernard Madoff said: 'This is my brother. He's the one who will keep you busy. I'm the easy one. Peter's the one who generates all the paperwork.'

Peter was much better looking than his older brother, Squillari thought, as they shook hands. Madoff was pleasant enough in appearance, with his wavy hair and brown eyes, but his lips were thin and his chin almost pointed. Peter Madoff reminded Squillari of Lee Majors, the actor who starred in the television series *The Six Million Dollar Man*. Bernard Madoff told Squillari: 'If you are loyal and dedicated, you'll go far here. And if you are good to us, we will take care of you.' Her starting salary was $160 a week. She was soon doing more than a receptionist's duties and helped the traders calculate their activities for the day. At the end of each day she totalled their trades on an adding machine. Elaine Squillari would work for Madoff until his arrest in December 2008.

These were exciting times to start a new career on Wall Street. The furore over pay for order flow was merely a touchstone for a much deeper unease among the Wall Street establishment. Even in the early years of the digital age, it was clear that in the world of high finance the old values of family connections, the right school, country club, and parents-in-law, increasingly counted for less than quick wits and an eye for the main chance. Wall Street, like the City of London, was being forced to adjust to a painful new reality of corporate raiders and determined asset-strippers. The 1980s were the decade of excess. In London, the British upper class, who for decades had run the City like a private club, was being upstaged by brash young traders. They spoke with raucous East End or Essex accents, and made unseemly amounts of money that they blew on champagne, cocaine, and worse. The era was immortalised in the film *Wall Street*, where Michael Douglas, playing Gordon Gekko, a ruthless corporate raider, proclaims: 'Greed is good'. Gekko's character was based in part on the Wall Street financier Ivan

Boesky, who famously told an audience of business students in 1985: 'Greed is all right by the way: I want you to know that I think greed is healthy. You can be greedy and still feel good about yourself.'

Boesky certainly did. He owned a 200-acre estate in Mount Kisco, Westchester County, twenty miles from Manhattan. He lived like the great *Yekke* banking families of a century before: his home had twenty bedrooms, a squash court, two swimming pools – outdoor and indoor – and a courtyard for his vintage Rolls-Royce.[6] Like Madoff's investment fund, Boesky's business empire was built on crime, in his case insider trading. His network of hundreds of contacts fed him information. They included businessmen, financiers, and industrialists; waiters, doormen, and chauffeurs, even an official at one of New York's airports who kept him updated on the movements of private jets. Boesky paid his tipsters in cash, business information, or with visits to an upmarket Manhattan brothel. Then everything collapsed. In December 1987 Boesky was sentenced to three years in prison.

In later years Madoff liked to portray himself as a great democratiser, the maverick trader who broke the grip of the NYSE establishment. On Wall Street he was a street fighter. Neither his carefully tailored suits nor his swish offices could ever completely disguise Madoff's *shtarker* heritage. It is true that the NASDAQ and electronic trading did open up Wall Street. They allowed major brokerage houses such as Fidelity and Charles Schwab to cut their costs and place orders with NASDAQ brokers. Such companies could now offer their services to people who would never have thought of using a stockbroker. Market-makers such as BLMIS also deserved some credit as they provided liquidity, using their own cash to actually make the trades, and so bore some of the risk. But if there were benefits to the general public from Madoff's business strategy they were incidental. The NASDAQ remained a very cosy cartel.

The cartel operated on two levels. Firstly, NASDAQ traders made their profit on what was called the 'spread'. The minimum spread then was known as an eighth, meaning one-eighth of a dollar or 12.5 cents. This was the difference between the buying and the selling price. The wider the spread, the greater the profits for the traders. Peter Madoff, the technology expert at BLMIS, developed software that let the company manage the risk so successfully that Madoff could afford to pay a cent for each share order and still turn a profit. But, although the minimum spread was one-eighth, stock prices were only ever traded in even eighths, or a quarter, a half, or three-quarters of a dollar. Nothing was bought or sold in odd eighths such as three, five, or seven-eighths. Traders colluded in keeping prices pegged in even eighths, which meant in effect a set spread of a quarter. If a trader dared to trade in odd eighths, he would be sent Chinese food, with a warning note that he was making 'Chinese markets'. 'Nowadays people think of Wall Street traders and they imagine Quant theorists who graduated from MIT,' says Ed Nicoll. 'Back then the traders came from Brooklyn and Staten Island. They wore gold chains and they were street guys. They made a lot of money and they were very protective of their turf. These guys were not polite.'

Secondly, only accredited dealers could trade on NASDAQ, which made the whole system opaque. Hypothetically, if Mr Smith wanted to buy 100 shares in Microsoft at a price of $25, he contacted a broker such as Waterhouse

Securities, who then commissioned a market-maker such as BLMIS to make the trade. Even though the actual buying and selling was now automated, it was still cumbersome, involving two lots of middle-men. This gave Madoff an advantage. It opened the door to what is known as a 'lay-off trade'. It works like this: the market-maker knows that Mr Smith wants to buy Microsoft at $25 a share, so he has a guaranteed buyer at that price. Instead of buying 100 shares in Microsoft at $25 for Mr Smith he buys them for himself. If the market goes up he makes a tidy profit of which Mr Smith sees nothing. If the market goes down, he can still sell at $25 to Mr Smith, because he has a guaranteed bid at $25. Mr Smith's bid protects Madoff's speculation. 'That is a nice deal and it was very powerful,' says Nicoll.

The deal always came first with Madoff, but it wasn't everything. He also had a human side, and could show great kindness. William Nasi worked for Madoff from 1968 to 1974, when the firm was based at 39 Broadway, as a messenger, delivering papers and security certificates. He left to study at university. In 1986 Nasi was hit in the face in a scuffle and he lost the sight in one eye, and by 1989 he was declared legally blind. Unsure of where to turn he went to visit the Madoffs, whom he had not seen for fifteen years. His old employers were very happy to see him, especially Peter Madoff who told him: 'We'll make you a job that even with an inability to read you will be able to do. Go down the hall to see Bernie and say hello.'[7]

Nasi was overjoyed. He stayed at the firm for nineteen years, until December 2008 when Bernard Madoff was arrested. He was well treated and Madoff often walked over to ask if everything was all right. 'It was the most work-friendly environment, a family environment.' If Nasi had a problem he would go straight to Madoff or Ruth for help. Nasi received a bonus of about $2,500 at Christmas and double that at Easter. Before he died in July 1972 Ralph Madoff, Bernard's father, would sometimes travel into Manhattan with Nasi. One day Ralph gave him advice from the heart: 'Never, ever, invest on Wall Street. It is run by crooks and SOBs [sons of bitches]. I don't trust them. Put your own money in a savings bank and you control it yourself. A dollar is worth a dollar, don't let greed get into your psyche.'

Behind the scenes the NYSE was working hard to bring down Madoff. On 2 October 1990, the NASD Payment For Order Flow Committee (PFOF) commenced its first meeting at the NASD's New York offices. The sustained pressure from the NYSE and its continuing protests that payment for order flow was unethical had finally forced a response. The committee was charged with recommending whether it should be allowed to continue. For Madoff the stakes could not be higher. If payment for order flow was banned his trading arm would be crippled. If he won, whole new worlds of business opportunity would beckon. Madoff knew that his response must be measured and carefully judged if the custom was to continue.

The PFOF committee was chaired by David Ruder, a member of the board of governors of the NASD and then a law professor at North Western University in Chicago. Ruder served as SEC chairman from 1987 to 1989. The committee had seven members, including senior employees of Merrill Lynch, Morgan Stanley, Charles Schwab, and the chairman of NASDAQ: Bernard Madoff. From the outside, and with hindsight, there seemed to be a massive conflict of interest. Perhaps that was inevitable as the NASD was charged with both operating and regulating the broker–dealer market. Ruder admits the situation was not ideal. 'Madoff sat on the committee but it was not his committee. Of course I felt uneasy about it. That's why I was particularly interested in the kind of explanation he gave.'[8]

Madoff had long argued that payment for order flow was essentially the same as using a team of salesmen to drum up business. BLMIS had no salesmen, and so used outside brokers to bring in business, paying them a commission. What was the difference? The strongest argument in Madoff's favour was that payment for order flow was just one of numerous inducements that brokers used to bring in business. The only difference was that it was paid in cash, instead of a barter for mutual services and back-scratching. Professor Ruder recalls: 'Madoff was charming, very persuasive and knowledgeable. He was treated by everybody on the committee as a trusted individual. He was quite laid back, a good contributor and a good questioner. He did not dominate the committee.'

Madoff had a point about other inducements. The committee's investigation into the grey area of mutual benefits discovered a host of equally questionable practices. 'We found that there were many different inducements for direction of order flow,' says Professor Ruder. As well as payment for cash flow, there was also swapping of order flow. NASDAQ members were both brokers and dealers, who both made a market (buying and selling) and executed the actual trades. So, for example, Firm A makes a market in a certain type of shares, and sends trades to Firm B for execution. Firm B makes a market in another type of shares, and in response sends trades to Firm A for execution. The crucial point was to keep the order flow flowing. The committee issued its forty-nine-page report in July 1991. 'Inducements for Order Flow' concluded that: 'cash payments for order flow are not sufficiently different from other inducements for order flow to justify separate regulation.'[9] Professor Ruder recalls: 'I came to the conclusion that virtually no execution transaction took place in the stock market unless there was an inducement for order flow. My conclusion was that if you cannot have any of these inducements the whole market will collapse. You would be in a regulatory morass that would be difficult to regulate.'

The committee's decision caused fury at the NYSE but was a stunning victory for Madoff. Madoff stepped up his attack on the NYSE, trading ever growing numbers of stocks through the 'third market', meaning those stocks that were listed on the NYSE, but which were traded outside the exchange itself. By 1992 BLMIS was trading with 350 NYSE members and executing 9 per cent of the daily trading volume of NYSE-listed stocks, in large part because of payment for order flow. BLMIS's forty traders were processing up to 25,000 trades a day, according to *Traders* magazine.[10] This was unprecedented. The NYSE was furious and continued pressing for payment for order flow to be banned. 'Who is Bernie Madoff and why is he driving the Wall Street establishment crazy?' asked David A. Vise in the *Washington Post* in 1993.[11] The NYSE argued that the practice was not in the customer's best interest as it prevented an auction on the floor of the exchange. It was compared to kick-backs in defence procurement. Madoff dismissed their claims: 'People would like to apply pejorative-type terms. I think people that use that kind of terminology are unhappy that they are losing business,' he said.[12]

Under pressure from the NYSE Congress called hearings on payment for order flow. Madoff testified and won again. The SEC finally legitimised the practice in 1995, as long as brokers disclosed to their customers that they received payments for orders. With hindsight, it seems likely that Madoff's ordeal by committees, especially testifying before Congress, gave him an imprimatur of legitimacy. He had been mauled by America's best, come out fighting and won. 'It may be that our report was partially influential in saying that he was OK,' says Professor Ruder. 'The whole system of payment for order flow was investigated, the report came out, Congress held hearings, the SEC looked into it. Madoff was under tremendous pressure and scrutiny. He handled it very well. Payment for order flow was not banned, and some of the trust that people had in him may have come from this.'

All this can only have reassured his investors and helped keep the money flowing into Madoff's Ponzi scheme. The more interesting question was why, after these important victories, he bothered with the fraud? Running a Ponzi scheme is complicated and immensely stressful. It demands a steady flow of new investors, immense organisation, a team of co-conspirators and great secrecy. It is a crime committed not in a moment of passion or anger, but steadily for months, years, and probably, in Madoff's case, decades. The whole edifice, no matter how carefully constructed, can crash at any moment. Madoff owned an extremely successful legal trading business, and was helping reshape the way Wall Street operated. He was wealthy and respected, beating the titans of the NYSE at their own game. But somehow, for the boy from Laurelton, it was not enough. It may have been the thrill of the crime, simple greed for more riches, the revenge of the *shtarkers* against the *Yekkes*, or most likely a mix of all these and more. After his arrest Madoff claimed that he had long wanted to shut down the Ponzi scheme but could not. Speaking in court in New York in March 2009, Madoff said: 'As I engaged in my fraud, I knew what I was doing was wrong, indeed criminal. When I began the Ponzi I believed it would end shortly and I would be able to extricate myself and my clients from the scheme. However, this proved difficult and ultimately impossible and as the years went by I realised that my arrest and this day would inevitably come.'

In the meantime, his Ponzi scheme kept growing and growing. And after his victories at the SEC and in Congress, Bernard Madoff and his firm had a virtual seal of approval from the US government.

6

When Bernie met Ezra

'It is not easy to stay on the sidelines when others are busy getting rich.'

Ezra Merkin, writing in *Security Analysis*, published in September 2008.[1]

Number 740 Park Avenue is what Americans call a 'storied' building, one with a rich history and legendary residents. On the corner of East Seventy-first Street, two blocks from Central Park, 740 Park is one of the most exclusive apartment buildings in the world. It was built in 1930 by James T. Lee, the grandfather of Jacqueline Kennedy Onassis, as an oasis of high living for America's old-money WASP dynasties, such as the Vanderbilts, Rockefellers, and Chryslers. A looming, austere granite façade belies an interior of extraordinary luxury, of marble bathrooms, high ceilings, and cavernous rooms. It is rare for properties at 740 Park to go on sale, but one was put on the market in June 2009. The lower floor was composed of enormous living and dining rooms, a library, kitchen, and breakfast room. The upper level had four bedrooms with en-suite marble bathrooms, and staff bedrooms, and bathrooms. Asking price: $26 million. A thirty-room duplex was reportedly on the market for almost three times as much, at $75 million.

Nowadays residents are expected to have at least $100 million in liquid assets, and the maintenance charge runs at an average of $10,000 – a month. But money alone is not enough to secure entrance. There are hordes of multi-millionaires and billionaires who would love to live at 740 Park but as in many expensive Manhattan blocks, would-be residents are interviewed by a board, to discover their 'suitability'. Suitability, in this part of the Upper East Side, means discretion, taste and, most of all, the right lineage. The nouveaux riches, and show business stars especially need not apply: Barbara Streisand, Joan Crawford, and Neil Sedaka were all reportedly turned down. In its early years 740 Park was almost exclusively WASP. Eventually the board surrendered to the inevitable and the Jewish power-brokers of Manhattan began to move in. By the 1990s 740 Park had numerous Jewish residents, including Ronald Perelman, a billionaire financier, who by 1989 was the richest man in America.

Ezra Merkin's background was the very epitome of Jewish respectability. He was a scion of one of the most respected Jewish dynasties of the Upper East Side, an *echte Yekke*. Ezra Merkin was accepted in his bid for a duplex apartment, and paid around $10 million for it in 1994. By then even the most exclusive sections of the Upper East Side were not immune to political correctness. Merkin is an Orthodox Jew and wears a skullcap. His head-covering seems to have speeded his purchase. When Merkin, who looks decidedly learned, appeared at his building admission interview, several board members thought he was a Rabbi. The story goes that the usually ferocious board was so afraid of offending him that they barely asked him any questions before accepting his application and nodding him through.

Ezra Merkin might have been able to buy his apartment without his connection to Bernie Madoff, but Madoff certainly helped him on the way. Merkin's funds, Gabriel, Ascot, and Ariel, were three of Madoff's most important feeder funds, channelling more than $2 billion to Madoff's Ponzi scheme. The funds made both Merkin and Madoff immensely wealthy. But Ezra Merkin provided Madoff with much more than money. Rich, respected, well connected, Merkin helped open doors to people and places to which Madoff would otherwise have been unlikely to enjoy access. Merkin was one of Madoff's entrées into the tight-knit network of Jewish educational, religious, and philanthropic institutions through which flow hundreds of millions of dollars. Madoff was soon catapulted to a whole new level. However, a person familiar with the situation argues that it is 'overstating the case' to say that Ezra Merkin used his connections to introduce new investors to Madoff. 'Ezra Merkin set up meetings for a number of investors in Ascot to meet Madoff and conduct their own due diligence on his operations. There were plenty of ways for people to meet with Madoff, it did not have to be through Ezra Merkin.'[2]

Ezra Merkin had a lot to live up to. Hermann Merkin, his father, was a *Yekke* among *Yekkes*: stern, devout, rigorous in his moral scruples and often distant. Born in 1907, Merkin fled Germany and arrived in New York in 1940. His native tongue, recent arrival from Nazi Germany, and sharp mind made him of great interest to the US intelligence services, where he served during the war. After 1945 Merkin started Merkin and Company, an investment firm. He was extremely successful. As a devout Jew, Hermann Merkin understood that wealth brings responsibilities, specifically the duty of *Tsedakah*.

Tsedakah is the Hebrew word for charity, but means more than merely writing a cheque every now and then for a good cause. *Tsedakah* means giving as part of everyday life, of a philanthropy that is woven into the very fabric of being, and which is a reason why wealth is earned. Presently American Jews, who comprise 2 per cent of the population, donate billions of dollars to charitable organisations every year. Only 20 per cent goes to specifically Jewish causes. 'American Jewry is the single most advanced Jewish community, with an organisation for everything. That is dependent on a high level of Jewish philanthropy,' says Steven Bayme, Director of the Contemporary Jewish Life department at the American Jewish Committee in New York. 'Giving is the very core of Jewish identity. It is not something casual. One gives until it hurts. Philanthropy is enormously significant, both institutionally and culturally.'[3]

Hermann Merkin supported two of the most important Jewish institutions in New York: the Fifth Avenue Synagogue and Yeshiva University. The Merkin family name was threaded into the history of both places. Hermann Merkin was one of the founders of the Fifth Avenue Synagogue in 1958. He served as president until 1976, continuing as chairman afterwards. The Fifth Avenue Synagogue was the synagogue of choice for many *machers* (community leaders). Its congregants include Elie Wiesel and Mort Zuckerman, the property magnate and publisher of the *New York Daily*

News, both of whom lost substantial sums with Madoff. Hermann Merkin also sat on the board of Yeshiva University and served as its vice-chairman, endowing the Leib Merkin chair in Talmudic studies and Jewish philosophy. The chair was named after his father. Yeshiva University, which also invested with Madoff, is the intellectual centre of the Modern Orthodox movement, meaning Jews who are devout but who engage in the modern world, in contrast to the ultra-Orthodox, who dress in the clothes of seventeenth-century Poland and spend their days cloistered in study. The Modern Orthodox are comparatively small in number, but are a powerful and influential segment of American Jewry.

Hermann Merkin took *Tsedakah* more seriously than most. He also gave money to tiny *yeshivas* – Jewish religious colleges – to hospitals, and cultural institutions. He endowed Merkin Concert Hall, on the Upper West Side, where the more artistic and liberal-minded middle-class Jews tended to live. There was money for a myriad of good causes, but a stinting attitude towards his own family, says the writer Daphne Merkin, sister of Ezra. 'Philanthropy was a way of cleansing the money, and it also became a form of power. There was an enormous emphasis on giving away the money in a hundred different ways. There was a withholding style in my family, that the money must go here, there, everywhere, everywhere except to us. It was all I heard about, to a degree that I felt charity should begin at home.' This sense of growing up among withheld riches created a 'curious sense of deprivation and anger all its own', says Daphne Merkin, wryly, 'with the added problem that the plight of the unprivileged rich is innately unsympathetic'.[4]

In the *Yekke* fashion, Hermann Merkin was strict and

often aloof with his children. There were few hugs or open displays of affection. Like every boy, Ezra sought his father's praise and acclaim. It was rarely given, to him or to any of his children. Instead Ezra found that a rich, successful father, prominent in public life, brings complex pressures and demands: to be equally successful, public, and even to perform. On Friday evenings at Shabbat dinners Ezra would expound on that week's portion of the Torah, the five books of Moses, in front of the distinguished guests who could include a visiting Israeli leader or New York Jewish power-brokers. The scene is echoed in Daphne Merkin's semi-autobiographical novel, *Enchantment*: 'Benjamin slides his chair back on the carpet and stands up. He is good at his appointed task; he pulls on his lower lip and adjusts his glasses like a professor, ostentatiously studious. Every Friday night Benjamin is called upon to trot out his erudition with an entertaining tidbit from the weekly portion of Torah that will be read in *shul* [synagogue] the next day. All the *parshas* run together in my mind, narratives involving flocks and shepherds, dispersals and betrayals, redemptions and abandonments. There are too many Big Themes, but Benjamin is able not only to remember which theme is exemplified in each portion but also to make it sound more diverting than it really is.

'"There is a question," my brother says in his best pedantic singsong, "in this week's parsha about the distribution ..."

'"*Der Junge hat einen guten kopf*," Mr Fischer says, nodding his head approvingly. (The young one has a good head).'[5]

The Merkins lived on prestigious Park Avenue, in a duplex. There was a chauffeur, a housekeeper, a cook and a laundress. But despite the live-in staff the Merkin children had austere childhoods. Daphne and her two sisters slept in one room, Ezra and his two brothers in another. Like her brother, Daphne went to the elite Ramaz day school. Many children at Ramaz came from wealthy families. Some were dubbed Jewish-American Princesses, or JAPs, a semi-derogatory term that implied being spoiled and over-indulged. Daphne Merkin and her two sisters were not JAPs. 'Even if I had wanted to be a JAP I could not have been,' she recalls ruefully. 'It was not my lifelong wish, but I was going to an American Jewish day school with indulged kids and I was always arguing with my mother about clothes. It was a very strange attitude, sort of "not for you, but for others".'

Money had brought the Merkins status in the community, but Hermann Merkin refused to discuss his own financial affairs with his family. 'Money was a secret,' says Daphne Merkin. 'My father was anyway a fairly unapproachable person. He was very straight, very German. He was not a group person, or a people person. If I asked him about money, he would ask me back why I was interested. The attitude to money was withholding, I would say.' Even summer fruits like cherries were a luxury, parcelled out in scanty handfuls. 'We used to argue about seconds, at the dinner table.' *Enchantment* includes an evocative description of a family barbecue. Barbecues are a great American institution: a cornucopia of freshly grilled beef, chicken, and hamburgers, piles of salads, washed down with beer or cocktails, a symbol of summer luxury and outdoor living. The barbecue portrayed in *Enchantment* is a meagre affair, with frozen and refrozen meats that taste of nothing, manufactured sauces, and sickly sodas. *Yekkes* and barbecues did not mix.

Ezra Merkin met Madoff either in the very late 1980s or 1990. 'I knew of his reputation on Wall Street. He was an acquaintance of my father's,' Merkin testified in January 2009.[6] 'My father had a very favourable opinion of him and at some point or other I found myself in his office discussing, broadly speaking, his activities in market-making and money management.' (Another well-informed source disputes this, saying that Madoff and Hermann Merkin were not friends, although they may have known each other. The source says that Madoff's name never came up in Hermann Merkin's office.) Michael Steinhardt, a retired hedge fund manager who moves in the same Jewish social and philanthropic circles as Merkin, says: 'Madoff came to Merkin in the best possible way, as a familial friend with a terrific reputation as someone who did 10 or 12 per cent of the business on the NYSE, one of the people who started the options business. He came with a wonderful imprimatur. So to expect Ezra to have done an amount of due diligence that no-one did is totally unreasonable.'[7]

Madoff and Merkin were divided by more than their fifteen-year age difference. Madoff grew up in Laurelton, Long Island, Merkin on Park Avenue, the very epicentre of the Upper East Side. Madoff went to Far Rockaway High School, spent a year at Alabama University and eventually graduated from Hofstra on Long Island. He dropped out of Brooklyn Law School after a year. Merkin went to Ramaz, and studied at two *yeshivas*, religious seminaries, in Israel. He majored in English and History at Columbia University.

Merkin then went to Harvard Law School. He graduated in 1979 and started his first job at an international law firm, where he specialised in corporate law, and bankruptcy cases.

As a child Merkin had excelled at parsing points of Jewish law at the family's Shabbat dinner table, under his father's stern but approving eye. But Merkin decided against a career in law and found a job as an analyst at an investment management firm in New York. One day in the early 1980s Merkin was sent to the Federal Court in Brooklyn to gather information about a takeover deal. There he met another financial analyst, called Victor Teicher, a colourful character with a rich vocabulary. Teicher would play an important role in Merkin's life over the following years.

Many sons want to follow in their father's footsteps, and Hermann Merkin was a powerful name on Wall Street. But in some ways finance was a curious choice for Ezra Merkin. Although he had graduated from Harvard Law School he did not have a certified Chartered Financial Analyst (CFA) qualification, the international professional designation. Nor did he have a Master of Business Administration (MBA), which is a virtual prerequisite for any Wall Street career. What he did have, however, was a brilliant sales *spiel*, the ability to persuade investors to put their money in the funds for which he was touting for business. Merkin exuded confidence, bolstered by his scholarly appearance, and his large frame. He could debate the finer points of Talmudic law and commentary with scholars and Rabbis, talk finance with Wall Street's finest, or politics and current affairs with university professors. Merkin is 'a complicated, highly intelligent and highly articulate person', says Michael Steinhardt. Despite his lineage and erudition, Merkin could even laugh at himself, and his engaging smile only helped persuade more investors to trust him with their money.[8]

Merkin also had Victor Teicher, who set up his own company that was managing various investment funds. The two men had stayed in contact. Teicher had become an expert in merger arbitrage, betting on one company taking over another, which brought his investors earnings as high as 25 per cent a year. Teicher was interested in Merkin's connections. Merkin was interested in Teicher's performance and introduced him to investors. By the late 1980s Merkin was still working as an analyst, at Gotham Capital, but he was looking for something larger, where he could properly showcase his sales talents. Merkin started two funds, Gabriel Capital, and the Ariel Fund. Merkin opened his office at 787 Seventh Avenue, in mid-town Manhattan, the heart of the financial district, where Victor Teicher had his offices. Merkin set up his own office on Teicher's premises.

Merkin had no employees, and Teicher's analysts and traders handled all aspects of Gabriel and Ariel's investment activity, according to the state of New York's claim against Merkin. (One of several lawsuits brought against Merkin by July 2009.)[9] Teicher was interested in more than money: when one young graduate applied for a job as an analyst Teicher took him by taxi to the Natural History Museum to demonstrate his knowledge of pre-Roman artifacts. But Teicher proved to be a problematic associate for Merkin. In 1986 he was investigated for insider trading in a high-profile case known as the 'Yuppie Five', as all of those involved were successful professionals under the age of thirty. He was indicted two years later. The case came to court and in 1992 Teicher was found guilty and sentenced to eighteen months in prison for securities fraud. He started his sentence in January 1994 and served ten months in a federal prison in New Jersey, and three months in a halfway house in New York City. While Teicher was in prison he was allowed to make unlimited fifteen-minute telephone calls to his colleagues. His firm continued to manage several funds that Merkin had given Teicher to look after, none of which had any monies invested with Madoff.

In 1992, Merkin set up Ascot, the state of New York's lawsuit says, for the 'sole but undisclosed purpose of serving as a conduit to Madoff'. From the late 1980s to 2008 Merkin's three funds, Gabriel, Ariel, and Ascot, channelled approximately $2.4 billion of investors' monies into Madoff's Ponzi scheme, while Merkin collected more than $470 million in management and incentive fees.[10] The New York lawsuit alleges that from 1988 Merkin occupied himself 'primarily with raising money for the funds using his extensive social and professional network', while relying on outside managers to run the investment activity, primarily, in the fund's early years, Victor Teicher. Merkin 'did little work for Ascot other than routine book-keeping and engaging in occasional telephone conversations with Madoff'. It accuses him of 'deceit, recklessness and breaches of fiduciary duty'.

Andy Levander, Ezra Merkin's lawyer, rejected the New York State lawsuit as 'hasty and ill-conceived' and 'without merit'. Ezra Merkin, Gabriel Capital and the funds they represent had fully cooperated with the investigation, providing hundreds of thousands of documents, he stated. 'Contrary to the Attorney General's allegation, investors in the Ascot Funds were well aware that the money was being invested with Madoff. Furthermore, investors in all of the

Funds expressly authorized Mr Merkin to allocate assets to third party managers such as Madoff, without giving them notice or obtaining their consent. Mr Merkin performed extensive due diligence on Madoff and his trading strategy, and in addition arranged meetings with Madoff for many investors to perform their own due diligence. Unfortunately, Mr Merkin's due diligence, just like the detailed investigations performed by countless others, including regulators, was thwarted by the intricate, fraudulent scheme perpetrated by Madoff.'[11]

Madoff claimed that he had invented a new way of trading, which brought his investment fund steady returns year after year, or so he claimed. Madoff's 'split-strike conversion' strategy was essentially a complex system of hedging bets. The strategy worked, Madoff claimed, by buying blue chip stocks in Standard & Poor's Top 100 Index. Madoff would buy a 'put' option to protect against the price declining, and simultaneously sell a 'call' option to fund the purchase of the put option. A put option is a contract between two brokers. One bets that the price will fall, the other that it will rise. A call option is the opposite of a put option and gives the buyer the right to buy shares at a specific price within a defined time period, irrespective of their market price. Madoff claimed the strategy worked regardless of market conditions, by putting a 'collar' on the price movements, so limiting losses. It did not, but that was irrelevant as his investment fund was a fraud.

Over the years Madoff claimed that his strategy evolved, the state of New York lawsuit records: 'He soon began to claim that he was using a larger "basket" of stocks selected from the [Standard & Poor] Index, combined with put and call options on the Index itself rather than on individual stocks. The positions were supposedly held for a short time lasting from a few days to no longer than about two months, then liquidated. Madoff claimed to execute the "split-strike conversion strategy" six to eight times a year. At some point Madoff purportedly adopted the practice of exiting the market at the very end of each quarter and putting all the funds in US Treasury Bills. For this reason, Madoff's quarterly statements to investors and the end of year audits of investor holdings would list only Treasuries.'[12]

This was unusual, to say the least. Victor Teicher warned Merkin that something was not right about Madoff's operation. 'He [Merkin] told me perhaps sometime in 1992 or 1993 that he was considering investing with Bernie Madoff. And he described Madoff in terms of what he was doing and the consistency of the returns and I just felt that was just not possible,' Teicher testified in January 2009, as a witness in New York University's lawsuit against Ezra Merkin, a separate complaint to that brought by the state of New York. Asked why he had these doubts, Teicher replied he had never seen such steady, consistent returns. 'It's possible to do 50 per cent a year. In some years you do more and in some years you do less. But just the nature of the business, you can't year in, year out, have such low volatility in the returns.'[13] Regarding the New York University (NYU) lawsuit, which claims that the university had no knowledge that its assets in Merkin's Gabriel and Ariel funds were being managed by Madoff, Levander said that Merkin had 'always acted in good faith and did not deceive NYU or any other investors'.[14]

Teicher was also concerned that Madoff self-cleared his accounts. Self-clearing means that the whole process of buying securities is handled by one firm, from initiating the sale, to purchase, to holding the securities. Self-clearing is legal, and not uncommon in trading. But one of the cardinal rules of *investing*, which all of Madoff's investors either chose to ignore or did not know enough to ask about, is that the investment manager should not hold the stocks and shares in which he is trading for the client. The actual securities should be held in a third party account (meaning, one owned neither by the investor nor the money manager) to give added protection. Or as Ed Nicoll says: 'It is a fundamental rule that you never give your money to the person managing your money. You separate out the custody function from the advisory function.' In Madoff's Ponzi scheme, of course, they were the same.

Even Ezra Merkin's best friends would not claim that he was a details man, poring over the micro-questions. He was more of a 'grand sweep of history', big picture type of person, bringing clients, friends and business contacts into his orbit and dazzling them so much that they forgot to ask those troubling, niggling questions. Merkin also tended to exaggerate, according to Victor Teicher. So much so that if Merkin said his wife was ill in hospital 'it might not necessarily be the case', Teicher testified in January 2009, based on his personal experience.[15]

Merkin's personal big picture was to make himself a connoisseur of art and good living. There was no fighting over seconds at Ezra Merkin's dinner table. Over the next few years, as Merkin's business grew, and his reputation spread, his apartment at 740 Park Avenue became a fixture on the Upper East Side social scene. He engaged a personal art adviser, Ben Heller, to teach him and his wife Lauren about art and culture. Under Heller's tutelage Merkin built up one of the world's largest private collection of paintings by Mark Rothko, worth an estimated $150 million. The dozen canvases include two nine-by-fifteen-foot studies for murals Rothko painted at the Four Seasons restaurant in New York, and another study for a mural at Harvard University. Heller advised Merkin and his wife how to redecorate their home at 740 Park to highlight the Rothkos with subdued lighting and rugs. Heller acted for the Merkins at auction. In November 2008 he purchased a Rothko for $7.9 million at Sotheby's in New York, almost double the $4.5 million estimate. 'Many of them are large and it achieves exactly what Rothko wanted, which was to defeat the wall,' says David Anfam, an authority on the painter. 'The paintings at the Merkins' make the walls dissolve. They become the environment.'[16]

All the while Merkin and Madoff grew closer. There was a Ying and Yang appeal, a certain chemistry where rough and ready Queens met the smooth privilege of the Upper East Side. The two men were very different but worked together well. And everyone, it seemed, was making plenty of money. Perhaps Madoff was even a kind of benignly patriarchal figure to Erza Merkin, speculates Daphne Merkin, a warm and cordial mentor, a counterpoint to the austere and distant Hermann Merkin. 'I wonder if that was some of the allure of Madoff in general, and for my brother in particular, that he was so much more personal and amiable.' Ezra Merkin was less amiable to those who could not help his business interests, or he considered beneath him, recalls Madoff's secretary Elaine Squillari. 'I never once saw Merkin smile or say hello; when he visited Bernie, he wouldn't even look my way.'[17]

As for Madoff, he soon realised that the Modern Orthodox *Yekkes* too lived in a *shtetl*, in the heart of Manhattan. Its central points were Yeshiva University, the Fifth Avenue Synagogue, the Ramaz school, while its extensive network of charities spread over the city, and across America. Once you were in, you were accepted and trusted. The *Yekkes' shtetl* was awash with money and Madoff began to gather it in.

7
Feeding frenzy

*'They were on the ski slopes; they were on the beaches.
They had great fun – dinners out at very expensive
places.'*

Sherry Shameer Cohen, on her former boss Walter Noel, of
Fairfield Greenwich Group, which ran a Madoff feeder fund,
and his family.[1]

Greenwich, Connecticut, is one of the oldest, prettiest,
and wealthiest cities in America. It was first settled in the
seventeenth century by Puritan refugees from Britain. Greenwich has its own symphony orchestra, a choral society, a
museum, long sandy beaches, a nature reserve, and excellent
private schools. About 60,000 people live in Greenwich,
about 90 per cent of whom are white. Greenwich's rich
cultural life and heritage make it popular with artists,
writers, and actors. Mel Gibson bought a twenty-eight-room
Elizabethan-style mansion, set in more than seventy acres of
manicured grounds. Greenwich is safe, orderly, and only
forty minutes by train from Grand Central Station in central
Manhattan. It is a popular commuter town for financiers

and bankers. Awash with money, inhabited by the status conscious, Greenwich was prime territory indeed for Madoff.

But how to get an entrée into Greenwich society? Madoff was not part of Ezra Merkin's world, but he was at least a native New Yorker. He understood the tribal codes of the Upper East Side and its finely calibrated judgments. He had ironed out some of his Queens accent, he dressed elegantly, and he was a player on Wall Street. In a city that worshipped money and success, that was enough to open many doors. And with Ezra Merkin at his side he was now plugged into the Fifth Avenue Synagogue network of Modern Orthodoxy. Greenwich, however, was another matter. Greenwich was WASP heaven. Its residents were a tribe, one that socialised, worked together, and inter-married. They socialised at the Round Hill Country Club, whose former presidents include Prescott Bush, the father and grandfather of two former presidents of the United States. They played golf at the Shinnecock Hills Golf Club, in nearby Southampton on Long Island, one of the best courses in America. They swam at the super-exclusive Bathing Corporation on Southampton Beach, part of the famed Hamptons resort. Their comings and goings, club memberships, and current addresses were recorded in the arcane 'Blue Book of the Hamptons', a finely delineated social chronicle of Hamptons' society whose entries are by invitation only. It was unlikely, even at the height of his riches and mystique, that Madoff would be invited to be listed.

Madoff's entrée to Greenwich was a man called Walter Noel. Like Ezra Merkin, Noel would have his life turned inside out by Madoff, and like Merkin, he would become extremely rich along the way. Noel ticked all the right boxes, both for Madoff himself and the extensive international network of clients he built up for him over eighteen years. Walter Noel was a charming, suave, international private banker from Nashville with the charisma of Rhett Butler in *Gone With the Wind*. He had a master's degrees in economics and had graduated from Harvard Law School. Noel had worked for Chemical Bank in Africa, Brazil, and Switzerland, dealing with private clients who were often extremely rich. He was tall and good-looking, sociable, and dressed well. His wife Monica was half Swiss, half Brazilian. Monica was part of the Haegler family, usually described as 'prominent' by those who take note of these things, with branches in Zurich and Rio de Janeiro. They were part of international society, whose comings, goings and parties were chronicled in glossy, self-worshipping magazines. In many ways Noel was a slimmer WASP version of Ezra Merkin.

Noel was very, very, presentable, says Sherry Shameer Cohen, who worked for him from 1987 to 1998. 'He's tall, very distinguished looking. And he has a nice voice for the most part. And he looked like a real southern gentleman. Not too much of a drawl. In fact, virtually no drawl at that point.'[2] The Noels seemed blessed. They lived well, but not flashily on Round Hill Road in Greenwich, a pleasant area of the historic town. They had five beautiful daughters, all slim, athletic, multi-lingual, and intelligent. Like the Merkin children, the young Noel daughters were also expected to sit at the table with adults for dinner and, on occasion, perform. Monica Noel, unlike the Merkin parents, placed more emphasis on appearance than intellectual fireworks. 'Mom would say to us, "Join in but think of something interesting to say, keep your posture straight – but first go upstairs and brush your hair again"',' one daughter recalled.[3]

The Noels holidayed in Brazil in the summer, and skied in Switzerland in the winter.[4] Monica Noel worked, and ran her eponymous children's clothing brand. But like Ezra Merkin, and so many of those who became involved with Madoff, the Noels wanted much more. The Noels' critics say they were intensely socially ambitious, hungry for status and the wealth that would allow them to move in the circles they sought. The family's defenders say there is nothing wrong with ambition. 'Walter Noel is an educated, successful man,' says a source close to him. 'He has a top tier resumé and has done well for himself. It is all tainted now because of Madoff's fraud, but that is not limited to Walter Noel. It has been visited on thousands of people, in the markets, on fund managers, on Madoff's own sons, his business and his family.'[5]

Noel's main line of business was marketing investment vehicles such as hedge funds, and he also managed a small amount of money for personal clients. It seems that Noel, like Ezra Merkin, was more skilled at salesmanship than the intricacies of investment strategies. Shameer Cohen told PBS that Noel's main research consisted of picking stocks each week recommended by Value Line, an investment research company. The source close to Noel denies this. Noel did review Value Line's recommendations, as do many investors, but was not picking solely on that basis. Noel would discuss investments with clients, and included their ratings on Value Line, as well as other factors. Noel made a good living, using his network of clients and contacts that he had built up overseas. In 1987 the stock market crashed. Some of the best investors on Wall Street were badly burned. Salvation came in the form of a lawyer and former trader called Jeffrey Tucker. Noel and Tucker complemented each other. Tucker had worked for the SEC's enforcement division for eight years, which gave him a rock-solid pedigree. Tucker was not interested in Greenwich society. He was a New Yorker and passionate about thoroughbred horses. But like all financiers, he was definitely interested in making much more money.

At the end of the 1980s Walter Noel met Madoff through Jeffrey Tucker's father-in-law. 'Madoff is not somebody that would have crossed paths with the Noels other than through a third party, such as Jeff Tucker,' says Shameer Cohen. At that time Noel and Tucker were looking for an investment vehicle related to options trading. Tucker's father-in-law was a client of Madoff, and promised to introduce both men to him. Soon after, Noel and Tucker met Madoff in his New York office. Madoff talked them through his investment strategies and showed them around. Noel and Tucker liked what they saw and heard. 'Madoff had a tremendous reputation, he was a giant, a pioneer of NASDAQ and electronic trading,' says the source close to Noel. 'He thought he had an edge, because of his electronic trading platform and he was achieving steady but not spectacular returns, all of which gave him credibility. He honoured his redemptions and he was under regulatory oversight.'

Noel and Tucker decided to make a test investment in 1989 of about $1 million. It was successful and soon after they created Fairfield Sentry, a new fund mainly for international investors, followed by Greenwich Sentry, mainly for domestic investors. The funds would grow into a complicated international network known as the Fairfield Greenwich Group. The Madoff connection and their steady annual payments

made the funds phenomenally successful at attracting investors. Shameer Cohen recalls: 'People were getting very excited
about that, because they were convinced they were going to
continue to have these wonderful returns.'

Walter Noel and Ezra Merkin were two sides of the same
coin, says one Wall Street investment banker. 'There is a
culture of salesmanship on Wall Street and they were both
salesmen. Merkin hangs out in the Fifth Avenue Synagogue,
Noel hangs out in country clubs. Their clients were all people
seeking something that was too good to be true.'[6] But while
bankers often look down on salesmen like Noel and Merkin,
they are as much part of Wall Street as the financiers inventing
new products to draw in investors' money, for the salesmen
bring in the clients that the financiers need to make money.
'Walter Noel did not claim to invent or implement a new
future options trading method or the "split-strike" strategy.
Not everyone is creating new algorithms, or electronic
systems or performing Quant analyses,' says the source close
to him. 'That was Madoff's business, not Noel's. Noel did
not claim he was Warren Buffet. He had business relationships and he was successful at making those managers
available to his funds.'

Noel was certainly a superb salesman. The Fairfield Group
would ultimately prove to be Madoff's most valuable feeder
fund of all, bringing in substantial institutional investors
from Europe and across the globe. By late 2008 the Fairfield
Group had $14.1 billion of assets under management, $6.9
billion of which was invested with Bernard Madoff.

There was one thing that scared Bernard Madoff more than
anything else: the Securities and Exchange Commission

(SEC), the federal body charged with protecting investors and maintaining orderly and fair markets. The SEC had the power to close down his business and wreck his life. Madoff was not a licensed investment adviser. He did not register as one until 2006. If anyone asked, he replied that he did not need to be registered as he was only charging commissions on his trades, not taking a fee or percentage of profits. Madoff knew at first hand about the SEC and how much trouble it could cause. Back in the 1960s the SEC had brought a lawsuit against Gibraltar Securities, the company registered in his mother's name, which it later dropped. If the SEC began an investigation into his investment business he had no defence. If it discovered he was running a Ponzi scheme he would go to prison.

In early 1992 the SEC launched an investigation into Frank Avellino and Michael Bienes for running an unlicensed mutual fund and selling unregistered securities, as their Madoff investment notes were deemed to be securities. Avellino and Bienes had closed down their accounting firm and moved to Fort Lauderdale, Florida, to focus on Madoff's investment fund. They were making so much money, both for Madoff and themselves, that they even had their own feeder fund. Telfran Ltd, run by two other accountants, one in New York and one in Florida, bought $89 million worth of Avellino and Bienes' investment notes. By 1992 Avellino and Bienes had invested about $454 million dollars with Madoff's investment fund for 3,200 clients. Madoff was a money machine and the funds just kept pouring in. It was, says Bienes, 'easy-peasy'. Bienes says that he saw the transaction sheets of stock being bought and sold, and the mechanics of the trading. But he admits that he never asked Madoff what his investment strategy was and how he could guarantee such high returns. 'Never. Why would I ask him? I wouldn't understand it if he explained it. Something with arbitrage between bonds and stocks and blah, blah, blah, blah, blah.'[7]

The SEC investigation was potentially catastrophic for Madoff. SEC officials believed they had stumbled onto an enormous fraud. As the *Wall Street Journal* reported in December 1992: 'The pair had promised investors hard-to-believe annual returns of 13.5 per cent to 20 per cent – to be obtained by turning the money over to an unnamed broker. Regulators feared it all might be a huge scam. "We went into this thinking it could be a major catastrophe," says Richard Walker, the SEC's New York regional administrator.'[8] Bienes later claimed that he and Avellino did not know that they had to be licensed. 'We were just a couple of accountants with a fund. We had a group together and we were doing the accounting and book-keeping and record keeping and tax 1099s for the group. We didn't know. We were naive, yes. Whether you believe it or not, we were unsophisticated and naive.'

According to Bienes, Madoff did not want the accountants to register with the SEC as investment advisers, even though Madoff must have known this was a legal requirement. With hindsight, it is likely that Madoff did not want Avellino and Bienes to register with the SEC because he was not registered himself. That would have demanded opening up his business to SEC inspections. Bienes admits he had occasional doubts which he raised with Madoff. Madoff told them that he knew the biggest lawyers on Wall Street and everything was OK. Bienes did not argue. 'We were captive to him. He owned us.' The SEC made repeated visits to Avellino and Bienes during the summer of 1992. The pressure ramped up and both men became increasingly nervous. Madoff recommended a lawyer to Avellino and Bienes: Ira Sorkin. Sorkin was a good choice – he had run the SEC's New York office between 1984 and 1986. He knew how it worked, from the other side. He had previously served as Assistant US Attorney in New York, prosecuting numerous cases including organised crime, conspiracy, drugs, and violations of the federal securities laws. Ira Sorkin would later defend Madoff himself.

Sorkin negotiated a deal. In late 1992 Avellino and Bienes neither admitted nor denied the SEC's allegations but consented to the SEC injunction. Bienes was terrified. Visions of bankruptcy, a media circus, or worse floated before him. 'We were so frightened, so scared ... And I wanted to run away and hide in a cave.' In spring 1993 the SEC offered terms to Avellino and Bienes: a total fine of $350,000 and the $454 million to be returned to 3,200 investors. When SEC officials saw that all the monies were invested with Madoff, the chairman of NASDAQ, their fears eased. Madoff returned all the $454 million in a little over a week.

In December 1992 Madoff had another problem. He had been named in the *Wall Street Journal* as Avellino and Bienes' money manager. The SEC's next step should have been to properly investigate Madoff, the recipient of these questionable millions. The SEC already suspected a Ponzi scheme connection, as what else could pay out between 13 and 20 per cent a year? The SEC was right, and the answer was right under its nose. Madoff admitted in March 2009 that his Ponzi scheme had started in the early 1990s, which means the fraud was probably in full flow by 1992 when the SEC were investigating Avellino and Bienes. Yet the SEC did not properly investigate Madoff. Madoff's trading operation's business practices had just been thoroughly investigated by the SEC's panel on payment for order flow and he had come through with shining colours. Madoff was a name, he was a player and that helped reassure officials. It helped that Madoff also had an answer for everything. He told the *Wall Street Journal* that he had no idea the money he was investing had been raised illegally. He insisted that his high returns were really nothing special, considering that Standard & Poor's 500 Stock Index had generated an average annual return of 16.3 per cent between 1982 and 1992. 'I would be surprised if anybody thought that matching the S & P over ten years was anything outstanding.'

The difference was, as the newspaper pointed out, that Avellino and Bienes were promising these returns in advance and most money managers trailed the S & P during the 1980s. The SEC's Richard Walker said of Avellino and Bienes: 'They took in nearly half a billion dollars in customer money totally outside the system that we can monitor and regulate. That's pretty frightening.' But not frightening enough, it seemed. A court-appointed trustee took over the Avellino and Bienes case, together with PriceWaterhouse. Madoff could not have been more helpful with their enquiries, reports *Fortune* magazine.[9] He spoke frequently on the telephone with his SEC-appointed counterparts, and provided them with investing records when Avellino and Bienes were unable to. Interestingly, Madoff himself handled requests for computer records, which would normally have been arranged by a junior staff member. Testifying to the US Senate Banking Committee in January 2009, Linda Chatman Thomsen,

Director of the SEC's Division of Enforcement, said that the SEC did not pursue fraud charges for several reasons: a court-appointed trustee found that all the monies existed and all the investors' funds were reimbursed; Avellino and Bienes and Telfran agreed to stop offering unregistered investment opportunities to the public, and both firms were fined $250,000 with additional penalties of $50,000 for their founders. The SEC sued the entities offering the unregistered securities, and neither Madoff nor BLMIS was named as a defendant in either case.[10]

Once Bienes' elation at the comparatively light penalties had worn off he became angry with Madoff. Sometime in 1993, Bienes and Avellino and their wives Dianne and Nancy met with Madoff at his office in the Lipstick Building in midtown Manhattan. The five of them sat in the conference room. Madoff was cold and businesslike. This time there was none of the charm that always disarmed troublesome SEC officials or others who had the power to make life difficult, nor any promises, such as Madoff had made at his son's bar mitzvah that they were all 'family now'. They were not family. Bienes and Avellino were not even friends. They had brought Madoff an enormous amount of business, but they had endangered him, exposed him to his greatest enemy: the SEC. Madoff treated them with near contempt, in front of their wives. He told Bienes and Avellino: 'It's over now. You fucking guys have to get yourselves in order.'

Bienes lost his temper. He told Madoff: 'All right, you son of a bitch, it's over now. We went through it. It cost us a lot of money and a lot of grief. And it's all your fault, Bernie. God damn you, it's your fault, because we asked you, "Should we be registered? Should we get registered?" We were willing to do it. We were willing to pay any lawyer any fee. And you said, "No, no, no, no, no, no, no." And now you are looking at us like we did something wrong.'

Madoff did not lose his temper. He stayed calm and waited until Bienes had finished. Madoff said: 'Look, I heard enough from you. Now I want you to stop. You are starting to get to me.' Bienes realised what was at stake. He had millions of dollars invested with BLMIS, which was paying double-digit interest. For a while Bienes had even believed that he and Avellino were Madoff's only feeder fund. But by now Ezra Merkin and Walter Noel and other funds were introducing Madoff to much larger, institutional investors. Bienes realised that Madoff could just tell him and Avellino to take their money and go. Bienes backed down. He told Madoff: 'Bernie, I'm sorry. I'm just a very scared person. And let's forget what I said and go on with this. I apologise.'

The urbane way Madoff had dealt with the threat of an SEC investigation only increased his standing. 'He was the guy with the big offices, two floors, over 100 employees, all kinds of awards ... We were a small component of his huge business. He could lop us and say "Forget it" or just make some calls and get other people to do what we were doing.' Madoff could turn Bienes' whole existence upside down. The stakes were far too high for grandstanding. 'He was a god. He was my life.'

Much of the money that Madoff had to return to Avellino and Bienes' investors anyway soon found its way back to him. According to Elaine Squillari, Madoff's secretary, Avellino and Bienes' clients started calling Madoff directly to invest – most of them had not known that their monies were invested with BLMIS until the news broke in the press.

Squillari asked her boss where the new clients were coming from. He told her that the SEC had shut down Avellino and Bienes, but did not really explain why, describing the problem as an 'accounting glitch', before ordering Squillari not to tell anyone about the new clients. She asked him who would care. Madoff replied: 'I just don't want you talking about it. I don't want to be associated with a firm that was shut down by the SEC, because my reputation is my business.' Madoff was so secretive that he ordered her not to mention the names Avellino and Bienes. They were to be referred to only under the not very original pseudonyms of 'A' and 'B'.[11]

A and B's investors contacted Madoff's office in droves, recalls Squillari. Many were retired and widows, who demanded to become clients of Madoff. In fact the investigation may even have increased the feeding frenzy. 'People thought there was something shady going on and they liked that,' says a Wall Street investment banker. 'Madoff would say, "I can't tell you what we do, but the situation is well in hand," or words to that effect. People thought they were on the inside track. It was the gentle perfume of the illicit.' After years of enjoying high interest rate returns A and B's clients took it for granted, indeed as their right, that the high payments would continue. 'They didn't call *asking* to open accounts; they called *expecting* accounts to be opened for them,' says Squillari. 'Now they put their money in Bernie's hands.'

The SEC's 1992 failure to probe deeper into Avellino and Bienes' relationship with Madoff, and to properly investigate Madoff himself, was one of the most important missed opportunities to shut down his investment arm. Madoff had been named by the *Wall Street Journal*, the American financial newspaper of record, as Avellino and Bienes' money manager, even though he had no licence to manage money. Yet no action was taken against him. Instead, Madoff's smooth handling of the fallout – deflecting it all onto Avellino and Bienes – only increased his standing among the regulators. In his private moments Madoff laughed at the SEC's half-hearted probe. The precedent had been set. Numerous other warnings about his investment fund, including a nineteen-page detailed, comprehensive exposé sent to the SEC in 2005, would all fail to close down his fraud.

8
A family affair

'Until your name is on that door you keep your fucking mouth shut.'

Bernie Madoff to his brother Peter.[1]

Simon Levy and his wife always enjoyed their dinners with Bernard and Ruth Madoff. The two couples had known each other for thirty years. Levy had built up a successful business before he retired. He and and his wife lived in a comfortable, spacious apartment on the Upper East Side. Levy had sold his company for a substantial sum and was looking forward to taking it easy and spending more time at their holiday home on Long Island.

The Levys and the Madoffs were eating at Primola, an Italian restaurant on Second Avenue, near East 64th Street. By the 1990s the Madoffs had left Roslyn for the Upper East Side. They lived in a duplex apartment at 133 East 64th Street, an elegant pre-war building with a grey stone façade. Madoff had finally arrived in the *Yekke* heartland, known as the silk-stocking district. With four bedrooms, as many bathrooms and a huge terrace, the Madoffs' home was sizeable by any standards and, by Manhattan's, enormous. The lounge was tastefully decorated in yellow and white, but cluttered, featuring an enormous Persian rug, antique lamps and furniture, Greek and Egyptian statues and a painting over the fireplace. The bedroom had brown walls, a four-poster bed topped with ruffles, and a fireplace on which stood antique Chinese porcelains.[2]

It was elegant, if a little showy. Madoff even had his picture taken by Karsh, the renowned Canadian portrait photographer. One night Elaine Squillari and her colleague Barbara, Madoff's secretary, had gone out after work and found themselves in front of 133. They stood by the uniformed doormen and the long green awning that reached to the street, to protect its residents from the rain. Barbara gestured upwards. 'You see that penthouse up there? That's Bernie's! Look how far he has come,' she exclaimed, her eyes shining.[3]

The Madoffs spent their weekdays in their duplex and weekends in their summer house on Montauk, on the eastern edge of Long Island, often with their sons. The five-bedroom property covers 1.2 acres and had cost $250,000 in 1980, but was now worth many times that. The Madoffs enjoyed an idyllic New York lifestyle, yet in Manhattan, especially on the Upper East Side, there was always somewhere larger and more expensive to hunger for. Number 133, while certainly 'Tony' enough, as Americans describe the fancy and expensive, is a good long block from Park Avenue, and stands by the corner of the less upmarket Lexington Avenue. As high as the building is on Manhattan's social scale, it is several degrees below Ezra Merkin's home at 740 Park Avenue, a brisk ten-minute walk away.

But for Bernie and Ruth the neighbourhood was home.

They often came to Primola for dinner, sitting at a quiet table at the back. Madoff was not much interested in food and usually had salad and chicken, sometimes branching out to sautéed artichoke hearts with balsamic vinegar. He drank diet cola or a glass of red wine. Ruth enjoyed fish or whole wheat pasta, and drank white wine. The Madoffs were friendly, in a distant New York kind of way, but never sociable, the waiters at Primola recall. They tipped between 15 and 18 per cent, standard for Manhattan. They were usually in and out in under an hour, but took their time with the Levys. The Levys were not close to the Madoffs – the relationship, after all, was based on money – but after thirty years of meeting three or four times a year for dinner they certainly had a friendly relationship. They chatted over dinner about their families, holidays, new places to go in Manhattan, everyday matters. Madoff was sometimes taciturn but Ruth was usually much more sociable and chatty than her husband. 'I think he enjoyed meeting us, otherwise he would not have bothered,' says Simon Levy.[4] The human connection was an important aspect of Madoff's appeal, muses Daphne Merkin. 'Now, in the wake of all these defrauded investors, you almost get the sense that this was a forced sign-up. But I think after all the cold and anonymous business of investing, there was a sense with him of *mishpocha* [family]. That fact that he looked so amiable and so casual was an enormous part of it.'

Ruth was a culinary aficionado. She loved to entertain, and the duplex at 133 was a perfect venue. It had a large designer kitchen, with white cabinets from floor to ceiling.[5] Ruth also knew about food and health – she had a master's degree in nutrition from New York University. 'Ruth is a smart woman, probably brighter than Bernie,' says Julia Fenwick, the former office manager at Madoff's London company, Madoff Securities International. 'She is not a silly trophy wife. She had a better education than her husband.'[6]

Together with Idee Schoenheimer, Ruth Madoff co-authored a cookbook, *The Great Chefs of America Cook Kosher: Over 175 Recipes from America's Greatest Restaurants*, which was published in 1996. The book gathered new recipes from America's best new chefs that kept to Jewish dietary laws. The profits were donated to the Jewish National Fund, a charity in Israel. A photograph shows the two women wearing pristine aprons, Idee in white, Ruth in blue, ready for some serious work over the chopping boards and hobs. The caption explained that Ruth Madoff had been 'happily sampling food and testing recipes from around the United States in preparation for this cookbook'. But her claim to 'Great Chefs Cook Kosher' was contested. The book's editor, Karen MacNeil, says that she wrote it. Ruth was 'interested in having something with her name on it that would allow for some sort of fun', MacNeil told the *New York Times*. 'My understanding was that she entertained a lot in New York and kind of wanted to test some recipes just as a social thing with friends.'[7] Ruth has denied this, and said that both she and Idee put a lot of work into the book.

Whatever the truth of Ruth's cookbook, Levy certainly trusted Madoff, who knew everything about his financial situation. Levy had invested everything with him. He was a personal client, not invested through a fund such as the ones run by Ezra Merkin or Walter Noel. Levy was a believer, happy with the steady returns Madoff paid. There were red flags, which Levy, like most of Madoff's investors, ignored.

Levy himself was an experienced businessman, but when he asked how exactly Madoff could guarantee such steady returns of 10 to 12 per cent a year, Madoff just brushed him off. Levy did not press too hard for an explanation. 'He did not want to explain it to me. He told me not to bother, because I would not understand it. But I trusted him absolutely, otherwise I never would have invested everything with him.'

When Madoff was arrested in December 2008 Levy's life was turned inside out. He lost all his investments, and everything he hoped to leave to his family. He was in shock for days and even in spring 2009 seemed dazed at his sudden change of fortune. 'I've known him for forty years. There are a lot of people who engage in illegal transactions but Bernie would have been the last one we would have thought of.' He had to sell his apartment. The prosperous retired businessman, looking forward to a comfortable retirement, was fragile and older, dressed in a sports suit, his face drawn as his apartment was packed up around him. Several months after Madoff's arrest Levy still struggled to process what had happened to him and his family. 'The impact is absolutely immeasurable. I just go up and down with streams of emotions, of realising that we went from 100 per cent security to none. When that happens you feel a fear. A fear that I won't be able to provide for my family.'

For all its personal pain, Levy's loss reveals much about Madoff: how he was able to build a bond of trust over the years, until Levy had staked his family's whole future on Madoff; how the personal connection and the regular dinners on the Upper East Side reassured Levy that everything was under control. Levy's tragedy shows that Madoff was a sociopath, someone lacking, empathy, scruples, or morals. With what we now know of Madoff's fraud, that is no revelation. But even among sociopaths, it demands a special kind of pathological case to sit opposite a man and his wife several times a year for decades, to break bread with them, to eat with them, to gain their trust, to look into their eyes, when all the while you are feeding their hard-earned money, with which they hope to provide for future generations, into the maw of a Ponzi scheme.

Bernard L. Madoff Investment Securities was a family affair and the chairman and CEO liked it that way. By 2000 its trading arm was ranked among the top 1 per cent of securities firms, and was one of the country's largest market-makers in off-exchange stocks, including the Standard & Poor's 500 Index and the top 200 NASDAQ stocks.[8] Those first dreams of Wall Street success, back in the early 1960s when Madoff and his wife ran his firm in between his lectures at Brooklyn Law School, had come true. Luxuriating in their duplex on East Sixty-fourth Street, the Madoffs had come a long way from their first tiny apartment in Queens. They had more or less lost touch with their old friends Joe Kavanau and his wife. But Kavanau was still proud in his friend's achievements. 'We were certainly aware of his success. We took pride in it, and we were thrilled whenever he was interviewed on television. We revelled in it and enjoyed it.'

The key positions in BLMIS's trading arm were all filled by family members. Bernard Madoff was the sole principal, meaning the owner and person legally responsible for the firm. Peter Madoff owned a nominal amount of shares and was overall head of trading, head of compliance, and in charge of computers and technology. Bernard Madoff's older son Mark was director of listed trading, stocks that were listed on exchanges, and his younger son Andrew was director of NASDAQ trading, both senior positions for two men still in their thirties. Peter's daughter, Shana, worked as an in-house lawyer, in charge of compliance with securities law. The Madoff children were expected to work in the family firm. Peter Madoff used to bring his daughter in while she was still a teenager so she could get the feel of the office. Peter's son, Roger, worked for Primex Trading, an alternative trading system composed of four investment banks and BLMIS. Shana Madoff said at the time: 'What's nice is that everyone has their own area. I have compliance, Mark has listing, Andy has NASDAQ. So even though we can all work together, we're not thrust into one position, fighting over something to do.'[9]

Bernard Madoff was proud of both his sons. Mark and Andy were both good-looking, intelligent, hard-working boys. Mark was two years older, and was more extroverted and sociable. Andy was quieter and more cerebral. Both did well at Roslyn High School, where Andy was editor of the school newspaper and was known as being extremely good at mathematics. They were excellent skiers. Mark went to the University of Michigan, not quite the Ivy League of Harvard and Yale, but still a highly regarded university. Andy graduated from Wharton School at the University of Pennsylvania, one of the best business colleges in the United States. 'Andy was very intelligent. He had great grades, was very smart, very friendly and was very popular in school,' recalls a friend, who grew up with the Madoffs in Roslyn. 'Mark was more outgoing and very social. Both of them were always focused on the family firm. They were in a nice situation, as their dad had a very successful brokerage business.' Mark and Andy went straight to work for their father. Mark told *Wall Street & Technology* magazine in 2000: 'What makes it fun for all of us is to walk into the office in the morning and see the rest of your family sitting there. That's a good feeling to have. To Bernie and Peter, that's what it's all about.'[10]

Despite his success Madoff made sure to keep a low media profile. If he had to speak to a journalist, it was usually a trade publication, such as *Wall Street & Technology*. Unlike now, there were no profiles of Madoff in *Vanity Fair* or *New York* magazine, Manhattan's most influential glossies. The only Madoff to be noticed by the glitzy media world was Shana, who was a designer clothes addict. Tall, slim, attractive, and rich, Shana was a natural for a feature in *New York* magazine on 'Extreme Brand Loyalty' in August 2004. Her loyalty was to the designer Narciso Rodriguez. (Michelle Obama wore a dress by Rodriguez on her first appearance as first lady-elect.) The article did not mention Shana Madoff's uncle, but did give a revealing insight into the world of Manhattan's super rich. Shana Madoff was divorced and lived on Park Avenue with her young daughter Rebecca. She was a very busy person, so a selection of Rodriguez's clothes and shoes were sent by messenger to her at the start of each season, and she was charged for whatever she did not return. At the time her Rodriguez collection included: three coats including a knee-length black leather coat, six dresses, and four pairs of shoes.

Shana explained: 'I just don't have time to shop. I get a little bit aggravated when I go into a store because I could be doing so many other things that are so much more productive. And the salespeople are around the clothes all day. They know them much better than I do.' One day the previous summer Shana was at the beach with friends, idly flicking through *Harper's Bazaar* magazine. She saw a picture of a Prada handbag that would perfectly match her Rodriguez collection. Shana jumped up and strode down the sands, telling her friends that she had to make a 'very important phone call'. The bag arrived two days later. Back then Shana Madoff's lifestyle, of a luxury apartment and messengered clothes, seemed the very height of Manhattan aspiration. But behind the gloss lay a family tragedy that would reveal another side of the Madoffs.[11]

BLMIS was spread over the 17th, 18th, and 19th floors of the Lipstick Building at 885 Third Avenue, in Manhattan's mid-town commercial district.[12] Completed in 1986, the curved, thirty-four-floor postmodern skyscraper, with its striking red granite and steel exterior, soon became an iconic New York landmark. Its oval-shaped design was modern, innovative, and iconoclastic, just as Madoff viewed BLMIS. Madoff's trading operation took up the whole of the 19th floor. Bernard Madoff had the largest office in the corner, by the lifts. Mark and Andy sat on a raised podium overlooking the trading floor and the fifty or so traders. Their immediate boss, Peter Madoff, had his own office, directly across from his brother and there was a large conference room in between.[13]

A circular staircase led down to the 18th floor. There was a reception area near the foot of the stairs, where Ruth Madoff kept her office. She returned to work in the 1980s, after Mark and Andrew grew up. Her unpaid role was to reconcile company and personal bank statements, checking the monthly statements against the cheques written, and she also worked on her cookbook and charity projects. Ruth did not play an active role in the company, says someone familiar with the matter, and never voted, attended a meeting or solicited business for her husband. During the 1990s she came in far less often. Shana Madoff, the firm's rules-compliance lawyer for the trading division, and the firm's separate in-house attorney, also had offices on the 18th floor.

So did Cohmad Securities. Cohmad Securities was a legally separate entity to BLMIS, but was so deeply entwined with BLMIS that 'they acted in many respects as interconnected arms of the same enterprise', according to the lawsuit issued by Irving Picard, the trustee for the liquidation of BLMIS, against Cohmad in June 2009.[14] BLMIS provided Cohmad with a computer network. The two companies shared some staff, including Shana Madoff, who was Cohmad's compliance lawyer, according to the Picard lawsuit against Cohmad. While Shana Madoff would doubtless have been aware that BLMIS was renting the 17th floor there was no reason for her to suspect that Madoff was running a fraudulent investment fund there. There is no evidence that she knew of or participated in the fraud. Shana Madoff, like Ruth Madoff, Peter Madoff, Mark Madoff and Andrew Madoff, has not been charged with or convicted of any crime.

Cohmad was an important feeder fund for Madoff. It took its name from its two founders: Maurice 'Sonny' Cohn, his former neighbour when he lived on Long Island, and Bernard Madoff. The two men sometimes commuted to Manhattan together by seaplane. Cohn, a retired former member of the

NYSE, also had his own office on the 18th floor. Cohmad was owned by Cohn, his daughter Marcia, Bernard Madoff, Peter Madoff, Robert Jaffe, and two others. Robert Jaffe is married to Ellen Shapiro, the daughter of Carl Shapiro, who back in the early 1960s had written Madoff a cheque for $100,000. When Peter Madoff applied for membership of the Trump International Golf Club, in West Palm Beach, Florida, he listed Sonny Cohn as a reference.

The 18th and 19th floors, which were open to visitors, were modern, light and airy with stylish office furniture. Everything had to be in its correct place, or Madoff would throw a tantrum. Madoff was obsessed with neatness and control. He decreed that all picture frames had to be silver or black, the window blinds had to be properly aligned, and that employees clear all their papers from their desks before they left for the day. The rules were well known and every now and then Madoff would patrol the office to check they were adhered to. Madoff was a bully towards all of his staff, whether they were family or not. He suffered from mood swings and had a mercurial temper. He was personally abusive sometimes, picking on an employee's most sensitive spots, such as their weight or appearance. When Madoff was in one his moods, sometimes his secretary, Barbara, would just pick up her bag and go home. Eventually, she left for good and Elaine Squillari took over her job. Madoff's word was law, recalls Nader Ibrahim, who worked for BLMIS's computer support department, from 2000 to 2003. 'If you had to deal with him, basically he says something and it's done. It's no questions, no back and forth. It's just, he needs something, you get it done right away.'[15]

William Nasi, Madoff's messenger, recalls that Madoff was

obsessed with cleanliness. So much so that Madoff often wielded the vacuum cleaner himself. 'I would open the office at 7.30 a.m. and sometimes I would see Bernie in there, vacuuming the floors, personally. He was a workaholic and a clean-o-phobe. Everything had to be clean, even if he had to do it himself.'[16] Madoff could also be generous. When Elaine Squillari asked for an advance against her bonus of $4,000 to add her children to her car insurance policy, the money just appeared on her paycheque. Neither Madoff nor his brother Peter would admit to knowing anything about the extra money. She was touched and stood between their offices to shout out her thanks.

Madoff's mania for order was probably overcompensation for the perpetual inner turmoil of running a multibillion-dollar international fraud. However long the Ponzi scheme had lasted, it could still spin out of control at any moment, in the (admittedly unlikely) event that the regulatory authorities should decide on a serious investigation. And there was no avoiding the routine SEC audits of the trading operation. When the SEC arrived Madoff put the whole operation on a virtual war footing. The auditors were assigned a single office where he could watch them, and were allowed out only to go to the toilet. Whatever they needed was supplied, so there were no opportunities to wander around. If the auditors asked to use the photocopying machine Madoff instructed Squillari to offer to make the copies for them, and to tell him what they were interested in. 'Bernie was having a fit when these people showed up. Everyone had to have his nose to the grindstone,' recalls William Nasi. The SEC were the enemy. The only time Madoff became stressed with Nasi was when he had to deliver something to the SEC. He made sure

Nasi demanded a receipt from the SEC. If Nasi was not back fast enough, Madoff would page him. When Nasi returned Madoff would be 'jumping up and down' shouting, 'Did you get it, did you get it?'[17]

Madoff never travelled when an SEC audit was scheduled. If he had to be out of the office when they were present he demanded to know the auditors' precise movements from his secretary. When did they arrive, when did they leave, and what were they doing all day? Each July Madoff invited all the employees out to his holiday home at Montauk, on Long Island, for a weekend party. When, one year, the SEC visit was scheduled for that month, he told the auditors that the company party was scheduled to start that particular weekend, so the auditors had to be finished by Friday, even though the party was actually planned for sometime later in the month. When one of the SEC auditors went to the toilet Madoff then panicked that someone would let slip that he had lied about the date. Madoff ordered Squillari to dispatch a male member of staff to the toilet to make sure that nobody gave the game away.[18]

Madoff's greatest fear, of course, was that the SEC auditors would stumble upon the 17th floor, which housed the Ponzi scheme. The 17th floor was completely closed off from the trading operation. Access was strictly controlled by key or card key. The client statements were generated on an old IBM AS/400 computer, an obsolete workhorse launched in 1988. The IBM was encased in glass, and was completely separate to the computer network on the trading floor above. The AS/400 was the heart of the Ponzi scheme, a Wall Street version of HAL, the omniscient computer in Stanley Kubrick's film *2001: A Space Odyssey*. Clerical staff seated nearby researched share prices from public media such as the Bloomberg financial news agency, the *Wall Street Journal*, and other sources. These prices were then used to create fictitious trades, which would, however, appear accurate if an investor actually checked their statement. The AS/400 would then generate false trade confirmations, for the trades which had never taken place, according to the lawsuit brought by Irving Picard, the trustee for the liquidation of BLMIS, against Cohmad in June 2009.[19] Significantly, even though Madoff was a pioneer of electronic trading at NASDAQ, his investors had no real-time electronic access to their accounts. They received paper trading statements in the mail. Customer transactions were kept on handwritten logs and entered manually into the system, according to the Picard lawsuit against Cohmad. The running balance of available cash was recorded on index cards and reported to Madoff. The lawsuit claims that several Cohmad employees, including Maurice Cohn, had access to the 17th floor. Steven Paradise, the lawyer for Maurice Cohn, says the Cohns disclaim any involvement with Madoff's Ponzi scheme. 'I can say unequivocally that the Cohns deny having any knowledge [of] or playing any role in Mr Madoff's Ponzi scheme. Unfortunately, each of the SEC and Mr Picard are judging the Cohns and Cohmad with the benefit of hindsight, which makes things seem much clearer and more apparent than what they were in real time.'[20]

The 17th floor was run by Frank DiPascali, a veteran Madoff employee who had joined the firm in the mid-1970s after graduating from high school. DiPascali and his staff had their own office, where they dealt with clients' accounts. DiPascali was a surly New Yorker, who refused to answer enquiries from clients about how the investment fund operated. He took frequent cigarette breaks and wore pressed jeans, a sweatshirt and white sports or boat shoes to work. Despite his peculiar business attire and lack of social skills DiPascali had prospered at BLMIS. The DiPascalis lived in Bridgewater, a pleasant suburb of New Jersey, in a fivebedroom house with a swimming pool, set in seven wooded acres, valued at $1.38 million. They owned two Mercedes cars and a 61 foot boat.[21]

The senior staff on the 17th floor were often rude to customers, who would then complain to Elaine Squillari. But Madoff would not hear any criticism of them, she recalls. 'If I mentioned this to Bernie, he would wave me off. "They're doing a good job down there. Most of these customers are a pain in the ass." He would never reprimand anyone on 17 – they were untouchable.' At the end of the month the ancient IBM generated and printed the investors' statements. It was the most sophisticated financial fraud in history and until 10 December 2008 it worked brilliantly.

9
Red flags flying

'Frank, this is a Ponzi scheme.'

Harry Markopolos, a portfolio manager at Rampart
Investment Management, to his colleague Frank Casey after
analysing Madoff's trading record.[1]

Charles Gevirtz was on the telephone to Frank DiPascali and wanted some information. He had invested a six-
figure sum and had been reading his statements in detail.
Each one showed more than thirty-five trades every month,
considerably more than 350 a year. Gevirtz was an engineer
in his early forties, who worked for the Ford Motor Company
and lived in Michigan. Like many private investors he had
been introduced to Madoff through personal contacts, in his
case the cousin of a family friend. Madoff's appeal was the
fund's steady, if unspectacular performance. Gevirtz also had
an MBA and knew how to read his monthly statements. He
wanted to know how the fund worked. 'I was asking questions early on. I thought how can they cover all these transaction costs and still make money? I thought maybe they are
taking all this money out of my earnings.' The secretary at

the Lipstick Building put Gevirtz through to DiPascali, the abrasive king of the 17th floor. He had a simple answer for Gevirtz's questions. If Gevirtz didn't like the fund, he should get out, DiPascali snarled.

Gevirtz was shocked. Investment firms did not usually treat clients who had just handed over hundreds of thousands of dollars like this. 'He was really rude to me. I said I don't want to get out, I just want to understand it. I called back and asked to speak to his boss. They told me that was Mr Madoff, and he would call me later.'[2] Madoff rang back that evening from his car. He turned on the charm, asking politely what Gevirtz's concerns were. Gevirtz said he did not understand how BLMIS could make so many trades and still turn a reasonable profit. Madoff replied that he owned the trading firm and was not especially interested in the investment side, he just ran it to keep some of his clients happy. Gevirtz asked some more detailed questions. Madoff told Gevirtz that he was the largest trader on Wall Street. He explained how his split-strike strategy worked, with its complicated system of 'puts' and 'calls'. He even claimed that he was thinking of closing the fund.

Madoff knew exactly what to say, and what not to say, subtly flattering Gevirtz and leaving space for him to construct his own fantasy, he recalls. 'I understood what he was talking about when he explained his investment strategy, and he asked me how, and what my background was. I told him I have an MBA. He didn't say anything directly, but he gave one or two hints to communicate the idea that I knew a lot, I understood finance, I had an MBA, maybe he had something for me. He was careful and subtle. He played with my imagination and knew how to push my buttons with a well-timed compliment. He indicated that he might be able to use me in his firm one day. He was very charming. I was like "Wow, he thinks that I am good enough to work for his company." I also told him that I was not treated very well by his staff on the 17th floor.' It was a bravura performance by Madoff. Gevirtz was flattered, charmed, and reassured. The conversation took place some time in 2001, after which he felt privileged to be a Madoff investor, believing that the firm's trading arm was subsidising the investment fund. 'I thought I was really getting a special deal, so I did not question it too much. I felt confident.' And the next time Gevirtz telephoned the 17th floor Frank DiPascali was friendly and confiding. 'Once he told me that his market timing stinks. I thought, my God, he is so candid, you would never get this from a Wall Street firm.'

Gevirtz later checked with a friend who confirmed that Madoff's firm was indeed large and well known. Madoff persuaded Gevirtz that his money was safe, but among some finance professionals there was a growing sense that there was something peculiar, if not criminal, about his operation. The biggest of numerous red flags was that Madoff simply could not properly explain, especially to other finance professionals, how he could beat the markets year in, year out and guarantee such steady returns. 'I thought he was ripping people off. Everybody on Wall Street thought he was ripping people off,' recalls Ed Nicoll, who has known Bernard and Peter Madoff for more than twenty years. 'We thought he was front-running, taking the information and profiting from it. That's the world he comes from, where you keep the customer's order in your back pocket and use it yourself. Trading on Wall Street is a rough and tumble game. There is no such thing as a sixth sense, or "natural ability". No successful trader trades successfully without an advantage. They trade because of information asymmetry, knowing something the other guy does not. I assumed Madoff was using the information from the market-making business and transferring it to the investment advisory business.'

Such suspicions were rarely discussed, at least in public. That would be a breach of etiquette, and anyway there was no proof that Madoff was engaged in criminal or shady activity. But Nicoll was right that many financiers shared his unease about Madoff's investment fund. A decade before Gevirtz trusted his money to Madoff, the chairman of one medium-sized Wall Street brokerage company which placed share orders with Madoff's trading operation found that he could not answer straightforward questions about how the investment fund operated.[3] The brokerage company had a social as well as a business connection to Madoff. The company president also lived on Long Island. Both he and Madoff were members of Fresh Meadow Country Club. The president had invested his own monies with Madoff and tried to persuade the chairman to as well. The president enthused: 'We have been doing good business with the Madoff people for a couple of years, they pay promptly and properly. I don't know if you know that Bernie Madoff personally manages money for individuals and institutions. He has a terrific track record, very consistent, with high returns in the low to mid-teens, year in, year out.'

The chairman was interested. He knew Madoff personally, and BLMIS's trading arm was swift and professional. 'We weren't friends but Wall Street is a small community and people get to know one another. Madoff was regarded very highly on Wall Street. He was a pioneer of spread trading and paying for order flow. Later on more people got into it and made lots of money but he reaped the rewards for being early. Nothing commands respect on Wall Street as much as money.' The chairman was also impressed by Madoff's quiet demeanour. 'Many people on Wall Street are very aggressive, very extroverted. Bernie was just the opposite. He was quiet, unassuming and that was unusual for the head of a successful firm.'

But when the chairman asked his colleague what exactly Madoff's investment strategy was, his doubts began. The president was not sure, but he thought that Madoff bought treasury bonds and sold options against them, meaning that he gambled on whether the price would rise or fall. 'I didn't understand this. I knew that you can buy and sell options on Treasuries, but I couldn't see how you could get double digit returns from this. The most you could get would be low single digits. He was a little confused himself. It was apparent to me that he was not digging too deeply into how Madoff made the money. It was good enough that he made it.'

However, this was not good enough for the chairman. He called Madoff to try to find out more. This put Madoff in a tricky position. The company was a valued customer of his trading arm, so Madoff could not simply brush him off, or use his usual psychological tricks. But the chairman was also a Wall Street player, with in-depth knowledge of investment and market strategies. He recalls: 'I told Madoff I heard that he was investing money and that I wanted to know more about it, that I might be interested in having him manage some of my money.' Initially at least, Madoff was receptive. 'I asked him how he went about the investment and what was the strategy. He explained that he bought very high quality securities, not just Treasuries, but also blue chip stocks. He would enter into various option strategies in connection with those securities. I told him that sounded interesting but I was confused. I didn't understand how he could generate these double digit returns like that. He down-played that, and said well, no, it's more like 12 per cent.'

Even so, a steady 12 per cent annual return was very respectable, the chairman told Madoff. 'I said that I had used this strategy myself with my own money, and I was not able to generate anything near that kind of performance, certainly not on a consistent year in, year out basis.' Madoff then offered a second, more complex explanation, of how the fund worked. The chairman listened, becoming increasingly puzzled. 'It did not make any sense whatsoever. It was bullshit that left me more confused than before.' He tried again, with no better results. 'The third response made even less sense than the first two. I told him that I did not need to know which specific stocks he was buying and selling but I needed to understand the principle.'

The principle was very simple: Madoff's investment fund was a Ponzi scheme and the chairman was asking too many questions. Madoff pulled up the drawbridge. 'He told me that I was a sophisticated Wall Street investor, and his invest-ment fund was not for me. I said, OK, Bernie, thank you. I never imagined that he was running a Ponzi scheme or embezzling people in any way, shape or form. I thought he had some secret strategy, and he was reluctant to reveal it.' Madoff's investors thought of themselves as a kind of elite club. 'There was this mystique around him, that you were not assured that he would take your money. He made it difficult, or appear to be difficult. People would boast about how he was managing their money. But I have never been one of those people with a compulsion to be accepted by someone that does not want to accept me.'

In Boston Frank Casey and Harry Markopolos were also asking difficult questions about Madoff. Casey and Markopolos both worked at Rampart Investment Management, an investment adviser firm. Casey was a business development manager, who raised institutional capital, while Markopolos was a portfolio manager and a Certified Fraud Examiner. Sometime in the late 1990s Markopolos told Casey that he had heard of a financier in New York who was investing in a fund that returned a steady 1 per cent a month, no matter what the market conditions. Markopolos was sceptical about how this could be done. Casey travelled to New York to meet the financier's boss, a French aristocrat called Thierry Magon de la Villehuchet, one of the cofounders of a company called Access International Advisors (AIA).[4] De la Villehuchet was reluctant at first to reveal the name of the investment wizard, but as both he and Casey were keen sailors the two men bonded and the French aristocrat revealed that AIA was a feeder fund for Bernard Madoff.

Casey quizzed de la Villehuchet about how Madoff's fund worked. De la Villehuchet gave what was by now the standard answer, about the famed split-strike conversion strategy. The French aristocrat boasted about how he was making between 12 and 15 per cent a year for his clients, whether the market went up or down. This only increased Casey's suspicions. De la Villehuchet tried to reassure Casey that AIA was indeed doing its due diligence as it received trading statements from BLMIS. He told Casey: 'I get reports every day of which positions are bought, which are sold, which options are purchased and which are sold.' AIA's clerks then logged the paper trading confirmations into a computer. Casey countered that logging Madoff's information was not any kind of due diligence. AIA was merely recording Madoff's statements, according to Casey, and its clerks made no effort to check whether the statements were true. 'It was due diligence to him.' Casey returned to Boston with records of Madoff's trading, and handed them to Markopolos to analyse. He told him: 'Harry, if you can do this for me, we can make a lot of money.' Casey strongly suspected something was wrong but like Ed Nicoll he thought that Madoff was engaged in insider trading, using advance information to pre-empt the market. But Markopolos showed that even with the best timing and information flow, it would still be almost impossible to make such steady returns.

The biggest red flag for Casey was that Madoff's fund actually took private investors in the first place. Why did he need them? If the famed split-strike conversion strategy brought such steady, guaranteed profits for the trading wing of BLMIS, then the simplest strategy would be to use the firm's equity to secure a highly leveraged loan, increasing several-fold the amount of money it could invest, and so multiplying the profit from the split-strike strategy. This would also eliminate the need to pay investors their 1 per cent a month, and would avoid all the troublesome admin-istration of keeping client accounts and records. The banks of course would require extensive documentation and would carry out due diligence before advancing the loan. But for some reason Madoff needed a steady flow of cash from investors who did not ask too many difficult questions. A second red flag was Madoff did not charge any fees for its money management. Other hedge funds charged up to 2 per cent of monies invested and 20 per cent of profits. Madoff claimed he made enough profit from the commission on the share trades. Combined with its market-beating returns, this made Madoff's fund irresistible to investors, but only increased Casey's suspicions.

Casey offered Rampart's services to de la Villehuchet, to help him diversify AIA's risk. He asked what would happen if Madoff turned out to be a fraud. But the French aristocrat was not interested. De la Villehuchet told him: 'He can't be. I've got all my money with him. I've got most of my family's money with him. Almost every royal family I know has got money with him.'

Casey's colleague, Harry Markopolos, investigated further. Markopolos saw that Madoff had made an elementary error in his performance presentation. He compared his fund to the Standard & Poor's 500 Stock Index, but his investment strategy supposedly replicated the S & P 100 Stock Index and there was a considerable difference in price returns between the two. As Markopolos told the US Congress in February 2009: 'This lack of sophistication was a recurring theme during the nine-year investigation. BM's math never made sense, his performance charts were clearly deceiving and his return stream never resembled any known financial instrument or strategy.'[5]

In May 2000 Markopolos wrote an eight-page report detailing his suspicions about Madoff's investment fund, the first of several he would write over the following years. Markopolos believed Madoff was making money by one of two methods. Either he was running a straightforward Ponzi scheme, and the claimed returns were fictional, or the returns were real and BLMIS's trading was making the trades by front-running, a version of insider trading. With the help of a SEC official called Ed Manion, Markopolos handed his report to the Boston office of the SEC. He waited for a response. None came. In September 2001 Manion called Markopolos. He thought that the Boston office had failed to pass the report to the New York office. Soon afterwards, Markopolos resubmitted his report, this time directly to the New York office of the SEC, with an extra three pages of mathematical analysis, including two pages entitled 'Madoff Investment Process Explained'. But Madoff's Ponzi scheme stayed in business. The SEC, it seemed, did not welcome outsiders investigating matters under its purview.

Meanwhile, Markopolos's colleague Frank Casey tipped off a journalist named Michael Ocrant that he thought something was awry at BLMIS. Ocrant worked for *Managed Account Reports* (MAR/Hedge), an influential trade magazine covering hedge funds. Ocrant started digging and asking questions. He published his article in May 2001, under the headline: 'Madoff Tops Chart: Skeptics Ask How'. Madoff was well known on Wall Street as a market-maker, wrote Ocrant, but who knew that he was also running one of the world's largest hedge funds? It was a 'safe bet that relatively few Wall Street professionals are aware that Madoff Securities could be categorised as perhaps the best risk-adjusted hedge fund portfolio manager for the last dozen years', with assets of between $6 and $7 billion.[6] But how did he make so much money? Those who had heard of Madoff were 'baffled by the way the firm has obtained such consistent, non volatile returns month after month and year after year'. Ocrant spoke to more than a dozen current and former traders, money managers, consultants, analysts, and hedge fund executives who were familiar with the split-strike conversion strategy. All questioned the consistency of Madoff's returns. Ocrant also examined Fairfield Sentry, the Madoff feeder fund run by Jeffrey Tucker and Walter Noel. For the previous 139 months Fairfield Sentry had generated net annual returns of around 15 per cent and had reported losses in only four months.

Ocrant raised numerous other red flags about Madoff's operation: his 'astonishing ability to time the market'; the way BLMIS was apparently making so many substantial share trades without noticeably affecting the shares' market prices; the failure of other firms to duplicate the famed 'split-strike' strategy if it was indeed such a guaranteed money maker; the failure of other firms, knowing BLMIS's strategy, to trade against it; and BLMIS's curious reluctance to set up its own asset management division and deal directly with investors. And why, as Frank Casey had highlighted, did Madoff not ditch the investors, leverage the firm's capital and keep all the profits for the firm's owners? These were all good, sharp questions that got to the heart of the contradictions of Madoff's investment operation.

But Madoff batted all of Ocrant's questions straight back, sounding, as Ocrant wrote, 'genuinely amused' at the attention. Madoff was cool, suave, and plausible. The lack of volatility was an illusion, Madoff claimed, as on a daily, weekly, or monthly basis the fund's volatility was 'all over the place'. As for the timing, BLMIS was an experienced

Wall Street operator which had pioneered the use of technology, had excellent market intelligence and solid 'gut instincts', Madoff said. He refused to discuss the specifics of the trading strategy, as he was not interested in 'educating the world' about how BLMIS worked. Nor would copying the split-strike strategy be nearly as simple as it might seem, as other Wall Street firms had discovered when they had tried to imitate competitors' tactics. And he was not interested in setting up a separate asset management division, as that would conflict with BLMIS's primary business, its trading operation's market-making. As for leveraging the firm's capital, Madoff said, 'the firm generally believes in concentrating on its core strengths and not overextending itself,' which, considering later events, is darkly ironic. 'The strategy is the strategy and the returns are the returns,' Madoff concluded.

Despite Madoff's smooth answers, the MAR/Hedge article caused ripples on Wall Street. Erin Arvedlund, a reporter at *Barron's*, a business magazine, was also working on an investigation into BLMIS. Like Ocrant, she had numerous questions about how the fund could produce such steady returns. She speculated that the market-making operation was subsidising the investment fund: 'It would work like this: Madoff Securities stands in the middle of a tremendous river of orders, which means that its traders have advance knowledge, if only by a few seconds, of what big customers are buying and selling. By hopping on the bandwagon, the market-maker could effectively lock in profits. In such a case, throwing a little cash back to the hedge funds would be no big deal.'[7] Arvedlund had spoken to numerous Wall Street insiders, many of whom, like those interviewed by Michael

Ocrant, expressed strong doubts about the fund's lack of volatility.

But those closest to the operation did not want to be interviewed. Madoff himself was not available. Jeffrey Tucker refused to talk about Fairfield Greenwich. He told Arvedlund: 'It's a private fund. And so our inclination has been not to discuss its returns. Why *Barron's* would have any interest in this fund I don't know.' *Barron's* was interested because it was an influential financial publication and by May 2001 the Fairfield Sentry fund was supposedly managing $3.3 billion in assets. Tucker's stonewalling only increased suspicions. The day the magazine went to press Madoff was suddenly available. He spoke to Arvedlund from a boat in Switzerland. He dismissed the idea that the market-making operation was subsidising the fund as 'ridiculous'. Madoff repeated much of what he had told Ocrant. He sounded reasonable and affable, but stonewalled over details.[8] She pressed him on why he did not charge fees or take a percentage of the 1.5 per cent that Fairfield Greenwich was charging for channelling investments. Madoff again claimed to be satisfied with the commission on trades that were supposedly being made using the split-strike strategy.

Arvedlund did some calculations which made for interesting reading. Suppose that Madoff charged 1 per cent of assets annually plus 20 per cent of profits. If Madoff's fund was worth $6 billion, and returning 15 per cent profits a year, that added up to $240 million a year in fees, $240 million a year that Madoff could be charging, but was not. Many were still asking why not? And while Madoff had handled the media attention very smoothly, back at the Lipstick Building the press interest was causing some concern, recalls Nader Ibrahim, who worked for the IT department at BLMIS. The traders on the 19th floor were talking among themselves about the *Barron's* article and the questions it raised. 'These employees have been asking these questions for God knows how long, depending on who you ask.' Meanwhile, Harry Markopolos's reports languished unacted on in desks somewhere in the SEC's Boston and New York offices.

10
Impossible returns

*'The temptation to speculate recurs regularly as animal
spirits send markets soaring beyond valuations that the
fundamentals would justify.'*

Ezra Merkin, Security Analysis.[1]

Desire, gullibility, greed, all of Merkin's 'animal spirits'
are as old as humanity itself. The book of Genesis records that
history's original great persuader was not a person, but a
snake, living in the Garden of Eden with Adam and Eve. The
first man and woman were permitted by God to eat the fruit of
every tree except the tree of knowledge, on pain of death. When
the serpent tried to persuade Eve to eat from that tree, she
refused, saying she would die. Not so, replied the serpent. 'For
God knows that in the day you eat thereof, then your eyes shall
be open, and ye shall be as gods, knowing good and evil.' The
lure of secret inside knowledge was, of course, too good to
miss. Eve succumbed to the serpent's siren call, ate the tree's
fruit and passed it to Adam. The snake delivered on his
promise: Adam and Eve did not die, and became worldly. They
realised they were naked and made themselves clothes.

But there were life-changing consequences. When God saw what they had done, he was furious. He cast Adam and Eve out of paradise and condemned the serpent to slither on his belly for eternity. Like many who later regret being charmed into decisions which have unwelcome consequences, Adam and Eve then played the blame game. When God asked Adam if he had eaten of the tree of knowledge, he blamed Eve, saying: 'She gave me of the tree and I did eat.' When God asked Eve why she did it, she blamed the serpent, saying: 'The serpent beguiled me and I did eat.' To be beguiled by a smooth talker, though, is never an adequate excuse. Several millennia later, many of Madoff's victims, quite as charmed by Uncle Bernie as Eve was by Eden's serpent, showed a similar unwillingness to take responsibility for their actions. If they lost money via feeder funds, they blamed the fund's managers for not carrying out sufficient due diligence while funnelling their money into Madoff's Ponzi scheme, even as they enjoyed its high returns. If they were personal clients, friends, or relatives of Madoff, they blamed the SEC for not investigating BLMIS and closing it down, while they were banking their steady 10 per cent. The one person investors usually didn't blame for believing that Madoff, like the tree of knowledge, held coveted secrets, that in his case let him beat the market decade after decade, was, of course, themselves.

In these times there is much talk of the wisdom of crowds, an idea explored in the book of the same name by James Surowiecki. He argues that large groups of people are smarter than an elite few, better able to solve complex problems, foster innovation and even predict the future. In fact centuries of human gullibility, of which the Madoff fraud is only the latest, prove precisely the opposite. Almost a century before Madoff's birth a Scottish journalist called Charles Mackay wrote the seminal work *Extraordinary Popular Delusions and the Madness of Crowds*. Mackay's book, first published in 1841, is still in print and it chronicles an eternal truth: collective manias and delusions are a permanent feature of human history.

The Middle Ages brought forth alchemy, the idea that base metals could somehow be turned into gold – a precursor of the Madoff investors' belief that there was a secret formula to beat the market and bring eternal wealth. The Crusades saw tens of thousands of men desert their work and families to go on bloodthirsty rampages through Europe and Palestine and attempt to capture Jerusalem from the Arabs. The hunt for imaginary witches saw countless innocent women across Europe burned alive or drowned for nonexistent sins of sorcery, while the mob cheered. Mackay wrote: 'We find that whole communities suddenly fix their minds on one object and go mad in its pursuit; that millions of people become simultaneously impressed with one delusion, and run after it, until their attention is caught by some folly more captivating than the first. Once an idea, no matter how illogical, took hold in the collective consciousness, it was almost impossible to shake off. Men, it has been well said, think in herds; it will be seen that they go mad in herds, while they only recover their senses slowly, and one by one.'[2]

As the world's economy became more sophisticated during the seventeenth and eighteenth centuries, so did financial upheavals. The Dutch Tulip Bubble, which swept through Holland in the 1630s, saw the price of a single tulip bulb soar to unprecedented heights, as a virus swept through the crop, increasing its rarity. A futures market developed where contracts to buy bulbs at the end of the season were traded. Growers hoarded their stocks, while buyers sold everything they owned to get hold of cash to invest. The Dutch described this as 'windhandel', meaning 'wind trading' as no tulips were actually changing hands, only future contracts. As more prudent investors began to sell, the price collapsed. (Recent research has challenged Mackay's account of the extent of the Tulip Bubble, but the episode is now embedded in Holland's collective memory.)

Early in the following century Britain was swept by a mania for shares in the South Sea Company, which had secured exclusive trading rights in the South Seas in exchange for financing the war debt. Lured by visions of gold, slaves, and precious stones from South America, investors rushed to purchase as much stock as they could. The company directors had little experience, but like Madoff made sure to rent impressive, spacious offices, which reassured doubters. The directors issued wave after wave of stocks, but did little actual trading. When they eventually sold their stocks, panic ensued, and the company collapsed. Isaac Newton lost £20,000, lamenting: 'I can calculate the motions of heavenly bodies but not the madness of people.'

The Dutch Tulip Bubble and the South Sea Company Bubble were early examples of what the economist Robert Shiller, in his book *Irrational Exuberance*, calls the 'feedback loop'. This occurs when 'investors, their confidence and expectations buoyed by past price increases, bid up specu-lative prices further, thereby enticing more investors to do the same, so that the cycle repeats continually, resulting in an amplified response to the original precipitating factors'.[3]

Or in other words, an extraordinary popular delusion. Social pressures are crucial in shaping our behaviour, says Professor Stephen Greenspan, author of *Annals of Gullibility*, a study of why people expose themselves to risks. Gullibility, he says, is 'an induced social' foolish action, in which peer pressure plays an important role.

Investors in Madoff's Ponzi scheme, both individual and institutional, were scared they would otherwise miss out on something, he argues. 'We tend to model our behaviour after others, especially those who have prestige. It's the "Emperor's New Clothes" syndrome, we stifle our doubts by looking at what other people are doing, which creates a bandwagon effect. The more pressure there is, the more likely you are to fall for it. With Madoff there was a combination of greed and fear. Fear that other people are making more money than you, and that you will lose out.'[4] The lack of social pressure is one reason, he explains, why so few people fall for completely absurd Nigerian email bank scams that promise great riches in exchange for personal financial information. The natural tendency to ignore the the email requests stems from the fact that recipients do not know anybody who has profited from them, in addition to the scheme's blatant implausibility.

Yet despite his pioneering work on the psychology of gullibility, Professor Greenspan lost about one-third of his retirement savings with Bernard Madoff. They had been placed in an investment fund that seemed solid, stable and enjoyed a good reputation. But that fund eventually fed into a Madoff feeder fund. Like numerous Madoff victims, he had no idea that his assets had been passed down a chain which ended in Madoff's Ponzi scheme. 'I did not know Bernie Madoff. I had never heard of Bernie Madoff. I invested in a $3 billion fund.

I trusted the individual who brought me to the fund, who was a true believer himself. Now I see that my gullibility was an abdication of my personal responsibility,' says Greenspan.

Madoff was not the only fraudster running a flourishing Ponzi scheme during the early 1990s. Numerous scams operated across Eastern Europe and Russia after the collapse of Communism. This was the time known as 'Wild Capitalism', of lax or nonexistent laws and regulatory authorities, widespread corruption, and an explosive hunger, after decades of privation, for consumer goods and Western luxuries. From the Baltics to the Balkans, just as on Wall Street and in the City of London, greed was good. For those running the scams, greed brought unimaginable riches. For most of their investors, it brought destitution. The post-Communist frauds showed that Professor Greenspan's basic principles of gullibility applied to the roughest hewn peasants and the most sophisticated investors. At the same time wars and political upheaval greatly amplified the 'feedback loop', fuelling the madness of crowds, first in Serbia, whose president was a former banker.

During the late 1970s, while Madoff was making waves at NASDAQ, Slobodan Milosevic was president of a conglomerate of nineteen banks, based in the capital Belgrade. He was always welcomed by Wall Street's grandees who hoped he would open up the creaking Yugoslav economy to Western investment. Milosevic certainly knew all about Ponzi schemes. He organised one which stole tens of millions of dollars of his own citizens' savings. The man Milosevic chose to run his Ponzi scheme was called Jezdimir Vasiljevic. His nickname was 'Gazda Jezda' – Jezda the Boss, a diminutive, which, like 'Uncle Bernie', fostered a cosy familiarity and, hopefully, warm feelings of trust. Gazda Jezda, like Uncle Bernie, loved money. 'Mr Vasiljevic is a great believer in money,' said one aide. 'He really believes you can get anything done and persuade people to do anything with money.' For a while, as long as he enjoyed Milosevic's support, Gazda Jezda was right. In 1990, Vasiljevic set up a credit and savings cooperative, which became known as the Jugoskandic bank, in Pozarevac, eastern Serbia, Milosevic's home town.

The following year war erupted. The Yugoslav army and Serbian paramilitaries attacked newly independent Croatia and set Bosnia ablaze. The international community responded with economic sanctions. The Serbian economy collapsed and hyperinflation made the local currency, the dinar, worthless. In 1993 a banknote was introduced with a face value of 50,000,000,000 dinars. Hyperinflation also brought strange benefits: utilities and telephone calls became free, in effect. Which is why Gazda Jezda, and Milosevic, wanted only foreign currency in Jugoskandic's accounts. Jugoskandic was a Ponzi scheme, which paid interest rates of up to 15 per cent a month on short-term foreign currency deposits, or 50 per cent every three months.

Encourage by the state-controlled media, Serbs rushed to invest everything they had. Every morning long lines of customers waited outside Jugoskandic's branches. Most families knew at least one person who had returned home with a tidy sum in Deutschmarks (DM) after having worked in the car factories of Germany. Unlike Madoff's clients, the investors at Jugoskandic were not after riches, only survival. A deposit of 1,500 DM would bring a return of 225 DM a month, enough to scrape by. The money poured in and

Jugoskandic was soon transferring substantial funds to the national bank. A complex industry worth hundreds of millions of dollars a year had sprung up to bring in illicit fuel and tobacco. For Belgrade's elite, war and sanctions were hugely profitable. Vasiljevic's interests expanded to shipping, trading, and the Belgrade race track.[5] Awash with cash, in autumn 1992 Vasiljevic sponsored one of the most bizarre events of the Yugoslav wars: a $5 million sanctions-busting chess match in the beautiful resort town of Sveti Stefan, on the coast of Montenegro, between Bobby Fischer and Boris Spassky.

Protected by Milosevic, Vasiljevic was untouchable. There were no independent regulatory authorities to speak of, no Serbian version of the SEC. Momir Pavlicevic, a director of the Serbian chamber of commerce, warned that it was all too good to be true, but no one was listening. 'Black market dollars are all making their way to Mr Vasiljevic and his Jugoskandic bank. I personally believe the bank is engaged in dangerous speculation and deals related to the armed conflict. It is offering hard currency interest rates of 10 per cent, which is incredible. I would not be surprised if a collapse happens.' It did. In April 1993 Vasiljevic closed his bank and fled to Israel, claiming that the government was extorting him and forcing him use the deposits to buy weapons. About 100,000 customers lost everything, and Jugoskandic left debts of at least $75 million, triggering fury and panic across Serbia.

Madoff managed to outwit the regulatory authorities for the lifetime of his Ponzi scheme. When Jugoskandic crashed there were, of course, no consequences for Milosevic. The Serbian state had organised the giant plundering of its own citizens' savings, says Dusan Mitevic, a former key adviser to the Serbian president. Mitevic's description of Milosevic's role in Jugoskandic has uncanny echoes of what we know so far of how Madoff's Ponzi scheme worked. Milosevic, like Madoff, was the enabler. It seems he had learned a great deal on his visits to Wall Street, knowledge which he passed on to his subordinates. Mitevic said: 'They were not real bankers, they were unsophisticated people. Milosevic gave the idea to them, he taught them how to do it and then created the environment in which it could happen. Milosevic was an absolutely key person for them. Without him they would not have been able to work for three minutes.'[6]

In Romania more than one million investors bought into the Caritas pyramid scheme, which in its early stages paid 800 per cent a month for deposits of three months. Caritas, which means charity in Latin, was founded by Ioan Stoica, an accountant. The scheme exploded when he combined forces with Gheorghe Funar, the ultra-nationalist mayor of Cluj, a city in Transylvania. With Funar's support Stoica opened an office in Cluj's town hall. Peasants and factory workers travelled to Cluj on chartered buses and even donkey carts to hand over their savings. At Caritas's height, in 1993, Stoica lined up his tellers in the local sports stadium, where they kept piles of banknotes behind their desks.[7] By October the local paper was printing forty-four pages of names of 'winners', as those who received their 800 per cent interest were known, a day. Warnings that Caritas would collapse, including a leaked report from the Romanian intelligence service, were ignored. By spring 1994 Caritas had gone the way of Jugoskandic.

Yet the spectacular failures of both Jugoskandic and Caritas, both of which were widely reported, did not deter

Russian investors from putting their savings into the MMM stock fund. By summer 1994 MMM had at least five million shareholders, all putting their faith in its brash version of capitalism. The stars of MMM's television advertising campaign, two potbellied men drinking beer in foreign capitals, became national heroes. Just as in Serbia and Romania a feeding frenzy erupted. MMM's end too came suddenly. By the end of July that year the share price had plunged more than 100 times, to about $1.60. The company refused to buy any of its shares back and collapsed soon after. Still the pyramid mania continued. During 1996 and 1997 Albanians invested in various pyramid schemes whose collapse brought the country to the brink of civil war. At one stage two schemes, Xhafferi and Populi, had almost two million investors – in a country with a population of 3.5 million. These and others competed wildly for funds: Xhafferi offered to treble deposits in three months, another scheme offered to double deposits in two.

The small Balkan nation was swept by a frenzy: houses were sold, livestock auctioned off, anything to get hold of cash. The government stood by, unable or unwilling to intervene. In January 1997 the schemes began to collapse. The government belatedly froze the bank accounts of Xhafferi and Populi, which held $250 million. The country exploded into violence. Soldiers and police officers deserted and gangs looted state armouries. More than one million weapons were taken, some of which were later used by Kosovo Albanian guerillas against the Serbs. The government lost control of the south of the country and about 2,000 people were killed. Looters burned down tax and customs offices and Albania descended into anarchy. The government eventually regained control and shut down the remaining schemes.

Albania is a long way from Wall Street but it is unfortunate that the International Monetary Fund's (IMF) recommendations on dealing with pyramid schemes were not sent to the SEC and acted on with regard to Bernard Madoff. The principles were clear and straightforward: 'Companies believed to be operating pyramid schemes should be investigated. By definition, the liabilities of pyramid schemes exceed their assets, and the schemes fund payments to investors out of new investment inflows. To determine whether a company is operating a pyramid scheme, it is necessary to find out if it has real investments and if these investments are likely to be sufficient to cover its liabilities. The investigation can be conducted by the police, a government ministry, or the central bank. The key point is that the investigators should be able to recognize financial fraud and also to assess the value of company assets.'[8]

After Madoff was arrested there was much excited talk in New York that he had done to the most damage to the Jews since Hitler. A profile of Madoff in *Vanity Fair*, by Elaine Squillari, his former secretary, and the journalist Mark Seal, opens with a long paragraph about Traudl Junge, who was Hitler's secretary.[9] On one level, the comparison is nonsensical, for obvious reasons, but that does not mitigate the intense sense of anger, hurt and, most of all, of betrayal. Hitler aside, it was a fact that Madoff, a Jew, had stolen the most money from other Jews and Jewish institutions since the Nazi looting during the Holocaust and the post-1945 Communist appropriations. Perhaps a more useful comparison, in terms of psychological insight to both the perpetrator of the fraud

Bernie Madoff in 2003 at the height of his riches and power. Madoff was the biggest financial fraudster in modern history. (Rex)

Ruth and Andrew Madoff on the beach by the family's summer home in Montauk, Long Island. (Getty)

The house where Bernard Madoff grew up with his sister Sondra and brother Peter in Laurelton, Queens, a suburb of New York City. (Stephen Wilkes)

Above: Bernard Madoff, his brother Peter and sons Mark and Andrew. Many of the senior positions in Madoff's legitimate share-trading operation were held by family members. (Getty)

Above right: Mark Madoff, director of listed trading, at his desk in his father's company. (Getty)

Right: Andrew Madoff, director of NASDAQ trading. Like his brother, Andrew started work for his father as soon as he graduated from university. (Getty)

Peter and Marion Madoff and their son Roger at Montauk. In later years Roger would bravely fight chronic leukaemia. (Getty)

Shana Madoff, Roger's glamorous sister, was a regular on the New York society circuit. (Rex)

Bernard and Ruth Madoff on holiday in Mexico. They enjoyed an opulent lifestyle. (Rex)

A portrait of Bernard Madoff on his 50th birthday by the acclaimed Canadian photographer Karsh. (Camera Press)

Left: Michael Bienes ran a feeder fund for Bernard Madoff until 1992 and became a renowned philanthropist. (Miami Herald)

Below: Thierry Magon de la Villehuchet. The French aristocrat also ran a feeder fund for Madoff but his involvement ended in tragedy. (Rex)

Above: Ezra Merkin, a highly respected figure in New York's Jewish community, was one of Madoff's most important business associates. (Getty)

Above: Harry Markopolos, the financial investigator who doggedly pursued Madoff over the years, testifies about his activities. (Getty)

The ultra-luxurious Palm Beach Country Club in Florida. Numerous members fell victim to Madoff's scam. (Rex)

The iconic Lipstick Building in mid-town Manhattan, where Madoff's company rented three floors. (Rex)

Bernard Madoff leaves court in New York in January 2009 after losing his plea for bail. He was ordered to be confined to his penthouse. (Getty)

Madoff arrives in court in March 2009. He pleaded guilty to charges of fraud and was taken to prison. (Rex)

and its victims, is to compare Madoff with the former Serbian president.

Their levels of criminality are different, of course. Slobodan Milosevic ignited and directed four wars and was indicted for war crimes and genocide by the United Nations tribunal. Madoff was a thief. But there were still numerous similarities between the two men; on a personal level, in their modus operandi, and psychological make-up. They were intellectually arrogant, authoritarian bullies who often humiliated their underlings. Madoff's financial empire, like Milosevic's Yugoslavia, was a one-man show, where decisions were taken at the top and expected to be immediately implemented. Both men believed they were outwitting the system: in Madoff's case the regulatory authorities and the SEC, in Milosevic's the international community that for years regarded him as part of the solution to the Yugoslav wars, even though he was the main problem. Both men were sociopaths, with no shred of human empathy for their victims, whether they were bankrupted by Madoff's Ponzi scheme, or displaced or killed by wars and ethnic cleansing. Milosevic was utterly unmoved by the human suffering that he unleashed, recalls one diplomat who negotiated with him. 'He gave the impression that he did not care about people as individuals. Nothing seemed to affect him emotionally, any kind of suffering. Apart from his family, people were nothing to him.' The same is true of Bernie Madoff, as Simon Levy, his investor and dining partner for decades who lost everything, can bear witness.

The plaintive stories of the victims of Jugoskandic, MMM, or Caritas, echo the accounts of those who lost money with Madoff. Life savings and family legacies vanished, pensioners who hoped to live off the interest were left penniless and families were left without money to pay for vital medical care. The collapse of the Eastern European frauds elicited much pontificating, some of it very patronising, in the Western press; about the lack of state regulation, a naive and financially unsophisticated population, the legacy of Communism and a failure to understand the harsh reality of capitalism. Caritas, wrote Jane Perlez in the *New York Times*, was partly about 'the unrealistic expectations of a people who have heard about capitalism but never experienced it'. To some extent this is true. Anybody with even the most basic experience of capitalism would be unlikely to hand over their life savings to a teller sitting at a makeshift desk in a sports stadium.

But the story is not quite that straightforward. Caritas and Madoff's scam share much more than hordes of unhappy investors who have lost everything. The key phrase here is 'unrealistic expectations'. Clearly, returns of 800 per cent over three months are unrealistic. But how realistic was it for Madoff's investors to expect returns of 10 per cent or more, not for one or two years, but for decades, whether the market went up or down? Some simply refused to be told that there was something fishy going on, says one Wall Street investment banker. 'A lot of people knew that something was wrong. My accountants had five Madoff clients and they warned them. But the clients told them they would fire them, they said, "you go before Bernie goes".' Many Madoff investors dealt with their secret inner doubts by bringing in friends and relatives to the scheme, which somehow subconsciously validated it. 'Since people know when they are getting something for nothing, when things are too good to be true, they become proselytisers for it,' says the banker. 'They convince themselves, that's why so many people dragged in other victims.'

Bennett Goldworth, an American real estate broker, brought in about another fourteen people. Goldworth first invested with Madoff in 2000, introduced by a BLMIS employee. Goldworth was then in his early forties and seeking financial security. 'Madoff was a closed fund and lots of funds are closed, so for many people investing with him felt like something prestigious. But I wanted to get in because I was tired of the roller coaster ride in the stock market. We are now being portrayed as just the opposite, but we were conservative investors. Technology stocks were jumping all over the place, but Madoff's return was relatively low, about 9 or 10 per cent.' Over the next eight years Goldworth invested a seven-figure sum with Madoff as a personal client. He felt completely safe. 'The statement came every month and most of the time you would make very little money. A couple of times a year you scored big. It felt secure. Madoff had a history going back to the 1960s, including 1987 when the stock market crashed. He even made money then, which reassured me.' Goldworth, who has an MBA, asked his contact how the scheme worked but didn't really get any satisfactory answers. 'It was presented in a way that is very complicated and no one really understands. Only a handful of people could analyse his statements and see through them. Many more investment professionals could not.'

Realism then is in the eye of the beholder. Caritas and Madoff both calibrated their returns for their investors' expectations. In post-Communist Romania everyone believed that capitalism was a giant casino with spectacular winnings. In New York the folk memory of the crashes of

1929 and 1987 had left a different legacy: a longing for the safe and steady. In both cases, the Ponzi principle is essentially the same: manipulating investors' belief, or rather, suspending their disbelief and critical faculties. Each fraud demands an imprimatur of legitimacy. It just needs to be tailored for the society where it is operating. After forty years of living in one of the harshest regimes in Eastern Europe, Romanians in the early 1990s still looked to the authorities for reassurance. Even under Communism the state had always provided work, homes, and food, however meagre, and the penalties for dissent were extremely harsh. So when the mayor of Cluj, the country's second city, allowed Stoica to open a Caritas office in municipal buildings, and then opened up the city's sports stadium for its tellers, everyone was reassured.

As a chairman of NASDAQ and a powerful figure on Wall Street, Madoff too had the imprimatur of legitimacy. His office in the Lipstick Building, a very imposing location, served the same purpose as Caritas' desks in the Cluj sports stadium: to impress potential customers with his firm's power and stability. Once the Ponzi scheme is apparently legitimised, whether by plush offices, an eminent founder, or powerful allies and contacts, the same principle applies. That barely suppressed panic, that someone, somewhere, is making more money, knows something, has an investment secret, was Madoff's most powerful recruiter. Nowhere was this fear more prevalent than in Palm Beach, the playground of America's ultra-rich.

11

The *shtetl* on the sand

'Money is the only thing that matters on Palm Beach.'
Lawrence Leamer, author of *Madness Under the Royal Palms.*

A pair of trousers are waiting for Bernard Madoff at a men's clothes shop on Worth Avenue, the most expensive shopping street in Palm Beach. The trousers are made of spun cashmere and cost $2,000. Madoff's size was not in stock when he last visited, so the trousers were ordered for him from Italy. By the time they arrived he had other things on his mind. Still, someone has to pay for them, perhaps especially on Palm Beach. When David Neff, owner of retail outlet Trillion, heard that Madoff had been arrested, he immediately charged the $2,000 to Madoff's credit card but it had already been cancelled.[1] Compared to most Madoff victims, Neff escaped lightly. Bernard Madoff blew through Palm Beach like one of the Florida hurricanes that sweep up boats, cars, and houses before pounding them to smithereens. Hurricane Bernard left a trail of financial devastation in its wake from which Florida's swankiest enclave will take a very long time to recover.

Palm Beach is one of the richest and most socially stratified places on earth. A small island off the coast of south Florida, thirteen miles long and barely a thousand yards wide, it is linked to the mainland by three bridges. To drive from the mainland, across Royal Park Bridge and over Lake Worth, is to enter a serene world of luxury and exclusivity. To describe someone as a mere millionaire is an insult. Out of season, about 10,000 people live on Palm Beach, a number that triples during the holiday seasons. Current and former residents include Conrad Black, Donald Trump, Estée Lauder, Ray Kroc, who founded McDonald's, the Kennedy dynasty, Jimmy Buffet, Rod Stewart, Rush Limbaugh, James Patterson, and numerous multimillionaires, including, until recently, Bernard and Ruth Madoff.

Palm Beach is so clean, beautiful, and tranquil that it barely seems to be in America. At times it barely seems to be alive. It is the ultimate gated community. The three bridges can be raised and the island made unreachable by land. The sprawling villas and faux-Hispanic haciendas are hidden behind high, carefully manicured hedges and the smooth, spotless pavements positively glow in the Florida sunshine. The long, sandy beaches are a pristine shade of cream, the sea a vivid turquoise. There is neither litter nor graffiti. The few people of colour are mostly Hispanic domestic servants. Even the house for sale signs must not be larger than twenty-four square inches. Many female faces over fifty are set in the rictus grin of botox and plastic surgery. Much of the population is elderly but there are no hospitals, cemeteries or undertakers on the island. Death, despite its inevitability, even proximity, is the great unmentionable. Lives on Palm Beach are measured by consumption and acquisition. As well as Trillion,

Worth Avenue boasts a Saks Fifth Avenue, Salvatore Ferragamo, Valentino, Hermes, Ralph Lauren, and a Gucci on the corner. The island's newspaper, the *Palm Beach Daily News*, is known as the 'Shiny Sheet', printed with special ink that does not rub off on readers' hands.

'People pretend that Palm Beach is about class and culture,' says Lawrence Leamer, 'but all that matters is your money. People look at you and they don't think how intelligent you are or how good a human being. They just want to know how much money you have.' Nobody can scan, process, and absorb social and economic signifiers faster or more accurately than Palm Beach's dowager matrons. In a blink or two of an eye, they evaluate hair, teeth, botox, facelifts, handbags, skin tone, posture, clothes, and accent. Those judged acceptable may, eventually, be admitted to the choicest soirées, but it will be a long and expensive process, demanding substantial donations to charity and endless benefit dinners.

'Every year you will see a bunch of new faces who have either just moved here or want to come to events here and get into Palm Beach society,' says one longtime resident, a former boyfriend of one of the richest women in America. 'Everything revolves around philanthropy. If you want to be accepted, you have to go to the benefits and make donations. You buy tickets to all the parties, either through a PR person, or through someone you know. If you give a lot of money, your social standing rises. You start getting better tables. The organisers want to raise the most money they can, so the Palm Beach charity business feeds itself.' Palm Beach considers itself so exclusive that local wits quip, when they drive to the mainland, that 'they are going to Florida', says Saul

Irving, a house restorer. 'As you come across those three bridges you enter into an entire different world. The whole place is just about showing off. When an exotic new car comes out it's here. It's all about money. But it is also extremely beautiful, the weather is intoxicating, the people are friendly, and the place has a certain charm, especially with some of the older houses.'

Perfect territory, then, for Bernard Madoff. By the 1990s the Madoffs had become very rich. He and Ruth were fixtures on the Palm Beach social scene. They played golf, sailed, shopped, brunched, lunched and had drinks in the lounge of the historic Breakers Hotel. Or they just stayed at home, where they lived in luxury. Their house, at 410 North Lake Way, had five bedrooms and seven bathrooms spread out over two floors, and a wooden deck overlooking the sea. The house cost $3.8 million but soon doubled in value. Madoff's ocean-going Rybovich fishing boat was worth more than $2 million. But on Palm Beach, just as on the Upper East Side, Madoff was careful to never appear too pushy. He and Ruth were not members of the 'blister pack', the ardent social climbers who elbowed each other out of the way as they moved up the society ladder. Unlike most Palm Beach matrons, Ruth did not drape herself in expensive jewellery. She still adhered to the cardinal rule of Our Crowd: 'don't be showy'.

The Madoffs were among friends on Palm Beach. Carl Shapiro and his wife Ruth lived in their own apartment at the Breakers Hotel. Frank Avellino lived nearby on Coral Lane. Walter and Monica Noel also owned a house on the island. The Madoffs' seal of approval, at least for their monied Jewish investors, was their membership of the Palm

Beach Country Club, the ultimate status symbol among American Jews who care about these things. The initiation fee is reportedly $300,000. The verdant, rolling golf course, dotted with palm trees, covers the width of the island from the Atlantic ocean to Lake Worth. The spa, swimming pool and gourmet restaurants are all world class. The club, like its WASP rivals the Bath & Tennis, and the Everglades country clubs, also has elaborate dress codes and rules, furthering its air of rarified exclusivity. No shorts are permitted less than four inches above the knee. Men are required to wear jackets and ties after 6 p.m.[2] Perhaps a third of the members signed up with 'Uncle Bernie'.

What this vast edifice of luxury, comfort and formality signifies, of course, is not security, but quite the opposite: the obsessive need to measure, judge, and exclude. The Palm Beach Country Club is a long way from the *shtetls* and ghettoes of Eastern Europe from where its members' forefathers originated. But for all its resplendent interiors and legions of uniformed staff, the club is essentially an ultra-luxurious *shtetl* by the sea. Bernard Madoff was its wise man, coveted for his secret knowledge, not of the Torah, the five books of Moses, but the stock market. Palm Beach is part of a continuum of American history, the part that has always sought validation in the acquisition of material goods and social status. Paradoxically, in America, the richest country in the world, that hunger for acceptance flourished as never before and, for some, it seems, could never be sated.

But this was nothing new in immigrant history. The Austrian author Stefan Zweig recalled in *The World of Yesterday*, his autobiography, how, before the cataclysm, the Viennese Jewish bourgeoisie loved to revel in social and economic one-

145

upmanship: 'We were always being told that these were "fine" people, that others were "not fine". Every friend's pedigree was examined back to the earliest generation to see whether or not he came from a "good" family and all his relatives as well as his wealth were checked. This constant categorisation which actually was the main topic of every familiar and social conversation at that time seemed to be most ridiculous and snobbish because for all Jewish families it was merely a matter of fifty or a hundred years earlier or later that they had come from the same ghetto.'[3] Zweig noted this phenomenon but he was not immune to it. Like the Upper East Side *Yekkes* of a century ago, he shared a disdain for the Jews of Eastern Europe. His family came from Moravia, he wrote: 'They were entirely free both of the sense of inferiority and of the smooth pushing impatience of the Galician or eastern Jews.'[4] Whether in inter-war Vienna or present-day Florida, the assessing, the calibrations, and the judgments all serve essentially the same purpose as Madoff's mania for tidy desks and regulation blinds at BLMIS's offices: keeping the vagaries of the outside world at bay. In his case, that meant the SEC. At the Palm Beach Country Club the enemy – Bernard Madoff – was already within.

Madoff was held in a kind of awe on Palm Beach, says Richard Rampell, a prominent Palm Beach accountant, several of whose clients invested in Madoff's fund. 'The country club was very important to Madoff. It helped give him the imprimatur of legitimacy. If you find a good money manager everyone wants to pile on, and he seemed to be one. This is country club investing. At the Palm Beach Country Club there are lots of very, very, rich people there, billionaires and centimillionaires. Big money. They had money that they would gamble with, and without too much investigation.' Rampell first met Madoff a decade or so ago at the Palm Beach Grill, a popular upscale place on Royal Poinciana Plaza. Heads turned when Madoff entered. He was spoken of with awe. 'I was having dinner there with some people when he came in. They told me, "That's Bernie Madoff, he is responsible for 2 to 3 per cent of all the trades every day at the NYSE".'

Madoff's Palm Beach network was a triangle built around three people. Two were investors: Carl Shapiro and Jeffrey Picower, while the third, Robert Jaffe, worked for Cohmad, Madoff's feeder fund that was based on the 18th floor of the Lipstick Building. For Madoff, his friendship with Carl Shapiro was priceless. Shapiro was widely respected in Palm Beach, both for his financial acumen and his enormous generosity. He had donated vast sums to hospitals and universities in the Boston area, including $25 million to Brandeis University, where three large buildings are adorned with his name.

Shapiro, it seems, regarded Madoff almost like the son he never had. Madoff attended the elderly tycoon's family celebrations and the two men were often seen together on Palm Beach. 'People heard about others investing and doing well, and for a very long period of time. If somebody has some kind of a good deal, everybody wants to follow on,' says Richard Rampell. 'They see that Carl Shapiro is making a lot of money, clearly, because he giving a lot away. That was the due diligence that the followers of Carl Shapiro did, that he had invested himself.' Perhaps they should have asked tougher questions. Shapiro lost about $400 million of his personal funds with Madoff while his charitable foundation lost up to $200 million. After Madoff was arrested, Carl Shapiro said in a statement: 'I also want to be abundantly clear that at no time did I ever formally introduce individuals as potential investors with Mr Madoff. In fact, we agreed when our friendship began that I would not introduce him to potential clients. I wanted to avoid putting him in the awkward position of having to say no to a friend of mine.'[5]

Jeffrey Picower and his wife Barbara were also immensely wealthy and well-known philanthropists. They lived in style in Fairfield, Connecticut, and in Palm Beach, where the Picower Foundation was based. The foundation was the seventy-first-largest charity in America. Until Madoff's arrest, it reported assets of almost $1 billion, all of which was invested with Madoff. The foundation closed soon after his arrest. Until then it had sponsored numerous good causes including the Picower Institute for Learning and Memory at the Massachusetts Institute of Technology, the New York Public Library, and the Children's Health Fund. In its last year of operation the foundation gave away $23.4 million, including $1 million to the Harlem Children's Zone. It had a high profile in Palm Beach, supporting the Kravis Center, an arts venue, and several children's charities.

In May 2009 Irving Picard, the Madoff trustee, launched a lawsuit against Jeffrey Picower and numerous trust funds and other bodies, seeking the return of $5.1 billion. The suit alleges that Picower made billions of dollars from Madoff's Ponzi scheme: 'Since December 1995 he and the other defendants collectively profited from this scheme through the withdrawal of more than $6.7 billion. The Trustee's investigation to date has revealed that at least five billion dollars of this amount was fictitious profit from the Ponzi scheme. In other words, Defendants have received, at a minimum, more than five *billion* [emphasis as original] dollars of other people's money.' In some years, the lawsuit claims, the defendants enjoyed annual returns as high as 500 per cent or 950 per cent.[6] William Zabel, a lawyer who represents the Picowers, rejected the suit's claims as 'inflammatory' and 'without any foundation'. In July 2009 Zabel filed a legal brief calling for Picard's complaint to be dismissed. The sixty-eight-page brief said that the complaint was 'dedicated to vilifying Mr Picower in order to justify the pursuit of funds from the defendants' and relied on 'baseless conclusions and idle speculation'. Zabel stated: 'The complaint is also riddled with significant factual errors, such as the claim that the Picowers earned returns of over 950%. These baseless charges are particularly unfair given that the Madoff fraud wiped out the Picowers' charitable foundation, which gave many millions to support medical research, the arts and education. In the Trustee's zeal to claw back money for other victims, he fails to recognise that the Picowers are honourable people who were deceived by the same fraud that for many years eluded thousands of other investors, financial professionals and regulators that had access to Madoff's files.'[7]

Robert Jaffe was vice-chairman of Cohmad, the feeder fun that Madoff ran with Sonny Cohn. Elegantly dressed, well coiffured, still dark haired in his sixties, Jaffe was a prominent figure in Palm Beach. He is married to Carl Shapiro's daughter Ellen, and they lived in a $17 million waterfront villa, on North Lake Way, near Madoff. Jaffe cultivated the air of a debonair English gentleman of leisure and considered himself quite the dandy. He drove a green 1954 MG convertible and loved to play golf and schmooze his way around Palm Beach society. The doors were usually open: Jaffe was Madoff's 'go-to' man in Palm Beach.

As in Greenwich, Madoff could not be seen to be openly soliciting for investors in Palm Beach. Such a déclassé tactic would remove the crucial air of exclusivity that he needed to keep the money flowing. Instead he used Cohmad and front-men such as Jaffe to 'subtly market his advisory business', according to the SEC's June 2009 lawsuit against Cohmad: 'Cohmad's representatives strategically circulated among wealthy individuals in various exclusive milieus – New Jersey golf clubs, Palm Beach Country Club, and the like – and offhandedly mentioned that they were affiliated with Madoff. The representatives projected themselves as individuals who became wealthy through B[L]MIS, had no need to work, and merely frequented country clubs. When prospective investors asked if the representatives could make an introduction to Madoff so they could invest with B[L]MIS, the Cohmad representatives would agree to try to put in a good word with Madoff and see if they could get the investors in. Cohmad and its representatives would then assist and arrange the opening of accounts with B[L]MIS.'[8] Jaffe's lawyers said in response that the SEC's complaint, which they learned about only from the press, 'smacks of impulsiveness and efforts at self-justification. It is unfair, baseless in the law and is inaccurate in its understanding of the facts and of Mr Jaffe.' Stanley Arkin, one of Jaffe's lawyers, said in January 2009: 'Bob Jaffe and his family are victims of one of the most willful and despicable frauds ever seen. The depth of betrayal of Bob Jaffe and his family by Bernard Madoff is stunning.'[9]

Like Madoff, Jaffe had come a long way from comparatively modest beginnings, and reinvented himself on the island's society, an investigation by the *Boston Globe* news-paper revealed.[10]

Jaffe grew up in New England and attended Suffolk University, where he graduated in business administration. He worked his way through college by selling designer men's clothing, developing a liking for expensive labels such as Brioni, and Zegna. Jaffe enrolled in an MBA programme but completed only a year before dropping out and marrying Ellen Shapiro in 1968. After twenty years or so in the brokerage business he moved over to Cohmad. It was easy work, schmoozing potential investors on the golf course or in the bars and restaurants. Jaffe became immensely wealthy and could afford plenty of designer suits. 'Jaffe had access to Madoff, and that made him a superstar. He was bigger than life,' said one Palm Beach resident. He fancied himself as a dandy, telling the *Daily Record*, an American newspaper about fashion, in 1998: 'The clothing I wear is more – dare I say – cutting edge. It's a few years ahead of the pack. Once you have had filet mignon you don't want to go back.'

Palm Beach certainly never looked back. This was not a place known for introspection. A little more than a century ago Palm Beach was still swampland, inhabited by alligators, snakes, and giant frogs. The resort was founded in the late nineteenth century by Henry Flagler, a millionaire industrialist who also built up Miami, about sixty miles north. Flagler was a visionary, who brought railways and infrastructure, and turned Palm Beach into a playground for America's super-rich. Its year-round warm climate, gorgeous setting overlooking the sea, and the fact that it was an island, separated from the mainland, soon brought the great WASP dynasties down from New York. The Rockefellers, Vanderbilts, and J.P. Morgan himself all holidayed on Palm Beach, alongside the Kennedys, European nobility, royalty, and numerous US presidents. Many stayed at Flagler's awe-inspiring new hotel, The Breakers, overlooking the sea. When the hotel burned down in 1925 seventy-five artisans were brought from Italy to work on the new structure, which was modelled on the Villa Medici in Rome.

Palm Beach's tropical location did not ease the East Coast grandees' carefully delineated hierarchies and social codes, all of which were anyway imported from the European 'society' that they mimicked so painstakingly. Henry James, America's great social chronicler, was impressed by their devotion to their social codes and European manners, but worried that America's nouveaux riches were so obsessed with their status and so unimaginative in their outlook that they boded ill for the new nation's future. The women were especially dull, he wrote: 'The women in particular failed in an extraordinary degree to engage the imagination, to offer it, so to speak, references or openings; it faltered – doubtless respectfully enough – where they for the most part so substantially and prosaically sat, failing of any warrant to go an inch further.'[11]

Where the WASP grandees went, the *Yekkes* followed. In its early years several of the great Jewish families winter holidayed in Palm Beach, such as the Lehmanns, Warburgs, and Seligmans, travelling down in their private train carriages, accompanied by numerous uniformed staff. The *Yekkes* were not especially welcomed, but they were accepted, however reluctantly. The *Yekkes* hosted dinners and lunches at The Breakers, played bridge, went shooting at the Gun Club and tangoed and tea-danced through the afternoon. Dressed in three-piece suits, they sat in wicker wheelchairs, pushed along the promenade by black servants. Several built or bought houses on the island. But just as on the Upper East Side, the *Yekkes* were discreet and tasteful about their wealth, and, muttered the WASPS, thankfully there were not too many of them.

A.M. Sonnabend, a Jewish businessman, helped change that. He opened up the island to Madoff's kind of Jews, the boisterous, successful, sometimes brash – in comparison to the *Yekkes* – entrepreneurs, the descendants of the Lower East Side *shtarkers*, who had prospered in America.

Sonnabend bought a property portfolio in the 1940s for $2.4 million, including two hotels, Henry Flagler's original mansion, a beach club, and a golf course. Sonnabend was not a rarified *Yekke*. He was a former fighter pilot who flew in World War I, a champion squash player, a Harvard graduate, and a tough businessman. Sonnabend was a *shtarker* in a suit, who knew a good business opportunity when he saw one. His arrival caused panic in the town's elite. The island's leading lights met at the Everglades Club, declaring that 'those people' must be kept out of Palm Beach, or it would become a second Miami.[12] Despite the WASPs' efforts, 'they' were not kept out. Worse, 'they' soon made a part of Palm Beach their own. Unwelcome at the existing country clubs, they founded the Palm Beach Country Club in 1952, which soon became the island's premier Jewish resort.

'Palm Beach has a history of anti-Semitism,' says Lawrence Leamer. 'Some places are still restricted. They say they just choose their members, and that you have to have a certain kind of class and culture, which is just a euphemism. They refer to Jews as "them".' According to the Anti-Defamation League (ADL), The Breakers Hotel openly discriminated against Jewish guests until the passing of the Civil Rights Act in 1964. Its rate card stated: 'The clientele of The Breakers is restricted and satisfactory social references must be submitted.' In 1960 the ADL wrote requesting rooms in the name of two guests, one with a Jewish-sounding name and one without. The Breakers told the first guest that the hotel was fully booked, although it offered rooms to the guest with the non-Jewish-sounding name for the same dates. This practice was widespread across Florida.

In 1965 the ADL filed a discrimination complaint with the Department of Justice against The Breakers, using its reservations letters as evidence. The ADL dropped the complaint after the hotel promised to stop its discriminatory policy. Bonnie Ruben, a spokeswoman for The Breakers, said that the hotel had no knowledge of or evidence that the hotel had 'ever declined reservations'.[13] The ADL has been meeting and holding conferences at The Breakers for more than twenty-five years. While open discrimination is now illegal, Palm Beach remains divided between Jews and WASPs. Many Jewish residents live in large apartment buildings on the south of the island. Their road is called 'Sloan's Curve' but is more usually known as the 'Gaza Strip', in what passes for irony. Most Jews would not feel comfortable at the Bath & Tennis, or Everglades clubs, and would not bother trying to join. The same holds true for the WASPs who would not join the Palm Beach Country Club.

Lord Jacobs first heard about Bernie Madoff while playing golf at Palm Beach Country Club. He was discussing investments with a close friend who had entrusted his money to Madoff several years earlier. The friend was satisfied. Madoff's interest rates had recently come down, but he was still paying a steady 10 per cent a year. With personal wealth of more than £100 million, the British peer was looking for investment opportunities, but he wanted consistency more than fireworks. Anthony Jacobs was a bastion of Britain's business establishment and was also well known in the country's Jewish community. He was an extremely successful businessman who had become immensely wealthy running the British School of Motoring, and in the fast food industry, launching the legendary 'Spud-U-like' brand.

Jacobs had been approached by several hedge funds to invest. But he disliked their volatility. Hedge funds can bring impressive, even spectacular returns but are largely unregulated. They rely on strategically placed bets to beat the average returns of the stock and bond markets. A fund that might return its investors 15 per cent, 20 per cent, or even more one year, might lose 25 per cent in another year if it makes a bad bet. Leverage is key to many hedge fund strategies: a client's $1 million investment can be used to borrow another $3 million, so a 10 per cent return becomes a profit of $400,000, after the cost of management and loan fees. But if a bet goes wrong or is too slow to realise, the penalties can be enormous. If half the original $1 million is lost, that translates into a $2 million loss – twice the original investment. Despite the risk, hedge funds are expensive. Managers usually charge 20 per cent of clients' profits and 1, sometimes even 2 per cent of the capital invested. Madoff did not take any commission, increasing his appeal. Jacobs thought some more about Madoff until a couple of months later, when he asked to see his friend's returns. 'I was interested, but I told him I was not sure if I was willing to take 10 per cent a year, just for the sake of consistency. This was a relatively modest return. The description of Madoff investors as greedy is the absolute opposite of the truth. I was a strongly risk averse investor.'[14]

Jacobs also considered himself – then – a sophisticated investor. Jacobs questioned Madoff in some depth about how his investment strategy worked. Unusually for Madoff, he answered Jacobs' questions. In Palm Beach's small and stratified society a wealthy British peer of the realm carried some weight. It would not do for Jacobs to tell his golfing partners that Madoff looked suspicious.

Madoff outlined his split-strike conversion strategy, which involved simultaneously buying 'put' and 'call' options on the shares. 'He was trying to match the balance of what he was investing against the proportion of the market in which he was investing. I went into some detail with him of how it works. What makes me look so foolish is that I was a fairly savvy investor. It may not look like it now, but I really was.'

Jacobs asked why the fund paid 10 per cent rather than 15, as previously. 'He told me that the stock market used to be much more volatile. He said when there are lots of ups and downs it was easier to make money.' Jacobs had never heard of Madoff's strategy, but it sounded plausible to him. 'It seemed clever to limit the ups and downs and accept a lower return because of that. But several things were attractive: there was no leverage and he was not borrowing on your money. You could get your money out in three to five days, he invested only in blue chip stocks and at the end of every year he went into Treasury bonds. The most persuasive thing was the consistency. Once you are willing to accept only 10 per cent on average you really had little to fear. The consistency was the most important thing for most people.' In 1999 Lord Jacobs invested $2 million with Madoff. More would follow.

There is another side, less often told, of the Madoff fraud. Numerous investors made vast profits along the way. Even if their original investment is now lost, and their last statement showing $X million dollars is worthless, many became very rich. One of Richard Rampell's clients, now deceased, certainly did. The client, who had first invested with Madoff in 1985, was getting a steady return in the low teens. This made him not happy but extremely wary, Rampell recalls. 'He was always suspicious of everything to do with money, so he asked me to call Madoff and ask him how come his account was going up by 13 or 14 per cent when the market was going down by whatever it was going down by. He thought Madoff may have been cooking the books.' Rampell made the call, and got the standard Madoff brush-off. 'He told me that he doesn't talk to people about his trading strategy because it's proprietary information. I thought that was a normal response. The propeller heads in the back room at Goldman Sachs don't tell anybody else their trading strategy either. He said: 'What I can tell you is that I can make money when the market goes up, I can make money when the market goes down. I just can't make money when the market stays flat.'

Rampell had seen one of his client's statements, and it showed a high level of transactions. Rampell concluded that there were two possibilities. The first was Madoff was probably doing some kind of day-trading, buying and selling enough volume to capitalise on the daily fluctuations in the stock market. Plenty of people on Wall Street made a respectable living by day-trading, and the more volatile it was, the more money they made. The second possibility was that Madoff was front-running, placing his own orders on the back of his clients', with the knowledge that their buying or selling shares would move the market up or down. This was illegal, but was harder to detect before the advent of automated computerised trading. Rampell outlined the two possibilities to his client. 'He told me, if he's front-running I don't want to know about it, because it's illegal. Ignorance was bliss, in that case.'

The client left his money with Madoff and became enormously rich. 'People lose sight of this. My client invested $5 million with Madoff in 1985. At that time a Madoff account was earning more than 20 per cent a year, a lot more than at the end. He let his account grow from $5 million to $10 million and did not take any earnings out. Once he got to $10 million he decided that was too high a concentration of his net worth in one place, so he took his income out every year. The money doubled in five or six years. He took out more than a $1 million a year and did this every year.' But the more money Rampell's client made from Madoff's fund, the more suspicious he became. Every now and then he would demand $3 million or $4 million back. He would place the money elsewhere for nine months or so, and then put it back in, never letting his account go higher than $10 million. 'Over the course of his lifetime, he started out with $5 million and he probably took out $15 million. So he did OK. There are a lot of people like that, who have been living off this money, over the long term.'

Meanwhile, as Madoff and Robert Jaffe were working the country clubs, Walter Noel and two more feeder funds were extending Madoff's empire far beyond the east coast of America. Associated Investment Advisors, run by Thierry Magon de la Villehuchet, and Bank Medici, founded in Vienna by Sonja Kohn, would bring in more than $4 billion for Madoff's Ponzi scheme.

12
Going global

'I want to take FGG [Fairfield Greenwich Group] to a whole new level. You can never make enough fees from rich individuals – I want to get institutions.'

Andres Piedrahita, son-in-law of Walter Noel, after he joined the Fairfield Greenwich Group in 1997.[1]

In Britain it's called the 'Curse of *Hello!* '. A glamorous couple will grant *Hello!*, a weekly celebrity gossip magazine, 'exclusive' (read: expensive) access to their home. The photographer will take numerous shots of the interior and the happy family relaxing and at play. The writer will chronicle the deep and enduring love the wife and husband have for each other. Some time later the couple will be back in the headlines: as warring parties in an acrimonious divorce. Another word, also beginning with 'h', can be used here: 'hubris'. For hubris runs like a dark thread through the Madoff saga, perhaps nowhere more so than Greenwich, Connecticut.

In October 2002 *Vanity Fair* ran a syrupy article about Walter Noel's five 'picture-perfect' daughters: Corina, Lisina,

Ariane, Alix, and Marisa, under the headline 'Golden in Greenwich'. 'They're well educated and well married, and they're raising a pack of multi-lingual children while keeping their string bikini figures intact,' gushed writer Kristina Stewart.[2] The occasion was a party for Marisa, then twenty-five, who was to marry an investment manager called Matt Brown. With her 'straight blond hair down to her waist and no make-up, she is a coltish mix of tomboy and glamazon', just one of the sisters who, *Vanity Fair* claimed, were 'shoring up the virtues of a nearly extinct aristocracy'. By then the Noels had added a whole new wing to their Greenwich house, large enough for their fourteen grandchildren, sons-in-law, and nannies. The Noels could not have wished for a more sycophantic article had they written it themselves. After all, as *Vanity Fair* noted reverentially: 'their ascent into the rarified social order of Greenwich was by no means assured.' The article did not mention Bernard Madoff but did mention the Fairfield Greenwich Group, which it described as an 'international hedge fund founded by Walter Noel'.

Four months after Madoff's arrest, in April 2009, the magazine published a long and highly critical examination of the family it had once lauded, much of it based on anonymous whispering. The author, Vicky Ward, listed the Noels' catalogue of sins: Walter Noel blurred the line between business and pleasure. Monica's natural Brazilian effervescence – hugs, physical contact – was not quite the thing among the air-kissing Greenwich WASPS. The Noels had bought houses in Southampton, in Palm Beach and a sprawling villa on Mustique. In the circles in which they now moved such wealth was not remarkable, but the Noels were showy. Yemanjá, their house on Mustique, was featured as a cover story, with the women of the family, in *Town & Country* magazine in 2005. This was considered a little too much, especially after 'Golden in Greenwich'. What may have worked on the Upper East Side or Palm Beach – the grand public gesture, the spread in a glossy magazine – did not play so well in the insular, rarified world of Greenwich.

And the Noels wanted everyone to know how well they were doing. They took out an entire page in the 'Blue Book', the select social register of the Hamptons, listing forty-three members of their family, every child and every mobile telephone number. They applied to join the Bathing Corporation, where the lissom Noel daughters apparently upset older members by wearing thongs and sarongs. Worst of all, Noel may even have *networked on the beach*. 'What I heard is he was actually selling the Fairfield Greenwich fund, or trying to encourage the other members of the beach club to buy it, because it was an incredible thing, and he was almost using that as currency, if you will, to garner a favour,' one resident grumbled.[3] The WASP grandees, none of whom of course would ever consider discussing business over the golf course, considered such behaviour 'pushy', two syllables that could spell the kiss of social death.

But the Noels carried on enjoying themselves regardless. Despite their curious hunger to be accepted in a world that, like Palm Beach, would value them only for their money, rather than themselves, Walter and Monica were very likeable, says Shameer Cohen. They enjoyed themselves and wanted everyone around them to have a good time and share in their delight. The Noels' daughters, and their husbands, were decidedly less engaging. 'They were sometimes arrogant. They had a tremendous sense of self-entitlement.

I wasn't the only one who thought that they were very, very aggressive. The younger Noels could not care less whose toes they stepped on ... I think that for the Noels, the unofficial motto was "If we act rich, we will become rich". It's a self-fulfilling prophecy.'

One day Noel asked Shameer Cohen to send him a set of BLMIS statements so he could better understand how Madoff's investment fund operated. Shameer was not impressed when the papers arrived. Corporate bank and brokerage statements were usually printed on thick, embossed paper, with a large logo, and large amounts of legalese in small print on both sides of the paper. Madoff's statements looked as if they were produced either on a typewriter or an ancient printer. Shameer was puzzled and decided to enter the BLMIS statement information onto a spreadsheet to analyse the portfolio. The share portfolio was conservative, like her own, but somehow was offering double the returns she was receiving. She could not see how or why Madoff's strategy worked. How could her bosses understand it? Both Walter Noel and Jeffrey Tucker understood how the 'split-strike' strategy worked. It was not that complicated and they were fully satisfied, says a person familiar with the matter.

Walter Noel moved Madoff's fund far beyond Greenwich, Connecticut. He recruited several of his five sons-in-law to sell Fairfield Greenwich around the world, using their connections. The rolling international circus of aristocrats and minor European royalty would prove a most fruitful source of income. It opened doors to wealthy individuals and institutional investors, not just for Fairfield's Madoff fund, but its numerous other investment vehicles. Noel's star salesman was Andres Piedrahita, who is married to Corina, the eldest

Noel daughter. Piedrahita is a short Colombian with an outsize personality. Like many in the Noels' world he enjoyed a gilded life of wealth and privilege. After attending a private school in Bogota he studied at Boston University, where he made many useful connections before gliding onto Wall Street. His investment career did not start well. Piedrahita's first job was to sell investments, mainly to South Americans. The funds went bust and Piedrahita moved on to a new job. Critics make too much of this, says a person familiar with the matter. 'This was a bump in the road. It was a time when the funds did not perform well.'[4]

After ten years working for various firms Piedrahita founded his own, Littlestone Investments, which he later merged with Fairfield Greenwich. He became rich. Piedrahita loved to live large and was a generous, even spectacular host. He and Corina moved to a large house on Chester Square in Belgravia, hosting parties that were flush with British aristocrats and European royalty. Piedrahita's friends looked on in wonder at his spending power. 'I've never seen anybody live like him and spend like him and I know billionaires who are ten times wealthier than he is. His job was to live grand,' said Fernando Botero, a Colombian friend.[5] In 2003 the Piedrahitas moved to Madrid. He commuted to London on a private Gulfstream jet. The Piedrahitas entertained the cream of international society at home in Madrid or on their hacienda in Majorca, including royals and supermodels. Fairfield Greenwich flourished as the money poured into its Madoff funds and other investment vehicles. Piedrahita is very good at his job, says a person familiar with the matter. 'He is a gregarious, warm personality, but there is much more to him than being a socialite and glad-handing. He is a very focused business person, with a great knowledge of the markets and financial acumen.' Piedrahita's main responsibility was to bring in investors, both individuals and institutions, for Fairfield's non-Madoff products, says the person. The advantage of institutions is that they bring an immediate portfolio of their own investment clients and so generate much more money than recruiting investors one by one. 'Piedrahita's job was to diversify Fairfield's operations. His primary focus was on Fairfield's fund of funds business. He attracted billions of dollars for that.'

As Fairfield grew, Piedrahita, Jeffrey Tucker and Walter Noel discussed floating the business. Fairfield hired a banker and searched for an investment bank to handle the flotation. A meeting was held at the end of 2007. Everything was looking good, apart from one thing: Bernard Madoff. He would not give potential buyers access to BLMIS's records, according to a lawsuit by Irving Picard, the Madoff receiver, against Fairfield Greenwich, and scuppered the deal. 'After FGG told them that BLMIS would not allow prospective investors to view its books, FGG was unable to find a buyer.'[6] The plans for the flotation fell through. This reasoning is incorrect, says a person familiar with the matter. The problem was Madoff's age, not his financial transparency. 'Madoff's position was that his trading strategy and algorithms were proprietary, which was not unique. He was almost seventy then and there was no guarantee that he or any part of his business would continue for any period of time.'

Fairfield Greenwich charged a 1 per cent management fee (after 2002), and a 20 per cent performance fee for providing access to Madoff's funds and for performing due diligence, which it claimed was extensive. Michael Steinhardt, the former hedge fund manager, is extremely critical of such charges. 'This is not money management. It's denigrating the profession. When I was a money manager I took a percentage of the profits and when there were no profits I didn't get paid apart from my expenses.'

By the summer of 2009 Fairfield Greenwich was facing several civil lawsuits, including claims from Irving Picard and the state of Massachusetts. None charged Fairfield with knowing that Madoff was running a Ponzi scheme. The Picard suit seeks the return of $3.2 billion that Fairfield Greenwich funds withdrew from BLMIS between 2002 and December 2008.[7] According to Picard, the Fairfield funds, and their managers, 'did little, if any due diligence, of BLMIS', while they 'ignored multiple red flags because with the Defendants' continued interest in BLMIS the investment manager of the Defendant's funds reaped massive fees, in excess of hundreds of millions of dollars purportedly for investment performance which had proved to be nothing but fiction.' The suit says that between 1996 and 2007 Fairfield Greenwich received consistent annual returns of between 10 and 21 per cent, despite the fact that the S & P trading index on which BLMIS purportedly based its trading reported far larger fluctuations. It also claimed that between 1998 and 2008 'more than 280 supposed trades by BLMIS were recorded on account statements at prices outside the actual trading range for those days, which could have been easily confirmed by any investment professional'.[8]

The Massachusetts lawsuit charges Fairfield with civil fraud. It claims that Fairfield Greenwich failed to make 'any meaningful check into whether Madoff was actually making the trades he said he was making or actually holding the assets he said he was holding on behalf of Sentry clients'. It claims that Fairfield never made 'basic checks' such as insisting Madoff supply the names of the parties with whom he was trading, so they could verify his claims. 'The Division's investigation attempted to discern how Fairfield could possibly not have discovered the fraud during their eighteen-year relationship. The answer, quite simply, is that they were blinded by the fees they were earning, did not engage in meaningful due diligence and turned a blind eye to any fact which would have burst their lucrative bubble.' The lawsuit quotes documents indicating in 2007 Andres Piedrahita earned more than $45 million and Walter Noel and Jeffrey Tucker each $30 million.[9]

Fairfield's lawyers reject all the lawsuit's claims. A seventy-six-page answer to the Massachusetts lawsuit describes the complaint as 'rushed' and 'filled with errors and factual distortions'. PricewaterhouseCoopers, retained by Fairfield Greenwich to audit the Sentry funds, consistently issued 'clean audit opinions', and the NASD and SEC provided additional oversight. Citco Fund Services, a hedge fund administrator, which Fairfield Greenwich retained for due diligence, had never indicated any concern about the Sentry group. The Sentry offering memoranda made it clear that Madoff held 'substantially all the funds' assets', and over the years Madoff had honoured $3 billion in redemption requests. The Massachusetts lawsuit was based on 'guilt by association' and 'fraud by hindsight', Fairfield Greenwich argued.[10]

In fact Madoff's returns were closer to 9 or 10 per cent, there were down months and up months, and Madoff was outperformed by other investment funds, argues a well-informed source. Fairfield employed six professionals in

Bermuda working on due diligence, including risk analysis, Quant analysis and spot checking share prices in relation to trades. The Picard lawsuit's claim that 280 trades outside their actual price range is using incorrect data. 'They are doing due diligence today for trades that took place years ago, without taking into account changes such as splits and other changes that would affect the price.' Fairfield Greenwich did receive trading confirmations which were then checked and it is not customary to give out the names of trading partners.

Walter Noel and Andres Piedrahita were not Madoff's only line into Europe's wealthy elite. Thierry Magon de le Villehuchet brought numerous investors to BLMIS, partly by using his connections to Europe's noble and royal families. De la Villehuchet was the French aristocrat who in the late 1990s had brushed off Frank Casey's concerns about Madoff, when the Boston-based investment adviser had suggested to him that Madoff's returns were unrealistic. De la Villehuchet had founded Access International Advisors (AIA), together with Patrick Littaye, another French banker, in the mid-1990s. The firm's New York offices were located at 509 Madison Avenue, a few minutes' walk across Park Avenue from the Lipstick Building. By the time of Madoff's arrest AIA had invested at least $1.4 billion with Madoff. Its clients reportedly included Liliane Bettencourt, the L'Oreal heiress who is the richest woman in the world, worth an estimated $22.9 billion and who was seventeenth on the 2008 *Forbes* list of the richest people in the world. Prince Michel of Yugoslavia was an investor relations adviser, according to AIA's marketing documents.[11]

De la Villehuchet had come to America in the mid-1980s and had fallen in love with its can-do spirit. He would often say that with hard work in America, anything is possible. He worked for Crédit Lyonnais Securities (USA), the investment arm of the French bank, before setting up AIA. He soon prospered. 'He loved finance and he loved his job. For him, America was the maker of finance. It was like an all-American dream,' recalls his widow, Claudine. They lived in a spacious house in New Rochelle, a historic town in Westchester County, New York, that was home to numerous multi-millionaires. Charming, elegant, and popular, de la Ville-huchet was a member of the New York Yacht Club and the Larchmont Yacht Club. As he became richer, he began to restore the family's chateau, near St Malo, on the coast of Brittany.[12] The Madoffs dined with the de la Villehuchets about three times a year. Like their dinners with Simon Levy and his wife, they were pleasant evenings, recalls Claudine. Madoff was 'very charming'. Her husband thought that Madoff was a 'genius of finance'. The two couples did not discuss business, but shared interests, such as films, France, and sailing. The Madoffs had bought an apartment at Cap d'Antibes on the French Riviera. 'We would talk about France, they loved the Riviera, of course.'[13]

The French aristocrat, like his American business associate, was a keen sailor, so they would also discuss their boats. Madoff had four, and his pride and joy, the *Bull*, his $7 million, twenty-seven-metre cruiser, was moored at Cap d'Antibes. If Madoff could not spend his spare time on one of his own boats he would socialise with some of his super-rich investors, such as Norman Levy. Photographs of the Madoffs taken over the last couple of decades often show them dressed casually in designer sports clothes, looking tanned and relaxed on a wood-panelled luxury yacht moored somewhere glamorous. Cap D'Antibes is a haunt of the world's ultra-rich such as Madonna, and Roman Abramovitch, the Russian oligarch. But it seems this was the one place where Madoff did not try to impress. The Madoffs' apartment, in the Château des Pins development at Cap d'Antibes, was surprisingly modest, at least compared to the sprawl of their properties in Manhattan, Palm Beach, and Montauk. Madoff owned the upstairs half of a white villa with terra-cotta roof tiles. It had three bedrooms, and the sea-view was partially blocked.[14] They often spent much of the summer there, staying several weeks, sometimes with their grandchildren, enjoying the sun, the sea and the excellent local restaurants.

When de la Villehuchet entertained potential clients the hospitality was not modest. AIA organised splendid dinners, with the finest wines and haute cuisine to entertain investors. But money managers and the super-rich are bombarded with such invitations to prise them from their wealth. De la Villehuchet brought something extra to the table: a touch of class, in the shape of minor European royalty or members of the aristocracy. Even the most jaded money managers, it seemed, could be seduced by the chance of exchanging pleasantries with a minor royal celebrity such as Prince Michel of Yugoslavia. The Prince is a regular on the international society circuit and trades enthusiastically on his royal heritage. Born in France, Prince Michel graduated from the European Business School and worked for Sotheby's International Realty in Palm Beach for fifteen years. Fluent in French, Italian, Spanish, Portuguese, and English, related, no matter how distantly, to all European royal families, he had connections that made him a useful asset for AIA.

Prince Michel set up a company called Belidvor Capital which markets his royal connections. Belidvor is based in Palm Beach and takes its name from Beli Dvor, the 'White Palace' in Belgrade, part of the Royal Compound, now home to Crown Prince Alexander. The company website, which appears not to have been updated since 2000, promises: 'It is an international corporate development company offering personalized marketing and promotional services . . . We integrate our customers into the targeted business cultures and environments they choose, using our network of worldwide connections.' Belidvor's previous events include several art shows in New York and Palm Beach, and a jewellery exhibition in Gstaad, Switzerland. Prince Michel's profile on Linked In, the international business connection network, describes him as an 'Independent Environmental Services Professional'.

Compared to, for example, Ezra Merkin or Walter Noel's social pulling power – at least until their fall – Belidvor is, at best, second division. Yet the lure of the crown – a picture of one is incorporated into Belidvor's logo – still resonated, it seems. 'AIA would say to potential investors, I have prince or princess such and such coming for dinner, why don't you join us, it will be a wonderful evening. The royalty were not there to invest, but to draw the others along. They were the bait, a part of the marketing. De la Villehuchet had a line into this world,' says James Mackintosh of the *Financial Times*. As the digestifs were served de la Villehuchet would steer the conversation to the real purpose of the evening: the

171

pitch. 'De la Villehuchet was selling his connections. He sold his aristocratic connections to Madoff, and his Madoff connection to the aristocrats. Madoff looked like a great product then, people wanted access to him.'[15]

In June 2002 Harry Markopolos, who worked with Frank Casey and who was convinced that Madoff was a fraud, landed a perfect opportunity to discover more about BLMIS. He travelled with AIA officials, including Casey's contact Thierry Magon de la Villehuchet, and Prince Michel on a ten-day business trip to Europe. AIA was marketing its funds, while Markopolos was selling a new Statistical Options Arbitrage Strategy for his employer, Rampart Investment Management. But Markopolos's real aim was to gather more information about Madoff's Ponzi scheme. At this time AIA was a $1.2 billion hedge fund, of which about 45 per cent was allocated to Madoff. Markopolos's itinerary for the trip details a whirlwind tour of fourteen meetings with high-powered bankers and financiers. In London he and AIA officials met with Barclays Bank; in Paris with AGF Asset Management and Société Générale, and in Geneva with HSBC, J.P. Morgan, and Banque Piguet.

Each client meeting began with AIA executives saying: Harry is just like Bernie Madoff only with higher returns and higher risk, before turning to the virtues of their own products, primarily Madoff's fund. The discussions with AIA often seemed to be more of a mutual congratulation session, as the clients also boasted of their contacts with Madoff. 'All bragged about how BM [Bernard Madoff] had closed his hedge fund to new investors but "they had special access to Madoff and he'd accept new money from them,"' Markopolos told Congress in February 2009. 'I came to realise that several European royal families were invested with BM. I met several counts and princes and it seemed they all were invested with BM or were marketing BM's strategies to noble families throughout Europe.'[16] For many in the close-knit world of Europe's royal and noble houses, the aura of a royal imprimatur combined with steady, market-beating returns proved irresistible.

Andres Piedrahita, Walter Noel, and Thierry Magon de la Villehuchet all had their reputations ruined by their involvement with Madoff and their lives turned inside out. But the French aristocrat would pay the highest price of all.

13
Plundering the *shtetl*

The most important men in town would come to fawn on me!
They would ask me to advise them,
Like a Solomon the Wise.
'If you please, Reb Tevye ...'
'Pardon me, Reb Tevye ...'
Posing problems that would cross a Rabbi's eyes!
And it won't make one bit of difference if I answer right or wrong.
When you're rich, they think you really know!

Tevye the milkman, singing 'If I were a rich man', in *Fiddler on the Roof*.

These were moments to savour. Bernard Madoff sat at the head of the table in his plush conference room and looked at the two rows of respectful, expectant faces. The boy from Laurelton, who dropped out of Alabama University and Brooklyn Law School and finally scraped a degree from the mediocre Hofstra College, was now holding court to an awestruck audience of professors and academics from

Yeshiva University, the alma mater of countless leading lawyers, financiers, and Jewish community leaders. All in the room were grateful to have Madoff as chairman of the board of the university's Sy Syms School of Business, where he led the search committee for a new dean. 'He was in charge without question. That was understood. He didn't shove it in front of our faces, but there was a lot of respect on everyone's part towards him in the faculty and among other board members,' says Professor Moses Pava, who teaches Jewish business ethics and sat on the search committee, which met on numerous occasions at Madoff's office before appointing a new dean in July 2007. The setting was almost intimidating, says Pava. 'The elevator stopped on his floor and you stepped out into this incredible office, I've never seen anything like it. Most search committees meet on the campus. This one did not. It met around his schedule, and that was clear.'

Madoff subtly dominated and controlled the proceedings, says Pava. Madoff would meet the candidate on his own before the committee sat, and then the other members would ask the candidate questions. After the candidate left the committee members would express their opinions. Madoff was the last one to speak, summing up the conversation, and steering it the way he wanted. When Madoff spoke in his soft, thoughtful voice, the others listened. 'He wasn't overbearing in any way, but people would not contradict him or have a direct confrontation with him,' says Pava. And Madoff was always polite to the university's administrative staff. On one occasion a secretary had forgotten to bring the candidate's CV. A board member screamed at her in public, humiliating her. 'Madoff would never have done anything like that. He was a gentleman, friendly and charismatic. He gave generously of his time. This was not something central to his being, but it was definitely something he took seriously. It was enjoyable, I learned from him, he asked good questions from all the candidates. He gets an "A" for what he did, not for the other activities, but for this one.'

Madoff had strong opinions about the new dean. As a pioneer of electronic trading and the NASDAQ he was focused on finance and analytical skills, as opposed to, for example, marketing. With his backing the committee appointed Dr Michael Ginzberg, an expert on management information systems. Madoff was especially impressed by Ginzberg's PhD from the Massachusetts Institute of Technology (MIT). None of the academics, of course, ever suspected that while Madoff held court, two floors below he was running the biggest investment fraud in modern history, a fraud that was also plundering the university's own endowment. On the contrary, Yeshiva relished its connection to Madoff. He was also treasurer of the university's board of trustees. When in April 2008 the Sy Syms Business School held a gala dinner to celebrate Ginzberg's appointment, Madoff, contributing to the school's website, wrote: 'It gives me great pleasure to partner with Dean Ginzberg and Yeshiva University to propel SSSB [Sy Syms School of Business] to higher levels of academic excellence and achievement.' Madoff also gave special thanks to his fellow board member Warren Eisenberg, who was honorary co-chair of the evening, as they 'looked to a future filled with promise'.

One reason both Madoff and Yeshiva University were looking to a promised-filled future was that both the university and, according to Bloomberg News, at least seven current or former board members' charitable foundations held substantial investments with BLMIS.[1] They were owned by, or affiliated with, some of America's wealthiest and most influential businessmen. David Gottesman was chairman of the university's board from 1990 to 1998 and remains a chairman emeritus. Gottesman is the founder of the First Manhattan Company, an investment advisory firm, and an associate of Warren Buffet. *Forbes* magazine estimates his fortune at around $2 billion. The Gottesman Fund, a charitable trust based in Washington, DC, worth $310 million, had an estimated exposure of $20.4 million, according to research by Benefit Technology, a computer software company, carried out for the *New York Times*.[2] Warren Eisenberg, a former university trustee, is the founder of the Bed, Bath & Beyond home furnishings company. The Mitzi and Warren Eisenberg Family Foundation, based in Union City, New Jersey, worth $105 million, had an estimated exposure of $5.1 million. Morry Weiss, chairman of the university's board of trustees, is chairman of the board of the American Greetings Corporation. The Sapirstein-Stone-Weiss Foundation, based in Cleveland, Ohio, worth $18.6 million, had a possible exposure of $4.1 million.

J. Ezra Merkin was not on the Sy Syms dean's search committee, but like Madoff he was a highly respected member of Yeshiva's board of trustees. His family ties to Yeshiva reached back through the decades. His father, Hermann Merkin, had served as its vice-chairman for many years. Hermann Merkin had endowed the Leib-Merkin chair in Talmud and Jewish Philosophy, and the Isaac Breuer College for Hebraic Studies, in memory of his father-in-law. Ezra Merkin endowed the Merkin Family Chair in Jewish

History and had been associated with the Rabbi Isaac Echanan Theological Seminary since the mid-1980s. Ezra Merkin was soon much sought after by Jewish organisations. He chaired the investment committee of both Yeshiva University and the UJA-Federation of New York, a network of Jewish charitable organisations. He was president of the Fifth Avenue Synagogue. He was a trustee of the Beyeler Foundation and Museum in Basel, where he could indulge his passion for modern art and enormous Rothko canvases. Widely acclaimed as a philanthropist and community leader, Merkin was an obvious choice to receive Yeshiva University's inaugural Presidential Medallion, one of four bestowed by president Richard Joel at the university's seventy-ninth anniversary Hannukah dinner, in November 2003 at the Waldorf Astoria, New York. Ruth Madoff helped arrange the dinner.

The medallion was appreciated, another accolade in the often incestuous and self-worshipping world of Jewish philanthropy. But the millions of dollars that Yeshiva University was investing in Ascot, Merkin's dedicated Madoff feeder fund, were far more welcome. Especially to Merkin, who was collecting a fee for managing money that he was channelling directly from Ascot to Madoff. The state of New York lawsuit against Merkin accuses him, in a likely reference to Yeshiva University, of breaching his fiduciary duty: 'Madoff and Merkin were friends and both were on the board of trustees of non-profit organisation A, which had a large investment in Ascot. Investors in Merkin's Ascot funds paid Merkin an annual management fee, but those who invested directly with Madoff did not. Merkin breached his fiduciary duty to non-profit organisation A by accepting its investment in Ascot, and the management fees that came with it, when Merkin and Madoff could easily have arranged for a direct investment with Madoff.'[3] The university conflict of interest requirements at the time asked only that those on the investment committee disclose each year that they were doing business with the university. According to the state of New York lawsuit, Merkin also failed to disclose his conflict of interest with regard to Spring Mountain and Millennium funds, and failed to recuse himself from discussions or voting on whether Organisation A should invest with those funds. Instead, he argued that the committee was benefiting from having some of New York's most successful fund managers sit on its committee. Merkin said: 'sometimes conflicts of interest are good because you want competent investment professionals to serve as committee members'.[4]

Yeshiva University invested in the Ascot fund with full disclosure to the board of trustees, says a person familiar with the situation. The university asked for and received a legal opinion that the situation was acceptable, and from 2007 Ezra Merkin agreed to make a donation to Yeshiva University equal to the fees he received. Andrew Levander, Merkin's lawyer, filed a thirty-seven-page motion to dismiss the New York State lawsuit on 1 July 2009. It argued that Madoff's operation appeared transparent to Merkin as Madoff had agreed to operate within the confines of a written trading authorisation; the funds received trading tickets and monthly statements from Madoff's brokerage; Merkin had regular discussions with Madoff about trading strategies and execution, and Madoff had a long history of paying all redemptions on time.[5]

Merkin's relationship with Madoff and his role at Yeshiva

are problematic, says Menachem Rosensaft, the former general counsel of a prominent financial services firm and adjunct professor of Law at Cornell University. 'Merkin was not acting as a money manager who was using his discretion and business judgments to invest funds. He was simply taking fees from people to take their funds which he then passed to Madoff. When you are a money manager and you claim to have a fund of funds, that does not mean you have a fund of fund, because that is not being a money manager.' (A fund of funds is an investment fund that invests in different funds; a fund of fund is an investment fund that invests in a single fund, in this case with Madoff.)

In addition, as an experienced investor, Merkin should have noticed numerous warnings, says Rosensaft. 'I leave it to the judicial process to determine what Merkin knew and did not know. I am not suggesting Merkin was culpable in Madoff's scheme. I have no idea what it is that he knew. But there are some real red lines and red lights, very bright flashing red lights, that should have put a sophisticated money manager on notice that there was something strange going on. There are enough institutions and potential invest-ors who met with Madoff and who asked the most basic questions and were told to go to hell.' Jewish institutions such as Yeshiva University that invested with Madoff are also at fault, says Rosensaft. 'It is a fact that some major Jewish institutions with sophisticated lawyers and business execu-tives among their trustees were not exercising due diligence. They have a fiduciary responsibility to the community which they did not carry out. This is not an issue of greed, or the collapse of Jewish values, it is an issue of failing to realise that the money is not yours to play with.'

Yeshiva University remains deeply embarrassed by its lengthy relationships with Bernard Madoff and Ezra Merkin, and refuses to discuss them. The author's requests for interviews with Richard Joel, the president, and Hedy Shulman, the director of media relations, were refused, and the university declined to answer questions. Bruce Bobbins, of Dan Klores Communications, eventually emailed the author a statement first issued by Richard Joel soon after Madoff's arrest in December 2008. (It is unclear why Yeshiva University is retaining a Park Avenue PR firm to email seven-month-old statements when it has its own Media Relations Department.) Joel said that the university had invested 8 per cent of its endowment with Ascot Partners, Ezra Merkin's feeder fund, which was valued at $110 million. The university was still strong, said Joel, and while 'these facts are disappointing we need to remain focused on the larger picture'. In fact it is unclear how much Yeshiva lost with Madoff. On 30 December 2008, after Joel issued his statement, J. Michael Gower, the university's chief financial officer, told Bloomberg Business News that Yeshiva's net investment was $14.5 million: 'Although the university has an estimated loss of $110 million, it now appears that any "profits" above $14.5 million were fictitious.'[6] Yeshiva has engaged Sullivan and Cromwell, an influential New York law firm, and Cambridge Associates, an investment adviser to non-profit organisations, to review its governance.

It is unlikely that any school, university, or charitable institution will ever again ask Merkin to sit on its board or subcommittees. By summer 2009 he was being sued by New York University, New York University law school, New York

State and Irving Picard, the Madoff trustee, among others. J. Ezra Merkin's name and reputation have been severely damaged by his involvement with Madoff. The fact that several of Merkin's investors were educational institutions and charities has left a sour legacy of resentment across Manhattan. Merkin was vice-chairman of the Ramaz day school on the Upper East Side, where he and his siblings studied, and where his own children attend. He also sat on the school's investment committee. Ramaz lost $6 million with Madoff.[7]

Many wonder what Merkin's father, the great Talmudist Hermann Merkin, would make of his son's tainting of the family name. For Michael Steinhardt, the former hedge fund manager who knows Merkin well, the issue is less that Merkin may have erred in his dealings with Madoff, and more to do with the fact that he took clients' fees for funnelling investors' money to Madoff's fund. 'When I was a money manager I was about as good as there was in terms of performance and I made oodles of mistakes, too many to recount, in judgments of people, facts, integrity. It's impossible not to have made a vast number of mistakes. I am extraordinarily familiar with the world of money management and decision taking and I don't think Ezra could be held to a higher standard than the one he used. I don't think that should have been expected.' Other issues take on a different character, says Steinhardt. 'These relate to what Ezra told his investors, how he dealt with some of his investors who were philanthropists, some of whom he was intimately associated with and sat on various boards with. These issues are what people find discomfiting. There is keen resentment in Yeshiva University and those circles.'

Steinhardt himself admits that he should have shown greater diligence in his dealings with Merkin. Since 1997 Steinhardt has served as chairman of New York University's investment committee and is responsible for overseeing the university's endowment, which is valued at more than $2 billion. As the university lost $24 million with Madoff and is now suing Ezra Merkin, clearly something went wrong. Steinhardt admits that he has some responsibility for the lost funds. He did not know that they were being channelled to Madoff. 'I did not know Bernard Madoff except in the vaguest reputational sense. All I knew about him was that he had been around for a long time and had a reputation for having consistent, low, double-digit returns. No one ever knew how he did it. The thought was that he did it through some sort of arbitrage, or special gimmicks, or he was front-running but no one really knew.'

NYU's investment with Merkin began in the early 1990s, several years before Steinhardt took charge of the university's endowment. Merkin's fund then brought good returns, he says. 'He was viewed very positively, he had good numbers, we even had him in to make a presentation to the entire committee.' Asked whether he sufficiently investigated NYU's investments when he took over, Steinhardt chooses his words carefully. 'I had known Ezra from the late 1980s and I became familiar with his investment. In retrospect I am not sure that I had a perfectly clear vision of what Ezra did. I thought he was a money manager who managed the money mostly himself. In retrospect I think he didn't do that.' Steinhardt knew Merkin well and simply trusted him. 'One believes what a money manager says. One sees the balance sheet and it was accurate and honest, and normally that is all one can do. I trusted him.'

Mort Zuckerman, it is fair to say, will never trust Merkin again. Zuckerman is a Canadian-born real estate dealer and newspaper owner, who publishes the *New York Daily News*, a tabloid newspaper, and *US News and World Report*, a digital magazine. Like Michael Steinhardt, this bullish billionaire is a strong supporter of Israel and conservative Jewish causes, as well as NYU, where he sponsors the Zuckerman Forum, an undergraduate public debate arena. Zuckerman and Merkin both moved in the same power-finance circles. Zuckerman is now suing Merkin, after losing about $40 million through Merkin's funds. Zuckerman invested $25 million from his charitable foundation and $15 million of his personal wealth. Zuckerman says he had no idea that the funds had been forwarded to Madoff. He had never heard of Bernard Madoff until he was informed that his investment had vanished. In an email to the author Zuckerman wrote: 'I have had no meetings with Mr Madoff nor did I ever hear his name until I was informed by one Ezra Merkin who was the manager of the Ascot Fund that, contrary to everything he had previously said to me, the Ascot Fund was entirely invested with Mr Madoff ... notwithstanding the fact that Mr Merkin was receiving a $27 million annual fee for such management of what was originally supposed to be a fund of funds and obviously, without anybody knowing it, turned out to be a fund of fund.'[8] Andrew Levander, Ezra Merkin's lawyer, said that Zuckerman's lawsuit was 'baseless and without merit' as the Ascot offering memorandum specifically warned about the 'lack of diversification' and did not constitute a 'balanced investment plan'.[9]

Not everyone in New York is sympathetic to Zuckerman. 'He is a very sophisticated investor, probably more so than most,' says one observer. I know he has daggers out for Ezra Merkin as the source of all this, but presumably he is capable of looking at his own records. Perhaps Mort Zuckerman has trouble accepting the simple ego-deflating fact that he made a bad decision.'

Despite the vast sums flowing back and forth across Madoff's world, it is a small one, where an intricate web of overlapping interests and connections link numerous players. William D. Zabel, like Michael and Judy Steinhardt, is a trustee of NYU. Zabel is a partner at the high-powered New York law firm of Schulte, Roth and Zabel, where he represents Jeffrey Picower. Picower is the immensely wealthy financier and philanthropist living in Palm Beach whose foundation was invested with Madoff. Zabel was also a trustee of the JEHT (Justice, Equality, Human Dignity and Tolerance) Foundation, a well-regarded charity that supported reform of the juvenile criminal and justice system, which invested with Madoff and has shut down. The foundation was run by Robert Crane and Jeanne Levy-Church. Jeanne Levy-Church is the daughter of Norman Levy, the property magnate and philanthropist whom Madoff had befriended, and the sister of Francis Levy. Francis Levy is cofounder of the Philoctetes Center which hosted Bernard Madoff in October 2007, when he lamented the onerous demands of SEC regulation, and mused on the possibility of programming computers to commit fraudulent trades.

Fake gods and false messiahs are perpetual motifs of Jewish history. Bernard Madoff is only the most recent supposed miracle-maker to exploit his co-religionists' trust and credulity. The book of Exodus records that when Moses ascended to Mount Sinai he left the Israelites for forty days and nights. A minority feared that Moses would not return and they would be abandoned in the desert, so they asked Aaron, Moses's brother, to make gods for them. Aaron gathered their jewellery, melted it down and made a golden calf. The idolaters celebrated, danced and made offerings before the golden calf. When Moses returned and saw what they had done he was enraged and smashed the idol. It was melted down and turned to a powder, which was mixed with water. The Israelites were forced to drink the mixture.

Several millennia later, a young scholar called Shabbetai Zvi began to gather followers across the Balkans. Zvi was born in Smyrna (present day Izmir in Turkey) in 1626. He was a devotee of Kabbala, Jewish mysticism. Zvi moved to the seaport town of Salonica, in present day Greece, where his lurches between extreme self-indulgence and asceticism soon caused unrest among the large Jewish community. He conducted a wedding ceremony with himself as the bridegroom and the Torah, the five books of Moses, as the bride. Expelled from Salonica, he moved to Palestine. There he met Nathan of Gaza, a well-regarded Jewish mystic who declared Shabbetai Zvi to be the Messiah. The endorsement of respected community figures greatly enhanced Zvi's standing, just as it did for Madoff. He rode around on horseback, and summoned a group of his followers whom he appointed as apostles, emissaries charged with recruiting new believers.[10]

They were wildly successful. Sabbatean communities sprang up across the Balkans and the Middle East, Italy, Germany and Holland. The Jewish world fragmented into two camps. Numerous respected community leaders and rabbis endorsed Zvi's claim to be the Messiah, and those who stood against him were brutally deposed. Zvi's name and picture, and kabbalistic formulas were printed in prayer books and new prayers were written to bless the new Messiah. Rumours and reports of miracles swirled. Eventually Zvi was arrested and imprisoned by the Ottoman authorities. Brought before Sultan Mehmed IV, he placed a turban on his head and agreed to convert to Islam. The news caused horror among many of his followers. Others sought to rationalise Zvi's adoption of Islam, arguing somewhat illogically that his conversion was proof of his divinity. Zvi was rewarded with a handsome salary and was allowed to go free.

Like Bernard Madoff, Shabbetai Zvi led a double life. He told the Sultan that he would convert Jews to Islam, and his fellow Jews that he was still a believing Jew. Eventually the Sultan tired of Zvi's intrigues and he was exiled to the Balkans, where he died, probably in Montenegro. The cult of Shabbetai Zvi was the greatest mass popular delusion in Jewish history, although, viewed from an empirical perspective, Shabbetai Zvi had as much claim to be the Messsiah as anyone else. His followers adopted a form of crypto-Judaism, mixing kabbalism, elements of Sufism, Islam, and Judaism, but consider themselves Jews. More than four centuries after the death of Shabbetai Zvi, Sabbateanism lives on in Turkey and other countries. The Sabbateans call themselves '*Ma'aminim*' meaning believers, and in Turkey are known as '*donmeh*' from the Turkish word to turn, a derogatory term.

The world of modern orthodoxy – Yeshiva University, the

Fifth Avenue Synagogue, the Ramaz school – were unlikely places for Madoff to find his *Ma'aminim*. Madoff himself was not Orthodox. He did not wear a yarmulke or keep kosher. According to Julia Fenwick, who managed his London office, he enjoyed fry-ups in a local greasy spoon and especially relished pork sausages. Madoff identified as a Jew, certainly, but in religious terms seems to have been a 'High Holidays Jew', at most, one who attended synagogue mainly on Rosh Hashana, the New Year, and Yom Kippur, the Day of Atonement. Madoff was a member of the Jewish Center of The Hamptons, a Reform congregation in East Hampton, says its former Rabbi, David Gelfand, now at Temple Israel on the Upper East Side. 'He was spoken of very highly by the lay leadership, many of whom invested heavily with him. Our synagogue there was very pluralistic, so it's fascinating that he was operating so successfully in the Modern Orthodox world. They are a minority within a minority, and he seemed to ingratiate himself there, and find a comfort level. The tough question is was it because there were people in that community who were willing to be his handmaidens?'[11]

There are perhaps 300,000 Modern Orthodox Jews in the United States. A Jewish traveller praying at a Modern Orthodox synagogue on a Friday evening in a strange town will always be invited home by one of the congregants for Shabbat dinner, and likely offered a bed for the night. Among the Modern Orthodox the moral values of the *shtetls* live on: trust, hospitality, and a powerful sense of community. On the east coast, especially in Manhattan, there is often only one degree of separation as so many Modern Orthodox Jews attended Ramaz day school and graduated from Yeshiva

University. 'Our community is one where people are affiliated with one another through our institutions,' says one source, who often prays at the Fifth Avenue Synagogue. 'If somebody is dating one of my children I can find out who they are with one or two telephone calls. You can walk into a synagogue anywhere in the world and you will probably know somebody. And if you don't the person you start to chat with will have a friend in common with you.'[12]

Modern Orthodoxy is more than a type of worship. It is a way of life. 'You have this religious affiliation but you also participate in the world. That brings a kind of duality that not many people can understand, except those who are in it.' Modern Orthodoxy has flourished as America has become more open. It was rare to see a yarmulke on Wall Street thirty years ago, but it is now unremarkable. Modern Orthodox synagogues are far noisier and more social than their Reform counterparts. People wander in and out of the services, walk up and down the aisles and chat, sometimes – even though it is forbidden – about business opportunities, such as the investment manager who, year after year, returned a steady 10 to 12 per cent, no matter how the market was doing. 'You develop relationships, even during services, that are important in your life. If you know the guy in synagogue, you take a leap of faith that otherwise you might not, because he is *unsere*, one of ours. The challenge with that is that you have a greater responsibility to people who trust you personally, and people are counting on that.' The communal grapevine is a very effective way to disseminate information, and a joke shows how: President G.W. Bush gathers his intelligence chiefs for a meeting. He is furious – whatever America's spies discover, the Israelis already know. How can this be, the president demands, when America has the CIA, the NSA, the FBI and all the other agencies? The Israelis use a special network, the chief of the CIA explains, the synagogues all over America. Bush demands to be taken to a synagogue. He puts a yarmulke on his head and sits in the back row where all the elderly men are gossiping. 'What's new?' he asks. 'Sssshhhh,' the man replies, 'President Bush is coming.'

Elie Wiesel certainly trusted Madoff. The Elie Wiesel Foundation for Humanity lost $15.2 million, most of its assets, and Wiesel personally lost much of his wealth. Wiesel, a Nobel laureate, was deported to Auschwitz as a teenager from his home in Romania. He survived the camps and went on to become one of the world's most influential Holocaust educators, lauded by the Jewish and secular world. He used his connections to the famous and glamorous, such as Oprah Winfrey or Nicolas Sarkozy, the French president, to raise money for his foundation, which campaigned on human rights issues. The foundation, for example, runs a programme in Tel Aviv for children of refugees from Darfur now living in Israel. Wiesel's losses have caused particular outrage, but his account of how he fell victim to Madoff follow a now familiar pattern. A friend who was one of Madoff's earliest investors arranged an introduction and Madoff made a very good impression, Wiesel recalls. 'I know that we checked the people who had business with him, and they were among the best minds on Wall Street – the geniuses in the finance field. I am not a genius in finances: I teach philosophy and literature. I don't know anything about the economy or financing ... so it happened.'[13]

Like Simon Levy, Wiesel had dinner with Madoff. Defrauding a Holocaust survivor and his charity, not through a feeder fund, but in person, over several hours, as they ate and drank together, took Madoff's fraud to a new level of infamy. Wiesel and Madoff did not discuss business, but Jewish education. Madoff wanted Wiesel to leave Boston University, where he has a chair in humanities, and relocate to Queen's College, part of the City University of New York, where Ruth had studied. Madoff promised that he could arrange a chair at Queen's for Wiesel and presented himself as a great philanthropist. Wiesel declined the offer but began investing his own money. Impressed by the steady returns and encouraged by others, he slowly began to feed in his foundation's funds. He recalls: 'Everybody told us, literally, everybody we know in the field of finance, they told us, come on, you can do much more, more projects, because of Mr Madoff, the saviour.'

Elie Wiesel, like Simon Levy, broke the cardinal rule of investing: diversify. Wiesel thought that Madoff would take care of everything for him: 'We thought he was God, we trusted him with everything.' Wiesel's losses are a sensitive topic among the New York Jewish community. Once the initial fury and disgust at Madoff's action had abated, some began to feel that Wiesel, like numerous other Jewish philanthropists, had been irresponsible in handing over all the assets of their charities to one man. 'Elie Wiesel is rightly an immensely respected figure. But to cast yourself as someone only concerned with literature and philosophy, as a naïf, to say you don't know about finances, is a nonsense,' says one senior figure in the New York Jewish community. 'The investor has a responsibility to know where the money is going. You don't have to be an expert, but you can't say

I don't know anything about it.' Wiesel says that the foundation's accountants checked their Madoff statements every month. 'He told us what he did with the money ... except it was all a lie.'

The best safeguard, says one Wall Street investment banker, is to avoid anyone who uses their ethnicity as a sales pitch. 'I met Madoff a couple of years ago with a client and I thought he was a pompous little man. He was dining out on being Jewish, with his mannerisms, his New York accent, his membership of the Palm Beach Country Club. The minute I see someone doing that, whether it's Jewish, Irish or whatever, I run in the opposite direction.'

Madoff performed a kind of psychological jiu-jitsu among his own co-religionists. Every community puts up defences against potential predators, walls of suspicion and distrust. But once a predator is through those walls, and accepted by his victims, he can prey freely among them. The walls that once kept the predator out, serve now to keep him in. 'If you are willing to do that, to financially murder people who are close to you, then they're the easiest access because they trust you,' says the Modern Orthodox source. 'There's an element of trust and closeness that makes them easier prey because they automatically take you at your word.' Even if suspicions mount, there is a communal reluctance to admit that a mistake has been made, because of the cost in pride and reluctance to believe in personal fallibility and gullibility. The smaller the group, the more intense the 'social-feedback loop', feeding off the respect and status of those either running or investing in the Ponzi scheme.

As J. Ezra Merkin once noted, with sufficient persuasion a gambler can even be persuaded to wager on blank dice. 'It's just like when Big Julie, in the classic Broadway musical *Guys and Dolls*, challenged Nathan Detroit to a game of craps played with dice that had no dots other than those Big Julie claimed he could see,' he wrote.[14] Across the Upper East Side few could see that Madoff's dice were blank.

14
Making merry in Montauk

'The whole thing was fabulous, like the wedding in the opening scene of The Godfather. *And he did it for everybody every single year.'*

Julia Fenwick, former office manager of Bernard Madoff's London operation, on the annual staff party at Montauk.

Like every benevolent uncle, Bernie Madoff was a generous host. Every summer he hosted a party at his house in Montauk, New York, for his staff and their families, a total of about 400 people. For the first few years the revelry took place at the family beach house, but the party was so lively that at the end of the weekend the floors and the deck onto the beach would have to be repolished, because there was so much dancing. So the party was relocated onto a long stretch of beach nearby. Mark and Andrew would come out and put down towels and chairs for the family, and arrange further rows of chairs in order of importance. The most important traders would be nearer Bernie and Ruth, radiating out to the service staff on the outer circles. Everything was carefully planned down to the last detail, in scenes reminiscent of *The Great Gatsby*, says Julia Fenwick. 'They had this whole thing set up, there was a huge barbecue, and games for the kids, we would sit on the beach and have a really lovely day.' In the evening the party relocated to the nearby yacht club under an enormous marquee. This was American hospitality at its most generous: unlimited first-class food and drink, in a beautiful setting by the sea. There was a full bar, oysters, lobster or fillet steak for dinner, and dancing afterwards.

Fenwick was privileged to be at Montauk, as the London staff were not usually invited to the annual shindig. But she and her husband Neil were flown to New York business class as a reward for her hard work. She got on well with her boss and worked for him for seven and a half years, until December 2008. When someone asked her why she was at Montauk, she quipped that she had 'sold her soul to Bernie'. He overheard and made her sit next to him for the whole evening. 'He was just very, very nice. He took the mickey, calling people a "shmuck", it was quite funny. He wasn't cruel, he was just sarcastic and cheeky, and used to wind people up.' Madoff was flirtatious with the women employees, but not overbearing and knew where to draw the line with her. Fenwick observed the interaction between Madoff and his sons. It was always clear who was boss. 'His sons were very much in their father's shadow. He was a real family patriarch and his whole family were to some extent beholden to him. He was the man, the big guy. He set up the business and made the money and they worked for him. They looked up to him, as did Peter. It was always, "Bernie did this" and "Bernie did that".'

In his London office in Mayfair, like the Lipstick Building,

Madoff was also a control freak, says Fenwick. The minimalist office with its black and grey office furniture did not really suit the house's style, but the London office was to be as similar to the New York headquarters as possible. Even the walls had to be adjusted to keep the boss happy. When a new video-conferencing system was installed into a semicircular wall Madoff sat staring at the camera. Semicircular was not acceptable, he announced, and the wall was duly filled in. Madoff usually visited London once or twice a year, and the staff worked for days beforehand to make sure everything was up to standard. Desks were cleared and organised – as in New York untidy piles of paper were strictly forbidden; blinds, pictures, computer screen were aligned so that their edges were the same height. The staff then scoured the doors and furniture for any traces of marks or scratches, before touching them up with a black marker pen.

Madoff always enjoyed his trips to London. He usually stayed at the Lanesborough, a classically elegant hotel on Hyde Park Corner, where each guest is allocated a private butler. His Savile Row tailors visited him in the offices, measuring him for new suits. If Ruth accompanied him they would dine at The George, a discreet private members' club in Mayfair. Julia Fenwick also had a special task: to supply Ruth with Boots No. 7 Protect and Perfect Beauty Serum, which Ruth had heard about on television in New York, but could not buy there. Madoff added to his collection of vintage watches, often buying something from George Somlo's store in Burlington Arcade on Piccadilly. The news that Madoff had been running the biggest Ponzi scheme in history came as a shock to Fenwick and the rest of the staff. 'We had no idea that he even had an investment business.'

One of Madoff's highest-profile victims was Nicola Horlick, the charismatic CEO of Bramdean Asset Management (BAM), which is the investment manager for Bramdean Alternatives Ltd (BAL). Horlick was dubbed 'Superwoman' by the British media for her ability to juggle a stellar career in finance with raising five children, while also coping with the long illness and death of her first child. A profile of her in the *Sunday Telegraph*, by Martin Baker, published in March 2005, was headlined 'The Mother of All Fund Managers'. The article described her as 'half Atomic Kitten's missing older sister' and 'half scrummy mummy'. Baker and Horlick married the following year.

In May 2008 Horlick took tea with Matthew Vincent, the money editor of the *Financial Times*, at the Wolseley in Piccadilly. The two discussed RMF Investment Management, which manages the hedge fund part of BAL's portfolio. RMF had invested $360 million in Madoff feeder funds on behalf of their clients. Horlick talked about Madoff and her interview is available on the FT Money Show webcast. 'There is a market-maker in the States, called Madoff, he is actually the largest market-maker in the States, and he is somebody who is very, very good at calling the US equity market. He has developed this product where he basically makes "calls" on the market and there are a number of funds that feed into his views, in effect,' Horlick explained. 'So if he is really negative or ambivalent about what is going to happen next, he will just put all the money into US T-bills. But if actually he is extremely positive about the market he will put on a derivatives trade and he will put on what's called a "collar". What that means is there is limited upside but also limited downside if he gets it wrong, so you are protected on the downside. This guy has managed to produce 1–1.2 per cent, per month, year in, year out, for years and years.'

Vincent was certainly impressed. Everyone should be interested in a fund like that, he said enthusiastically, and asked more about the feeder funds. 'This particular one, because there are various feeders, is called Defender,' Horlick replied, naming one of the Bramdean funds that invested with Madoff, through RMF. Unfortunately Madoff demanded a minimum investment of $1 million, she explained, but Bramdean Alternatives Limited (BAL) offered a way in.[1] BAL lost $20 million with Madoff, via RMF. After Madoff was arrested, Horlick, like so many defrauded investors, savaged the SEC: 'It is astonishing that this apparent fraud seems to have been continuing for so long, possibly for decades, while investors have continued to invest more money into the Madoff funds in good faith. The allegations appear to point to a systemic failure of the regulatory and securities markets regime in the US.'[2]

As Horlick is a media figure BAL's losses gained wide publicity. In some parts of the City, which remains a profoundly sexist institution, there was gloating, although overall RMF's fund selection performed creditably. BAL's losses of $20 million were a drop in the ocean, compared to the financial tsunami that hit the investment world after Madoff's arrest. Numerous major international financial institutions together channelled billions into his Ponzi scheme through feeder funds. The initial roll call of casualties included: HSBC with an estimated exposure of £1 billion; the Man Group at $360 million; Nomura Bank in Japan at $303 million; BNP Paribas at $468 million; and Reichmuth & Co., a Swiss private bank, at $325 million.[3] Clients of Union Bancaire Privée (UBP), another well-known Swiss private bank, lost $700 million. UBP's internal due diligence was 'conducted and evaluated in a professional and detailed manner', said Jerome Koechlin, UBP's Head of Corporate Communications.[4]

Numerous Madoff investors magnified their losses by leveraging their investments through bank loans. For example, if a bank lent a customer $10 million to invest with Madoff, he could use that sum as security to borrow twice as much again, all of which would be invested with Madoff. Instead of receiving Madoff's steady 10 per cent interest a year, the investor would get 30 per cent. The downside was that when Madoff was arrested, the investor was not $10 million down, but $30 million. 'People were very greedy,' says one Wall Street investment banker. 'I have a client who lost $175 million. He was borrowing heavily, because he wanted the 30 per cent return. I suggested that he buy a nice unleveraged commercial property which would bring him 8 or 9 per cent. He said, no, why would he do that when he was getting 30 per cent with Madoff. There was no point arguing with these people, they were believers.'

Madoff's institutional investors were also victims of an affinity fraud. This one was more geographically diverse than Madoff's Manhattan network. It was spread around the world but the principles were precisely the same. As the SEC says: 'These scams exploit the trust and friendship that exist in groups of people who have something in common.' Just as Palm Beach socialites clamoured to invest with Madoff because of Carl Shapiro, numerous reputable banks believed that BLMIS was secure because their rivals were also among his clients. Madoff's institutional investors shared a common culture of mutual reinforcement, says the Wall Street investment banker. 'These institutions are not endowed with any great wisdom. They are only as clever as the people who work there. They have a culture of charging fees, these were easy pickings and they are highly culpable.'

Société Générale, a French bank, was less credulous. In 2003 its investment bank sent a team to New York, part of whose mission was to investigate Madoff's fund. A growing number of the bank's customers, likely enthused by feeder funds salesmen for Walter Noel's Fairfield Greenwich and Thierry Magon de la Villehuchet's AIA, were demanding access to Madoff's fund. Three people from Société Générale's team met with Madoff. He outlined his strategy, but when they backtested it, it did not work. The French bankers were also troubled by the fact that Peter Madoff was the firm's chief compliance officer, reported the *New York Times*.[5] Société Générale placed BLMIS on its internal blacklist, banned its investment bank from doing business with the firm and strongly discouraged private clients from investing with him.

In Vienna, Sonja Kohn was one of Madoff's most successful advocates. Kohn was the founder of Bank Medici, a small investment bank, in Vienna. Bank Medici entrusted Madoff with up to $3.2 billion of its clients' money. Like Thierry Magon de la Villehuchet and Prince Michel of Yugoslavia, Kohn played on the aristocratic connection as she wooed investors, except in her case it was fictitious. Bank Medici's logo resembled a coat of arms, with two lions holding a shield with a crown on top. But the logo was completely invented. Bank Medici had no connection to the historic

Italian banking family. The family name was not copyrighted, so Kohn simply appropriated it. Nor did Bank Medici have much of a history. Kohn's investment house, Medici Finanz Beratung (Medici Finance Consulting), was founded in 1994 and received a banking licence only in 2003.

Kohn was born in 1948 to Orthodox Jewish Holocaust survivors, who moved to Vienna, where she grew up. Her contemporaries remember her as a diligent and intensely ambitious student but not especially gifted. She and her husband Erwin set up an import-export business and moved first to Milan, then Switzerland, setting up a network of contacts that would later prove extremely useful. By the early 1980s the family had moved to the United States. They settled in Monsey, a small town thirty miles from Manhattan that is home to a large ultra-Orthodox Jewish community. It seems that while in Monsey Kohn became much more religious. As her children grew and left home, Kohn decided to start a new career in investment. Bright, determined, and tenacious, she taught herself the basics, and passed her first broker's exam in 1984, according to an investigation by Bloomberg News.[6] Around 1990 she met Madoff, and began to market accounts for BLMIS. By now Kohn was travelling the world, building up a network of investors in cities including Zurich, Vienna, Milan, Moscow, and Jerusalem, where she could use her multitude of languages that include English, German, Italian, and Hebrew.

The Kohns returned to Vienna in the early 1990s. Like her business associate Bernard Madoff, Kohn sought respectability by building herself into the financial establishment. She played hard on her Wall Street connections, which seemed to open numerous doors in the still-provincial world of Austrian finance. The staid Viennese bankers seemed mesmerised by this human whirlwind, with her relentless self-promotion and talk of hedge funds and Wall Street. Kohn's return was well timed: the early and mid-1990s were an era of intense expansion for Austrian banking. The collapse of Communism had suddenly opened up half a continent for investment and business opportunities. Many foreign firms sought out Austrian banks for their regional expertise and historical connections with the new democracies of Eastern Europe. For many, Kohn was the future: a brash figurehead for the thrusting new world of Austrian banking, with Vienna as the regional hub for international investors.

Inside the close-knit Viennese financial world Kohn had a powerful protector among senior officials at Bank Austria. Bank Austria took an ownership stake of 25 per cent of Bank Medici. Dissenters within Bank Austria, who asked whether it was sensible for the country's biggest lender to be so deeply entwined with a parvenu like Bank Medici, were quickly silenced, according to one well-informed source in Vienna's financial community. 'They were told this is the way it is done, and that is that.' Bank Medici opened an office opposite the State Opera building, bedecked with antique furniture and Persian rugs. Kohn held court at the historic Hotel Sacher, with breakfast meetings at 8 o'clock, a habit probably picked up in Manhattan but unusually early for Vienna. Favoured employees were given a whole Sacher torte, a signature Viennese chocolate cake. In London she stayed at Claridge's hotel, receiving visitors in her suite.

Within the small Viennese Jewish community, just 7,000 strong, Kohn kept a comparatively low profile. She was not part of the charity circuit, which held benefits for favoured causes such as the Hebrew University in Jerusalem. She prayed with her husband at a small *shtibl*, an ultra-Orthodox synagogue in an apartment in a baroque building on Gruenangergasse, a cobble-stoned alley near St Stephen's Cathedral, in the heart of old Vienna. 'The *shtibl* is just a couple of modest rooms, but its congregants are some of Vienna's wealthiest Jews,' says one source close to the Jewish community. 'They are very religious. The congregants include more than one private banker and other members of wealthy families. These are highly respected people.'

But in the world of international finance Kohn was a relentless self-promoter. Bedecked in heavy designer jewellery, crowned with an auburn *sheitl*, the wig worn by strictly Orthodox women, Kohn became known as the woman who would not take no for an answer. Kohn was a dedicated networker. Two former government ministers took seats on Bank Medici's supervisory board. Bank Medici advised the Ministry of Economics and the Foreign Ministry. Kohn supported two events at the Kunsthistoriches Museum, the city's largest museum. Her relentless power-schmoozing worked: in 1999 Kohn was given a state honour: the Medal of Honor. Not everyone was applauding her rise. Bank Medici was a one-woman show. Kohn's word was law and her confrontational approach raised hackles in Vienna, a city which, since 1945 especially, has been built on compromise and consensus. Kohn was prone to temper tantrums and sometimes treated service staff like flunkeys. 'She was a player, and she was important. But she was convinced she was a genius. She was arrogant, obnoxious, full of herself and pretending to be someone special,' says the source in Vienna's financial world. 'She projected the Madoff mystique. It was a word of mouth thing, that there is this special fund, and if you can get in, then you have really got it made.'

Kohn was also an enthusiastic backer of the city's campaign 'Vienna: Your Investment Capital', which sought to raise Vienna's financial profile, although she complained that the city's learning curve was still too slow. 'It is very hard to launch exotics, and there will be a learning curve. The regulator has not yet authorised hedge funds,' she told the *Financial Times* in June 2008. But Austria at least was a 'commonsense environment'. She said: 'Here you are not guilty until you are guilty, which is not really typical of what you find everywhere else.'[7] Over the years Kohn's determination brought handsome returns for Bank Medici. The bank managed two funds, which invested a total of $2.1 billion with Madoff. Bank Medici also managed the Thema Fund, which had assets of $1.2 billion in November 2008, according to data compiled by Bloomberg Business News.[8] In November 2008, one month before Madoff's arrest, Bank Medici's impressive fund performance brought a major accolade: the bank won first prize in the German Hedge Fund Awards for the 'Single-Hedge Fund Multi-Strategy' category.

According to the state of Massachusetts lawsuit against Cohmad, the Madoff feeder fund based in the Lipstick Building, Kohn received about $526,000 from BLMIS via Cohmad. The suit noted that although Kohn was not registered in 'any capacity' with Cohmad, 'payments from Madoff to her were filtered through Cohmad and represented a proportion of the income it stated on its financial statements'.[9] Kohn is also mentioned in the lawsuit issued by Irving Picard, the receiver for BLMIS, against Cohmad, under the headline 'The Curious Case of Sonja Kohn'. The lawsuit includes an extract from a 2004 Cohmad document: 'Note: Payments from Madoff includes payments to SK in the amt. of $87,792.' A draft schedule of Madoff payments to Cohmad for 2006 includes the name 'Sonya Cohen' for the amount of $87,792.[10] Kohn has repeatedly denied any knowledge of Madoff's fraud or wrongdoing and said that she was also a victim of his fraud. Madoff was not a friend and did not confide in her. 'Having fallen victim to a company supervised by a US regulator, as did many of the world's most illustrious financial institutions, does not ease the pain,' she told *Bloomberg News*. 'Reading that some voices believe that I should have known better makes the pain even more unbearable.' Madoff had been trusted by the 'best and smartest'. 'The Madoff fraud destroyed lives, life savings and companies that were the result of decades of hard work.' Madoff's firm 'was not an obscure hedge fund; it was a 48-year-old, highly visible firm with approximately 200 employees and over $600 million in capital'.[11]

A spokesperson for Bank Medici said that the bank and Sonja Kohn were victims of Madoff. 'Both Bank Medici and the Kohn family had substantial investment in the Herald Funds. Bank Medici was active in institutional business and only eight customers of Bank Medici AG were invested in Madoff funds. Their combined total investment is a one digit million Euro sum.' The bank had faced high legal and other costs. 'Due to the fact that the equity base of Bank Medici went down below five million euros in May, the Austrian Financial Market Authority redeemed, in accordance with Bank Medici, its banking license. You can see, the company was heavily affected by the fraudulent activities of Mr Madoff and false accusations.'[12]

15

A *mensch*, sometimes

'The one thing we could all agree on is that we should curse the Madoff bloodline.'

Roger Madoff, son of Peter.[1]

The East Hamptons Jewish Center was crowded all week. Rabbi David Gelfand and the synagogue staff had organised a bone marrow registry for the Gift of Life Foundation, Bernard and Ruth Madoff's favourite charity. Congregants lined up to have a swab of cells taken from the inside of their cheeks. The donors were then entered into a registry for potential matches with patients suffering from leukaemia or lymphoma. If the cells matched, the donor could provide either bone marrow or blood stem cells. It was tiring but satisfying work. 'We really scoured the community and did a great deal of work,' recalls Rabbi Gelfand. 'We organised it in the synagogue because I wanted people to know that this was part of the community's responsibility, that there was a Jewish context, and Jewish values.' Ruth Madoff was very involved, making sure that the registry would be successful and was extremely grateful for the synagogue's support, says Rabbi Gelfand.

Her husband was less personable, merely watching as Ruth and Rabbi Gelfand encouraged the congregants to have their samples taken. He was aloof and seemed almost uncomfortable. He said nothing, except, 'It's a nice thing you are doing.' But Madoff may have had family matters on his mind. Roger Madoff, his brother Peter's son, was diagnosed with leukaemia in 2002. Roger had worked for Primex Trading, a firm connected to BLMIS's trading operation, but began a new career as a reporter with Bloomberg Business News. He loved the outdoors, and dreamed of starting his own bottled water company. Roger was bright, personable, and popular, and deeply in love with his wife Jennifer. He chronicled his battle with his illness in his book *Leukemia for Chickens*. It's a poignant chronicle that opens a different window into the world of the Madoffs, far from power deals on Wall Street, apartments on the French Rivera, and luxury yachts. The book recounts the devastating effect of an insidious disease on a close-knit family and their determined attempts to do everything they could for a much-loved son, brother, nephew, and husband, as he slowly wasted away.

As a schoolboy Roger had loved to go to work with his father. He recalled the thrill of the journey to Manhattan as Peter Madoff steered his Porsche 911 along the sweep of the Long Island Expressway before the dizzying panorama of Manhattan came into view: 'From the crest of the elevated highway, looking southwest, I could see the horizon.'[2] Roger was especially close to his sister Shana, who had just gone through a difficult divorce. Throughout Roger's illness Shana was a devoted sibling. She was a fixture at his bedside. She brought board games, a laptop computer with speakers and pictures drawn by her daughter Rebecca, who was not allowed to visit the leukaemia floor in case she brought in germs. Behind the designer façade, Shana is a sweet person, says Julia Fenwick, who became friends with Shana on her visits to the Madoffs' London operation. 'I had to be nice to her when I met her, but then we got on really well. She does love to shop but she is also very kind and generous.'

In spring 2003 Andrew Madoff joined Roger in the treatment room. He had contracted a form of lymphoma and underwent a course of aggressive treatment. He continued to work at BLMIS between sessions. His father did not let his emotions show, but after Andrew's diagnosis he would emerge from his office every day to spend time sitting next to his son on the trading floor. 'I noticed how he would stare at Andy, as if he was trying to absorb every expression that came across his face,' recalls Elaine Squillari.[3] Roger and Andrew were not close, separated by eight years, but they got on well. Andrew lived with his wife Debbie and their two young daughters in Manhattan. He was more cerebral and less gregarious than his brother Mark, and was obsessed with gadgets and new technology. Andrew and his wife 'seemed a very down to earth couple', Roger wrote. Cancer ran through the Madoff family. Peter Madoff had been diagnosed with bladder cancer in 2002. One of his great-nieces had also been diagnosed with a type of blood cancer. 'The one thing we could all agree on is that we should curse the Madoff bloodline,' wrote Roger.

These events were one reason why Bernard Madoff was a strong supporter of the Gift of Life Foundation, which is based in Boca Raton, Florida, a short drive from Palm Beach. In 2006 the Madoff Family Foundation gave $1 million to the Gift of Life, more than one-third of the charity's support for that year. The contribution resulted in 50,000 new donors joining the registry and 200 bone marrow transplants. It is thought that Madoff encouraged Yeshiva University to set up a campus recruitment programme for the registry. It was so successful that the foundation gave Yeshiva an award in 2008, as the institution which had facilitated the most bone marrow transplants. The Madoff Family Foundation also supported the Lymphoma Research Foundation (LRF), where Andy Madoff served on the board of directors, before becoming its chairman. In 2007 the Madoff Family Foundation donated more than $1 million to the LRF, which had no investment with Madoff. 'It was never even suggested,' said Suzanne Bliss, the president.[4] It seems the Gift of Life also did not invest directly, but it was affected as Madoff was such an important benefactor. After his arrest the charity announced a shortfall of $1.8 million.

Until his arrest Madoff was known in the world of Jewish philanthropy as a *mensch*, a Yiddish word meaning someone of strong ethical character, who is trustworthy and generous. To be a *mensch* is an accolade. 'Madoff built his career by hanging around Jewish social and philanthropic institutions. On one hand he was running a kind of Jewish country club, where he met people socially, on the golf course or in the gym, and those social networks led to other people making recommendations. The social aspect was enormously important. But Madoff's association with philanthropy is a key aspect of what gave him credibility,' says Steven Bayme of the American Jewish Committee. 'He heavily invested his time going to board meetings, getting involved in educational and charitable institutions. In some respect giving his time was at least as important as giving money, because people like him have no time. He was not seen as a Machiavellian financier, but someone who is interested in the betterment of the Jewish people and of society in general.'

American Jews' extreme generosity to charities and universities is part of the complicated relationship between Jews and money, says Daphne Merkin. 'There is a mystique, almost a stigma attached to making money, which I don't understand. Jews are good at many things, so why wouldn't they be good at making money?' Madoff understood the complicated psyche of his upwardly mobile co-religionists: their reverence for education and hard work; their desire to make the world a better place; their nagging unease, even guilt, about the material success that followed. Madoff deftly exploited his clients' mix of innocence and grandiosity, argues the writer Marie Brenner. 'A not inconsiderable part of his victim pool came from a group who thought of money with a complex tangle of shame and attraction, as if they believed that *understanding* money would drag them back into the stereotyping of their immigrant roots.'[5] Uncle Bernie, they believed, would deal with these complicated, perhaps even tainted matters for them.

All American philanthropy, like America itself, is intensely competitive. Charities have carefully calibrated donor structures, dependent on how much money is given. To British eyes the American tendency to adorn buildings, lecture halls and libraries with the donor's name may seem ostentatious. Maimonides, the greatest Jewish philosopher in history, argued in Spain in the twelfth century that the finest charity is donated anonymously. But naming donors brings results. 'Sure, it's distasteful to see lists of names and board members, in different categories as supporters or pillars and so on. But it's enormously effective because it's human nature,' says one source. 'If you see everyone else has given $10,000, then who are you if you haven't as well? If you are running a charity and you don't do that, sure you have a higher moral standard, but you will get less money. What's all this about? Getting the money.'

The yearning for legitimacy is also a factor. Like Madoff, many New York Jewish philanthropists traced their roots back to the Lower East Side. The *shtarkers*' sons and daughters were now successful and prosperous. Public charity let the world know. Michael Steinhardt, the former hedge fund manager, is one of American Jewry's most generous benefactors. His father, Sol Frank 'Red' Steinhardt, was not only a *shtarker*, but an associate of Meyer Lansky and other mobsters. When the Italian gangster Albert Anastasia was shot in the barber shop of the Park Sheraton Hotel in 1957 Red Steinhardt was picked up for questioning as the two men had been out gambling the previous night. During World War II, Red Steinhardt made money by buying up gold jewellery which he then melted down and sold to the government. That was the start of the Steinhardt financial empire, recounts Michael Steinhardt in his autobiography, *No Bull*.[6] Among his numerous donations, Steinhardt has endowed the Steinhardt School of Culture, Education and Human Development at New York University. 'America is a more public society. I don't put my name on many things. There are pluses and minuses. A plus is the ego – that your name will live on in perpetuity. Maybe you will inspire others but I am not sure I believe it.'

The *shtarker–yekke* divide also shaped Jewish

philanthropy. Madoff was an investment adviser to the American Jewish Congress, the historic rival to the American Jewish Committee. The Committee in its early years was dominated by the *yekke* establishment. The Congress, rooted in part in the Lower East Side's vibrant labour movement, was far more muscular and politically liberal. Its founder, Rabbi Stephen Wise, was one of the first American Jewish leaders to loudly protest against the Nazis and was a strong supporter of Zionism. Unfortunately for the American Jewish Congress, it seems Madoff's main advice was to invest around $21 million in his Ponzi scheme.

As Roger Madoff battled his illness, in Boston, Harry Markopolos was pushing the SEC into investigating Madoff's operation. Markopolos was the fraud investigator who believed Madoff was probably running a Ponzi scheme. He had submitted reports to the SEC in May 2000, September 2001, and October 2001, alerting them to his concerns. No action was taken. Over the next few years Markopolos followed up the reports with numerous telephone calls and emails but was stonewalled and ignored. In June 2005, Markopolos's colleague Frank Casey alerted him that Madoff was trying to borrow money at European banks. Markopolos believed this was a sign that the Ponzi scheme could be running out of funds. He set to work again. In November 2005 Markopolos submitted a densely argued nineteen-page memo to the SEC. The title made his conclusions clear: 'The World's Largest Hedge Fund is a Fraud'. The memo listed twenty-nine red flags including: evidence that the 'split-strike' strategy was 'mathematically impossible'; Madoff's 'perfect market-timing ability'; other suspicions of fraud harboured by major financial institutions that did not invest with Madoff; and the fact that only family members were 'privy to the investment strategy'. Markopolos concluded: 'In my financial industry experience, I've found that wherever there's one cockroach in plain sight many more are lurking behind the corner out of plain view.' Markopolos also attached a summary of the Fairfield Sentry funds' performance data from 1990 to 2005.

The SEC finally lurched into action. It began investigating Madoff's relationship with Fairfield Greenwich. The SEC arranged interviews with senior staff at Fairfield. Madoff was extremely alarmed by all this. On 19 December 2005 he spoke on the telephone with Amit Vijayvergiya, Fairfield's Chief Risk Officer, and Mark McKeefry, its General Counsel, about the SEC's interest. The three men discussed Fairfield's upcoming interview with the SEC at some length. It began as follows:

> MADOFF: Obviously, first of all, this conversation never took place, Mark, OK?
> VIJAYVERGIYA: Yes, of course.
> MADOFF: All right . . .

Except it did. Vijayvergiya taped the conversation. The sixty-six-page transcript is included in the state of Massachusetts' lawsuit against Fairfield Greenwich and makes intriguing reading. Madoff gives long, rambling explanations and instructions about what his firm was doing and not doing, and what line to take with the SEC investigators. The key point, he said, was that BLMIS was not acting as an investment adviser to Fairfield's funds, but was acting under

Fairfield's instructions. 'So the issue is, look, as far as you're concerned ... you've approved the parameters of the strategy and I've agreed to follow those.'[7] Meanwhile, everyone should be calm and casual with the SEC, and avoid mentioning any written instructions, as the investigators would immediately ask for copies.

The taped conversation, which has been widely reported as evidence of Madoff's manipulative skills, needs to be seen in context, says someone familiar with the matter. Vijayvergiya taped the conversation because Madoff spoke extremely quickly, too fast to take accurate notes. Madoff was known at Fairfield to be hyper-secretive and almost paranoid about releasing any information. This was just Bernie being Bernie. Such behaviour was typical among many hedge fund managers, who were unwilling to release details of their funds' investment strategies as this was proprietary information, so Vijayvergiya had no reason to be surprised about Madoff's behaviour. In addition, the Massachusetts lawsuit fails to mention that Fairfield asked the SEC in advance for permission to have the telephone call with Madoff and, despite Madoff's suggestion, informed the SEC about the telephone call after it was concluded, says a source close to Fairfield Greenwich. Fairfield responded quickly and accurately to all of the SEC's requests for information. McKeefry was not interviewed by the SEC, but did participate in the request of the SEC to have the call with Madoff, and in Fairfield's full disclosure to the SEC after the call.

The reason why Madoff could not allow the SEC to know that he was acting as an investment adviser was that he was not registered as one. Even though Avellino and Bienes had closed down in 1992 as a Madoff feeder fund, and the money trail led back to BLMIS, he had simply stayed in business, unbothered by the regulators. Arguably, without Markolopos's determination, the SEC would not have acted at all. By now Madoff's investment fund was the biggest open secret on Wall Street – if not most of the world's financial centres – yet the fact he was unlicensed as an investment advisor did not seem to bother the numerous feeder funds channelling billions to him. The counter-argument is that Madoff maintained for years that he did not need to register as an investment adviser as he was executing trades, and so did not meet the regulatory definition of an investment adviser, says a person familiar with Fairfield Greenwich's thinking. Madoff did not charge Fairfield for investment advice – he charged a commission on the trades he made.

The SEC launched its investigation into BLMIS in January 2006. It had two aims: to see if Madoff was acting as an investment adviser to hedge funds, in violation of the registration requirements, and to see if he was engaged in any 'fraudulent activity'. In May 2006 SEC lawyers interviewed Madoff in his office at the Lipstick Building. He was nervous beforehand, irritable with his staff. Once the interview began it seems he put on a bravura performance, answering the lawyers' questions with his usual calm confidence. The SEC eventually found that Madoff was indeed in violation of the law, acting as an adviser to hedge funds and high-worth individuals without being registered. It also found that Fairfield's disclosures to its investors did not adequately describe its relationship with Madoff. Fairfield revised its material and Madoff registered as an investment adviser. But crucially, there was no evidence of fraud, the SEC said. The case was closed.[8] Madoff later admitted that he told detailed lies under oath to the SEC investigators.

The failure of the SEC to close down Madoff's Ponzi scheme at this stage is one of the most extraordinary aspects of the Madoff story. The case for the defence is that the SEC, like all regulatory bodies, is understaffed and underfunded. The SEC has 3,500 staff of whom 1,000 work in the enforcement division. They are responsible for policing 11,300 investment advisers, 4,600 mutual funds, more than 5,500 broker dealers (including 174,000 branch offices and 676,000 registered representatives) and 12,000 public companies. Madoff's trading arm was repeatedly investigated by SEC staff to check it complied with the necessary rules and was not engaged in front-running, most recently in 2004 and 2005. Some frauds will inevitably fall through the cracks. Like every government bureaucracy the SEC is riven by turf wars. Markopolos was dealing first with the Boston office, then the New York office. Neither, it seemed, welcomed outsiders telling them how to do their job. Markopolos was extremely driven, with occasional tendencies to over-dramatisation, which could irritate those he dealt with. And the financial world was evolving at lightning speed, spawning all manner of new products as trading times were sliced to fractions of a second.

The sharpest minds were working on Wall Street, making millions, not sitting in government offices. The laws governing securities trading were written decades ago for a world of long Wall Street lunches and deals sealed with a handshake on the golf course. 'The Markopolos claims were made over a long period of time. They were very intense memos, and it may be that the SEC did not have staff who could understand if he was right or not,' says Professor David Ruder, who was chairman of the SEC from 1987 to 1989. 'If someone comes and says this fraud has been going on for years and nobody has found out about it, I want to ask why not. It's like being a policeman. You know there are lot of robberies but it's hard to stop them before they begin. You need a complaint.'[9]

Which the SEC had. Several, in fact. None of the above explains how, once the SEC investigators went to work, they failed to close down Madoff's fraud. The SEC had contact with Madoff in 1992, 1999, 2005, and 2006, says Harvey Pitt, chairman from 2001 to 2003. 'It had a specific roadmap to the fraud that he was committing and it still didn't catch him. I attribute that to human failure.'[10] Testifying to the US Senate Banking Committee in January 2009, Linda Chatman Thomson, Director of the SEC's Division of Enforcement, said that the SEC is deluged with complaints and tip-offs. 'We get telephone calls, handwritten letters, thick bound dossiers with numbered exhibits and extensive accounting analyses, complaint forms from the Enforcement Division's Office of Internet Enforcement, newspaper articles with company names circled in red ink, formal referrals from other regulators, informal referrals from other Offices and Divisions of the SEC, notes from reformed fraudsters, anonymous scribbling, seemingly random pieces of a company's financial statements, and occasional lengthy and disjointed diatribes that make no discernible securities-related claims.' The SEC lacks the resources to properly investigate each one. 'Every investigation we pursue, or continue to pursue, entails opportunity costs with respect to our limited resources. A decision to pursue one matter means that we may be unable to pursue another. No single case or investigation can ever be considered in a vacuum, but rather must be viewed as one of thousands of investigations and cases we are or could be pursuing at any given time.' Ms Chatman Thomson said she could not comment on any past SEC investigations of Madoff or his firm or associates as the SEC's Office of the Inspector General was 'actively investigating' the previous probes.

It also helped that Madoff made himself an insider at the SEC, says Ed Nicoll. 'He ran a very successful firm, and that is very powerful when people know that you are making millions of dollars. He devoted a lot more time than most executives do to Washington. And he could do that over a long period of time. In firms like Goldman Sachs or J.P. Morgan the chief executives come and go. But Bernie was running a family firm. They knew him, they trusted him, he'd been through ups and downs and he had their ear. He had enormous access.'

Human failure, it seems, also accounts for another major lapse: the role of Madoff's auditors. Lawsuits against Ezra Merkin, Cohmad, and Fairfield Greenwich all highlight this. Madoff's auditors were a firm called Friehling and Horowitz, which he had retained since 1991. Friehling and Horowitz had one working partner, David Friehling. It operated from a small office in a shopping mall in New City, a suburb of New York City, in Rockland County. The equivalent would be Nicola Horlick using a one-man operation in Watford to audit her blue-chip City investment company. According to the state of Massachusetts' lawsuit against Fairfield Greenwich, in 2005 Jeffrey Tucker asked for more information on the firm after an enquiry from a Fairfield customer. Dan Lipton, Fairfield's Chief Financial Officer, called Friehling and Horowitz to find out more for Tucker. He had a conversation with someone there, probably Friehling himself.

Lipton was apparently happy with what he heard. He sent the following email to Jeffrey Tucker on 12 September 2005: 'Friehling and Horowitz, CPAs [Certified Public Accountants] are a small to medium-sized financial services audit and tax firm specialising in broker/dealers and other financial services firms. They are located in Rockland County, New York. They have hundreds of clients and are well respected in the local community.' Lipton added details of the firm's professional registration and qualifications, before opining that expertise, not size, was the most important factor. 'As we know just a few years ago it was the "Big 5" and Arthur Andersen was an extremely highly regarded firm.'[11] Gordon McKenzie, another Fairfield employee, was also looking into the firm. Two days later McKenzie emailed Tucker, Lipton, and others that it appeared Friehling was the firm's only employee, and attached a business background report.

Lipton later testified to securities officials about his dealings with Friehling and Horowitz:

Q: How did you determine they had hundreds of clients?
A: That's what the partner said on the phone to me.
Q: Did you corroborate that in any other way?
A: No.

Lipton was also asked:

Q: How did you determine that they were well respected in the local community?
A: That's what our conversation – my conversation with

one of the partners at Friehling and Horowitz, that's what was told to me.

Q: So he told you they were well respected in the local community?

A: That's correct.

Q: And that's what you based this statement on?

A: Plus I had looked up on the Internet to see if he was in good standing with the CPA licence, which he was and it listed that he – or members of the firm were members of the local chapter of the CPA.[12]

The lawsuit further notes that when Amit Vijayvergiya, Fairfield's chief risk officer, was asked how he knew that Friehling and Horowitz were independent auditors, he testified that, 'on the front of the report it said independent auditor'. Vijayvergiya also said he made a note to himself to do some research on Friehling and Horowitz but never got around to it.[13] In its response to Massachusetts, Fairfield Greenwich say that this information has been taken out of context, so fails to provide an accurate picture. Securities officials refused to provide transcripts of the interviews with Fairfield staff, so the accuracy of the transcripts cannot be confirmed.[14] Others familiar with the matter argue that it's only now, with hindsight, that Friehling and Horowitz are being portrayed as a massive red flag. It is not customary for financial institutions to audit their associates' auditors. Fairfield used their own auditors for their Sentry funds and while Madoff was handling large sums of money, his trading operation was straightforward and could be handled by a small firm.

By July 2009 David Friehling was the second person to face criminal charges in connection with the Madoff fraud.

Federal prosecutors accused him of securities fraud, of helping Madoff defraud clients, and filing false reports with the SEC. Friehling also faced a civil lawsuit from the SEC. The lawsuit said that Friehling had falsely informed the American Institute of Certified Public Accountants that he was not engaged in audit work, so as to avoid reviews by other companies. This information was available to all Madoff's feeder funds, had they chosen to check. Friehling and family members had held accounts at BLMIS since 1980, and since 2000 alone had withdrawn $5.5 million. The SEC complaint said that 'Friehling and F&H obtained ill-gotten gains through compensation paid to them by Madoff and BLMIS and also by withdrawing millions of dollars from accounts held at BLMIS in the name of Friehling and his family members'.[15] Friehling pleaded not guilty to the criminal charges in July 2009. Friehling's lawyer did not reply to emails from the author enquiring about Friehling's plea or his response to the SEC suit.

With his family's love and encouragement Roger Madoff fought hard against his leukaemia. He endured numerous sessions of chemotherapy, with its debilitating side-effects and secondary infections. His hair fell out and his weight plummeted. His moods lurched between hope and despair. Yet there were times when he could live an almost normal life. Roger kept a diary, recording his treatment and his reactions to the powerful drugs that the doctors were pumping into him. He bought new clothes, visited friends, and enjoyed Manhattan. With the help of steroids his appetite returned. He would order two main dishes for dinner at restaurants, followed by a 'magic bar', a dense concoction of coconut, condensed milk and chocolate chips. 'I ate like a madman, although I could not gain much weight,' he wrote. Roger and Jennifer became close to Monica Lewinsky, who lived in the same building. Monica was very kind and frequently brought hot chocolate from the nearby Starbucks. 'Lots of our neighbours made goodwill gestures, but Monica's small acts stand out.' Roger and Jennifer took Monica on a double date with a friend, although it did not lead to anything.

Roger's hope was that Shana would be able to provide him with a stem cell transplant. On the eve of Rosh Hashana, the Jewish New Year, in 2003, Roger and Jennifer drove to his parents' house on Long Island with their dog, Milo, for a festive dinner. Shana and her daughter Rebecca came with Shana's boyfriend. It was a warm but poignant evening, as the family all wondered what the next year held in store for Roger. The next day Roger and Jennifer attended services at the Village Temple, a bohemian synagogue near their home in Greenwich Village. They took a trip to Lake Placid in upstate New York for a few days, enjoyed the beautiful scenery and tried to forget Roger's illness. Yet it was always there, the ghost in the room. When Jennifer discussed over dinner how a friend of hers was having trouble making some decisions about her life, Roger became irritated. 'Great. And I'm dying of leukaemia,' he snapped. Jennifer dropped her fork. Roger tried to reassure her that it was just a 'pressure release'.

Shana was accepted as a stem cell donor for her brother. For several days before the harvest Jennifer gave her daily injections of Neupogen, a drug which stimulated stem cell production. The harvest was scheduled for 13 October 2003.

Roger was not allowed to see his sister while she underwent the procedure downstairs – she had a cold and he was vulnerable to infection. He wrote: 'The harvest required that Shana be poked in each forearm with a large needle. It took about three hours to cycle Shana's blood through the aphaeresis machine, which filtered out the magic stem cells that would be inserted in me the following day. She seemed a little worn out from her cold, but otherwise expressed nothing but pride in being able to do this for her brother.' Shana later boasted to Roger how the doctors had complimented her on her large veins. That night was the annual Light the Night Walk, organised by the Leukemia and Lymphoma Society, which is held in cities across America. Roger could not attend but was represented by a legion of Madoffs, who walked back and forth across Brooklyn Bridge carrying a pen-light and a red balloon.

Shana's transplant failed. Sepsis set in, an infection of the immune system, followed by numerous complications. Roger spent the next few years in and out of hospital. He began to lose the battle against his illness and suffered greatly. His skin tightened, became ulcerated, and began to peel off. One day a doctor came into Roger's room to find his father applying ointment to Roger's feet. On the journey home to Long Island, Peter Madoff would weep silently as his chauffer-driven BMW swept along the Long Island Expressway, the road he used to drive his young son into New York.

16
Countdown

'Our firm is very dependent on its relationship with your firm. You are our most important business partner and an immensely respected friend.'

Jeffrey Tucker, of Fairfield Greenwich, writes to Bernard Madoff on 10 December 2008, one day before he was arrested.[1]

It was an elegant wedding, stylish and understated. The flowers were white, the table linen crisp, the silverware gleaming on the long table. A cool breeze blew over the terrace, scenting the autumn air with champagne, perfume and cigar smoke. That Saturday evening, 29 September 2007, Bernard Madoff had come full circle. His grandparents David and Rose Madoff and Benjamin and Gussie Muntner had arrived in New York from Eastern Europe a century ago. They and their children had worked diligently to escape the Lower East Side, so Bernie's generation could pursue the American dream of prosperity and success. The dream had come true and here he was again, back in the Bowery where he had spent his childhood, scampering through his grandparents' *shvitz*. The super-chic Bowery hotel, to be precise, where Shana Madoff was celebrating her wedding to Eric Swanson. Irony was added to irony – Swanson was a former senior official at the SEC.

Madoff put his arm around Neil Fenwick, whose wife Julia ran Madoff's London office. 'See them?' he asked, gesturing to the other side of the room, at a group of stylishly dressed guests gathered around the groom. 'That's the enemy,' Madoff said, laughing. Bernie was his usual friendly, charming self, that evening, recalls Fenwick. 'He was surprisingly accessible for someone who was such an investment guru and sage-like figure, very chatty and open. He said that as a joke, the enemy over there, but I don't think he was particularly serious. In retrospect of course, it takes on something different.'[2] Shana and Eric were married on the terrace, in front of the guests. A champagne reception followed, then dinner, speeches and dancing. 'It was very tasteful and understated,' says Julia Fenwick. 'The family were not show-offs and they were subtle. Bernie was wearing a black tie and a tuxedo and Ruth was dressed very simply. Her necklace was worth a fortune but you would not have known that.' Later that night Madoff sat outside on the terrace, a cigar in hand, its smoke wafting over the maze of streets and back alleys where he had played as a child. He was surrounded by acolytes, friends, and relatives, many of whom had invested almost everything they owned with the wizard of Wall Street. All were grateful to be allowed into the inner circle. Madoff's friends were virtually sitting at his feet, admiring him, recalls Julia, and that was how Bernie liked it.

But for all the evening's elegance and joy, the wedding was marked with grief, especially for Shana and her parents. Roger's condition steadily deteriorated after the failed stem-cell transplant. The steroids that had given him a burst of energy caused cataracts, and he had two operations to remove them. He required large doses of painkillers and contracted pneumonia. Roger and Jennifer moved to a new apartment in spring 2005 where they planned to host a Seder, the festive meal for the Passover holiday. Roger spent the holiday in hospital, gasping for breath with the aid of an oxygen mask. Most seriously, his body had reacted against the transplants. He had severe GvHD – Graft-versus-Host-disease, one of the worst cases doctors had ever seen. Roger and Jennifer sought a second opinion in Seattle: the doctors said it could take three to five years for his body and immune system to be able to tolerate one another. His body turned into a battleground and he needed constant doses of methadone to manage the pain. He lost much of his eyesight. On the last lines of his book, he wrote: 'I would try to find richness in every day I had in front of me. I had always tried to live this way and I would reserve my strength for the moments that mattered, regardless of how small they were and how often they came.'

In March 2006 Roger returned to hospital with a cough and a wound on his lower leg. It slowly became clear that he would not recover. He passed away on the night of 14 April surrounded by his family.

In Palm Beach Lord Jacobs was thinking about investing some more money with Madoff. Jacobs had realised a very large sum from the sale of a property in France. By spring 2008 he had been a Madoff client for a decade, and was very satisfied with his investment. The monies earned steady interest and all of Jacobs' redemption requests were speedily met. Every month he received a statement, and everything looked reasonable and legitimate. He and his son Simon discussed Madoff's fund in detail before they decided how to proceed. Simon asked his father if Madoff could be running a Ponzi scheme. Lord Jacobs was doubtful. 'I said to him, and I blame myself for this, that there has never been a Ponzi scheme that lasted twenty-five years, because the nature of Ponzi schemes is to run out of money,' he recalls. 'But what I didn't know, or had not thought through, was that if the return was only 10 per cent, you could keep it going if you keep bringing in enough money. And he didn't actually pay out 10 per cent a year, because a lot of investors did not take the money out. It never occurred to me that you could make a Ponzi scheme last that long.'

Several weeks later Lord Jacobs and his son travelled to New York. They met Madoff in the Lipstick Building to discuss investing the proceeds of their house sale. Madoff was his usual friendly self, ready to answer all of Jacobs' questions. 'He was an easy guy to talk to, so I told him that I didn't understand something. He was averaging a return of 1 or 0.5 a per cent, but in the last month of the year he went into treasuries, where he was lucky to earn a sixteenth of 1 per cent. I asked him why he bothered.' Madoff had a well-rehearsed answer, honed in response to numerous clients who had asked the same question. BLMIS had numerous institutional investors, he explained, who wanted to see an absolutely clean balance sheet and so they liked to show that their holdings were all in treasury bonds.

The answer left Lord Jacobs uneasy. It didn't really make sense. Treasury bonds were the dullest, safest investment. Why would major banks pay commission to an investment manager to buy them? Jacobs concluded that it was a ruse, and Madoff wanted to keep his investment strategy secret. 'I said to Simon, I don't think that's right, or true. I thought he didn't want the auditors to see how it worked, because it was really proprietary, so he covered it up by pushing it into treasuries. But I knew that the SEC examined his books, so for me that was a seal of approval.' Lord Jacobs and his son probed further. 'We examined it more and more to see if we had missed something. We came to the conclusion that we were absolutely safe.' They invested the house sale money.

Lord Jacobs was not the only investor to be reassured by the SEC's annual audits of BLMIS's trading arm, especially as the sub-prime mortgage crisis began to bite, sending share prices tumbling. That summer Bennet Goldworth tried hard to persuade one of the fourteen investors he had brought in to Madoff's fund to increase his holdings. Goldworth, a retired real estate broker, had invested 95 per cent of his assets with Madoff. He could see that there was an economic storm brewing but the Madoff fund was holding steady. For Goldworth, Madoff was a safe haven in uncertain times. 'People say now that we should have done much more due diligence, but the best due diligence is to look at past performance. Madoff had thirty years of performing consistently with the SEC's stamp of approval. There wasn't anything more anyone could have done. Only a handful of people could analyse his statements and see through them. Many more investment professionals could not.' Goldworth's friend rejected his advice and refused to put more money into Madoff. 'I am very grateful that he did not listen to me.'

Andrew Madoff recovered from his lymphoma, but the

illness was a life-changing experience. Like his cousin Roger, he tried to 'find richness in every day'. He began to lose interest in the high-stress world of market-making. He and Deborah separated. Andrew's new passion was fly-fishing, a pastime he and his brother Mark had enjoyed since child-hood. He bought part-ownership of Urban Angler, a fash-ionable fly-fishing store in downtown Manhattan in 2007. This was where Wall Street's movers and shakers bought their rods and tackle, and Bernard Madoff was especially proud of his son's new business.[3] 'Andrew's priorities shifted after his illness and he didn't want to be part of his father's business any more,' says Julia Fenwick. 'He didn't enjoy it any more and he wanted to do something completely dif-ferent. When I saw him after he bought into the fishing business he was totally different, so much happier like a huge load had been lifted.' Urban Angler brought Andrew a whole new life. He fell in love with another part-owner, Catherine Hooper, and they became engaged.

Andrew's older brother Mark, his father's heir apparent, had also divorced. Colleagues recall that he took the breakdown of his marriage very hard. But Mark remarried several years later and bounced back. His new bride, Stephanie Mikesell, worked in the fashion business and Mark enjoyed her entrée into a new and glamorous world. He began to relish his wealth and like his father enjoyed spending his money. 'Mark was much more like Bernie,' says Julia Fenwick. 'Of the two brothers, he was more of a show-off. He liked the glamorous things in life. I think he wanted to be his dad, very much so.' And like his father, Mark Madoff also spent a considerable amount of time on charity work. He was a devoted supporter of two theatres, especially active in their programme for inner-city students.

He could afford to be. Both Mark and Andrew became immensely wealthy working for their father. Before the fall, they reportedly earned as much as $4 to $5 million a year. Bernard Madoff himself reported a gross income of $13.2 million for 2007. Bernard Madoff merged company money with his own, using BLMIS to fund the family's luxurious lifestyles, court filings released in May 2009 allege. BLMIS's corporate American Express bill for January 2008 was $100,121.99. Peter Madoff charged $4,924.32, including $1,564 for a meal at Bistro Chez Jean, in Palm Beach. Ruth Madoff charged $29,887.94, including $69.50 for cinema tickets, $5,015 to the Montauk Yacht Club, $396 to Tiffany's, $2,001 to Giorgio Armani in Paris, and $15,200 of donations to charities in New York and Florida. Andrew Madoff charged $8,273.39, much of which was for airplane tickets. Mark Madoff charged $29,776.96, including $8,400 for one night at the Hotel Esperanza in Santa Monica, and $2,879 for a meal at Pica's, a Mexican restaurant in Wyoming. This was quite an achievement for a restaurant whose daily specials cost around $12. Shana Madoff was the most frugal, charging just $27.93 for the *Wall Street Journal*. Bernard Madoff charged $470, most of which was the card renewal fee.

Bernard Madoff also used company funds to issue loans to several family members and related companies, court documents record, noting that BLMIS received 'no apparent benefit' from these loans. In December 2007, BLMIS made an unsecured loan of $9 million at an interest rate of 4.13 per cent to Peter Madoff. The money came from a BLMIS account. In June 2008 Bernard Madoff authorised a loan of $6.5 million from BLMIS funds to Mark and Stephanie Madoff, at an interest rate of 3.2 per cent. The monies were sent to a law firm in Nantucket, Massachusetts, which represented Mark and Stephanie Madoff in their purchase of a house there for that sum. In neither case is there any record of any interest or principal being paid back to BLMIS, the court filing records. In September and October 2008 BLMIS sent $4,485,000 to two New York law firms, one of which represented Andrew Madoff in his purchase of an apartment on the Upper East Side for $4,378,475. Mark and Andrew received a total of $31.5 million in loans from their father, says a source familiar with the matter. Unlike gifts, loans can be offset against tax.

The court filings record that BLMIS funds were also channelled through a web of shell companies set up to purchase assets for Madoff's 'personal enjoyment and that of his family', including two yachts which 'served no apparent business purpose'. BLMIS paid $471,000 to a marina in Long Island, where the Madoffs had a holiday home. Between 1996 and 2008 BLMIS paid $947,703 to four different country clubs, including the Palm Beach Country Club, and the Trump International Golf Club, on behalf of Bernard, Ruth, and Peter Madoff and his wife Marion. Bernard and Ruth Madoff's housekeepers and their boat captain, who also had a company American Express card, were all on the company payroll. Marion Madoff received an annual salary of $165,500 from BLMIS, the document records, 'although there is no evidence that Marion Madoff performed work for BLMIS'.[4] Marion and Shana Madoff are 'among the many victims' of Madoff's Ponzi scheme, said John R. Wing,

Peter Madoff's lawyer, as they invested millions of dollars with Bernie Madoff. 'Any suggestion that Peter Madoff knew his brother was engaged in this Ponzi scheme is therefore absurd.'[5] Unbeknown to Mark and Stephanie, as they moved into their new house in Nantucket, indeed to all the Madoffs, their life of luxury was about to end. Ironically, it would be destroyed not by the SEC, but by some of the poorest people in America.

In the autumn of 2008 Madoff spent more and more time closeted in his office with Frank DiPascali. Squillari noticed that her boss's behaviour was changing. He was cranky and bad tempered, and spent long periods staring into space, telling her not to disturb him. When Madoff was nervous he had a mild facial tic, which got worse that autumn. But he was not the only stressed-out financier on Wall Street. There were growing fears of a global economic meltdown. Over the previous few years American lenders had freely lent to borrowers with weak credit ratings to buy property, known as 'sub-prime mortgages'. The borrowers were dubbed 'Ninjas' – no income, no jobs or assets. But with interest rates as low as 1 per cent in 2004 none of that seemed to matter. The lenders believed that as house prices rose, the Ninjas could re-mortgage their homes, using their rising equity to pay for the new loan, in a perpetual loop of financing and refinancing.

The sub-prime bubble was essentially a twenty-first-century version of the Dutch Tulip or South Sea Bubble. It was far more financially sophisticated but the same essential principles of human nature applied. Again, the madness of crowds flourished, fed by greed and easy money. Debt was no longer an obligation to be paid off, but had mutated into an asset that could be used to leverage even more loans. The banks packaged the sub-prime mortgage loans into mortgage-backed securities, known as Collateralised Debt Obligations (CDOs). Numerous hedge funds and several blue-chip investment banks, including Bear Sterns and Lehman Brothers, eagerly bought up the CDOs.[6] For while it looked like the good old days of 1980s excess were back. Salaries and bonuses soared. But the bankers had failed to account for a crucial factor. Interest rates rose. The Ninjas could no longer pay their mortgages. They defaulted on their loans and simply abandoned their homes. Property prices spiralled downwards across America. The banks had lent billions of dollars to purchase inflated assets that nobody wanted to buy. The party was over.

Bear Sterns was the first significant casualty. In spring 2008 its share price fell from $169 to $2. The bank faced collapse. If Bear Sterns sold its CDOs, it would drive down their price even further, affecting the solvency of other US banks. Backed by the US Federal Reserve, America's national bank, J.P. Morgan bought Bear Sterns for a fraction of its value. Lehman Brothers, the fourth-largest investment bank in America, was next. Like Bear Sterns it had heavily invested in CDOs. In summer 2008 Lehman reported its largest net loss in history, of $7.8 billion, and said it had another $54 billion in exposure to mortgage-backed securities. Its share price dropped by 95 per cent, from $82 to $4. On 15 September 2008 the bank collapsed. With public anger rising at the bankers' greed and incompetence, there would be no federal money for Lehman Brothers funded by tax payers. It was an ignominious end for one of the best-known financial institutions in the world, founded by *Yekke* immigrants more than 150 years earlier.

But any *schadenfreude* that Madoff might have felt at Lehman Brothers' collapse was tempered by its consequences. The stock market plummeted and numerous hedge funds closed down. Madoff's investors began to ask for their money back. He could meet requests for hundreds of thousands of dollars, even millions. But the millions became hundreds of millions and then billions. As autumn turned into winter, Madoff's behaviour became more erratic. Uncle Bernie turned into Grandpa Bernie. His voice, which was usually powerful, still tinged with the remnants of his Queens accent, became weaker. He no longer stopped at Elaine Squillari's desk to review the day ahead, she recalls, but rushed straight to his desk. The once open door to his office was now closed. Squillari found it hard to get Madoff's attention, and told employees who wanted to talk to him that 'he seems to be in a coma'. He checked and re-checked his blood pressure. He complained of back pain and lay on the office floor, with his eyes closed.[7]

As the financial crisis worsened through the autumn of 2008 Amit Vijayvergiya, Fairfield's Chief Risk Officer, was fielding increasingly concerned enquiries from investors and trying to find answers. Madoff held $6.9 billion of Fairfield's assets, almost half of its total of $14 billion. Fairfield sent Madoff a questionnaire in mid-September with a series of detailed enquiries about BLMIS's operations. Madoff refused to adequately answer numerous questions, the Massachusetts lawsuit records. Fairfield asked for a list of personnel involved in the split-strike conversion strategy and their roles. Madoff replied: 'The people involved in the SSC are traders, systems, analysts, programmers and operations people. No names given.'

Walter Noel, Jeffrey Tucker and Mark McKeefry, Fairfield's General Counsel, met with Madoff on 2 October to discuss their concerns. Madoff continued his stonewalling, the lawsuit records, and the Fairfield personnel 'did not push for answers'.[8] This is a misrepresentation, says a person familiar with the matter. Madoff behaved at the 2 October meeting as he always had done: he answered every question, in some areas he was less specific, as the information was proprietary. He supplied information and was much more forthcoming than most hedge funds.

Either way, it seems Fairfield's founders were satisfied by what they heard. Fairfield itself had recently withdrawn $1.2 billion from BLMIS. For Fairfield, the fact that while the world faced financial meltdown Madoff had honoured these redemptions proved his solidity. In response, as a token of their good faith, Fairfield launched a new product, the 'Emerald' fund. Emerald was discreetly marketed to selected investors as a modified version of the Sentry funds, with higher returns but greater risk. All potential investors were required to sign non-disclosure agreements before they received any written materials. The Emerald fund was not properly put together, according to the Massachusetts lawsuit against Fairfield Greenwich, and lacked an auditor, a custodian, or offering documents. Nonetheless, Fairfield's owners rallied, and raised $14.8 million, much of which was their own money.[9] The fact that they personally invested in the Emerald fund, at a time of economic meltdown, is a powerful argument that they had no idea that Madoff was committing fraud, say those familiar with the matter.

The $14.8 million was a tiny drop in an ocean of withdrawals. Madoff pressured his veteran investors for more funds. At the beginning of December Carl Shapiro wrote Madoff a cheque for $250 million.[10] That too vanished into the maw. Within a few days Madoff was facing demands for $7 billion. He began to panic. On 8 December he threatened Jeffrey Tucker of Fairfield that he would close Fairfield's account, warning that there were plenty of other institutions that could take its place. Even by the rough and tumble standards of Wall Street, this was strange behaviour. Now Fairfield was worried. Two days later Jeffrey Tucker wrote to Madoff, apologising and trying to reassure him of Fairfield's continued loyalty. 'We fully understand the frustration of your traders in this unique time,' he wrote. Tucker apologised for not keeping Madoff adequately informed of redemptions in Fairfield's funds and proposed a series of initiatives to raise money, and boost investment in the Emerald fund. Fairfield, he promised, would devote itself to BLMIS in 2009. 'As a firm we are prepared to commit to dedicating ourselves exclusively to Sentry and Emerald. Throughout 2009 we will engage in no other fund-raising initiatives.'[11]

Finally, Tucker proposed that he, Walter Noel, and Andres Piedrahita visit Madoff the following week. By then, of course, it was too late.

Everyone at BLMIS was looking forward to the office Christmas party at the Rosa Mexicano restaurant on 10 December 2008. 'Business could not have been better, and we all felt so fortunate to have secure jobs in the light of the depressing economy,' recalls Elaine Squillari. 'After all, Bernie Madoff had never had a down year.'

Bernie, Peter, Mark and Andrew were all meeting in Bernie's office, but there was a strange atmosphere, not celebratory at all. Peter looked as if 'all the air had been sucked out of him'. When the meeting ended Mark and Andrew looked anxious as they helped their father into his coat.

They had cause to be worried. Madoff had just told his sons that he wanted to pay millions of dollars in bonuses two months early. His reasoning was the business was profitable and now was a good time to distribute those profits. Mark and Andrew challenged this. It did not make sense. Was there a problem with the business? What was the matter?

Madoff replied that he did not want to talk about it in the office. He was not sure that he could 'hold it together'.[12]

Now Mark and Andrew were really worried. The three of them left. 'I'm going out,' Bernie told Squillari, without looking at her. Her boss's behaviour was getting stranger by the minute, she thought. She tried to reach him all day, but his phone was switched to voicemail.

Bernie, Mark and Andrew went to his apartment. And there, finally, he stopped trying to hold it together.

Afterword to the Paperback Edition

'We are never deceived: we deceive ourselves.'
Johann Wolfgang Von Goethe (1749–1832).

Inmate number 61727–054 at the Butner Federal Correctional Complex mixes freely with the other inmates, many of whom are white-collar criminals, during the daily recreation sessions in the prison yard. Sometimes he watches a game of dominoes, or just strolls around, wondering at the twists of fate that have brought him to Medium Security Facility No. 1. He knows that he will likely never see Wall Street again, nor enjoy a round of golf at the Palm Beach Country Club, or feel his yacht cut through the waves of the French Riviera. Still, life at Butner, in North Carolina, is certainly more comfortable than at the Metropolitan Correction Centre in Manhattan, where he shared a cell with several others and was locked up for most of the day. There is light, air and greenery. He spends much time in the prison library and watches films. Occasionally he dispenses financial advice to other inmates, pointing them towards funds that track the S&P 500 index of stocks, and advising them away from riskier investments such as day-trading.[1] He is half an hour from the state capital, Raleigh, if and when his relatives come to visit. And despite lurid predictions that prison gangs would turn on him, he is respected by many inmates for his refusal to implicate others in his fraud. Whatever else he is, Bernard Madoff is not a snitch.

But for many he remains the most vilified man in New York. There was a whiff of mob vengeance at his sentencing in June 2009, when numerous victims testified to the misery Madoff had caused them. Judge Denny Chin described his crimes as 'extraordinarily evil' and sentenced him to 150 years in prison. His projected release date according to the Federal Bureau of Prisons is 14 November 2139. Mort Zuckerman, the publisher of the *New York Daily News*, who had lost millions through Ezra Merkin's Ascot fund, was jubilant: 'Burn, Bernie, Burn', his newspaper declared, proclaiming: 'Madoff Will Get Punishment Only When He is in Hell'. It described him as a 'planetary pariah', whom nobody had come forward to defend – although with headlines like this, it was hardly surprising. It was left to Frank Rich, an acerbic columnist in the *New York Times*, to point out that the missing $65 billion – most of which never existed and was accounted as fictional profits of the Ponzi scheme – was 'flim-flam' compared to $2.5 trillion that the government had paid to bail out the economy by July 2009, thanks to the bankers' greed and incompetence.

Madoff will probably die in prison, but he no longer has to pretend, or to hold it together and that brings a kind of calm. He and Ruth attended the office Christmas party the evening of that fateful day, 10 December 2008. But Mark and Andrew did not join the revelry. Their father had confessed to them that his investment fund was 'one big lie' and a 'giant Ponzi scheme'. He would pay out the bonuses and then hand himself in to the authorities a few days later, he explained.

Mark was enraged, Andrew stunned. They walked down Lexington Avenue in a daze. That afternoon they met with a lawyer, Martin Flumenbaum, who called the offices of the SEC and the United States Attorney to arrange interviews for them. Bernard Madoff was arrested the next day. He was held under house arrest at his apartment on East Sixty-forth Street until 12 March 2009 when he appeared in court to plead guilty. He admitted that he had run a vast Ponzi scheme. He apologised, saying he was 'deeply sorry and ashamed' for his crimes, but gave nothing away about who had helped him commit them. 'As I engaged in my fraud I knew what I was doing was wrong, indeed criminal. When the Ponzi scheme began I believed it would end shortly and I would be able to extricate myself and my clients from the scheme. However this proved difficult and ultimately impossible and as the years went by I realised that this day would inevitably come.'

Madoff's refusal to reveal the detailed mechanics of his fraud, and the names of his co-conspirators, inevitably triggered an avalanche of speculation about the possibility of involvement by his sons and wife, or at least their knowledge that something was wrong. Donald Rumsfeld once opined: 'There are known knowns. These are things we know that we know. There are known unknowns. That is to say, there are things that we know we don't know. But there are also unknown unknowns. There are things we don't know we don't know.' Rumsfeld's epigram can be useful here.

We know that Mark and Andrew Madoff worked for BLMIS since leaving college. We know that Mark and Andrew were based on the 19th floor of the Lipstick Building and held senior management positions. We know that BLMIS also rented space on the 17th floor, where access was restricted. We know that any intelligent person working for a large, successful Wall Street operation would wonder about what was going on in a separate, secretive operation two floors down – especially if their father kept attending business meetings there and that only a select group of staff moved back and forth between both floors. Yet none of that logically demands that Mark and Andrew should have concluded that their father was running the biggest Ponzi scheme in history. They worked for a legitimate firm with an excellent reputation that was regularly audited by the SEC. Bernard Madoff owned the company and took all the decisions. He was a powerful and domineering personality, in a tough, hyper-competitive business. This was Bernie's world, and if part of it unfolded two floors down, then those who valued their places in it, and the riches they brought, did not ask questions.

Mark and Andrew's world has been turned upside down, says someone close to them. They have lost their livelihoods and their income. Both had deferred compensation accounts with BLMIS, worth about $40 million. They could face years of legal bills. Neither Mark Madoff nor Andrew Madoff has been charged with or convicted of any crime. There is no evidence that they knew of or were complicit in their father's fraud. No one has come forward to say that they invested in the Ponzi scheme through them. In October 2009 Irving Picard, the Trustee appointed to liquidate the Madoff business, sued Mark, Andrew, Peter and Shana Madoff for $199 million. The civil lawsuit alleges that the family members were 'completely derelict in their duties and responsibilities and as a result failed to detect or failed to stop the fraud,' and that BLMIS was 'operated as if it were the family piggy bank' to fund 'personal business ventures and personal expenses such as cars, homes and boats'. The lawsuit claims that Peter Madoff improperly received more than $60 million paid to himself, family members and entities on his behalf and that customer funds were used to purchase properties on Park Avenue in Manhattan and in Palm Beach. Mark Madoff is alleged to have improperly received $66.8 million, Andrew Madoff $60.6 million and Shana Madoff is alleged to have improperly received $10.6 million including almost $3 million to purchase a house in East Hampton.[2]

Four months later, in February 2010, Mark, Andrew, Peter and Shana Madoff voluntarily agreed to an asset freeze. Under the terms of the consent orders the four 'shall not incur any debt, obligation or other liability, directly or indirectly, beneficially or otherwise, beyond $1,000 without the written approval of the plaintiff, except for the ordinary use of credit cards and as permitted elsewhere in this Order'. Mark, Andrew, Peter and Shana Madoff all deny any liability or culpability for the allegations in the Picard lawsuit. In March 2010 all four filed court papers to dismiss Picard's lawsuit. Lawyers for Mark and Andrew argued that the brothers had immediately reported their father's crimes to authorities and so saved $170 million in funds from being dissipated; that they worked for the market-making business, not the investment fund, so had no legal duties towards the funds' customers and that they had no compliance duties at all at

BLMIS, let alone at the investment fund.[3] As the Trustee had sold their market-making business for $25 million Mark and Andrew should also be counted as victims. Their lawyer Martin Flumenbaum has stated: 'Mark and Andrew Madoff had no prior knowledge of their father's fraudulent activities and contacted the US Department of Justice and the SEC immediately after their father told them he had defrauded his investment advisory clients. They continue to cooperate fully with the authorities in their ongoing investigations. Mark and Andrew Madoff are among the many victims of this scheme. They are devastated by what their father has done.' Charles Spada, a lawyer for Peter Madoff, told the *Wall Street Journal* that the lawsuit was 'a sensationalistic attempt to lump together members of the Madoff family and create liability by association'.[4]

The newspaper also reported that Peter Madoff is the subject of a criminal investigation by the US Attorney's Office in Manhattan, although as of March 2010 he had not been charged criminally. The federal investigation into the Madoff fraud is ongoing. Asked whether it encompasses Peter, Mark and Andrew Madoff, Janice Oh, spokeswoman for the United States Attorney's Office in the Southern District of New York, said that its policy was to neither confirm nor deny the existence of investigations. Asked about the *Wall Street Journal* report that Peter Madoff was the subject of a criminal investigation, Ms Oh said: 'No comment'. A lawyer for Shana Madoff did not reply to the author's emails. Charles Spada did not respond to emails asking about the reported criminal investigation of Peter Madoff.

As for Ruth, we know that she was married to Bernard Madoff for almost fifty years, that she was better educated than him, probably more intelligent and helped him start his business. We know that Ruth also had an office on the 18th floor of the Lipstick Building, where she worked on her private charity projects and the now notorious cookbook. As with Mark and Andrew, only hindsight, that clearest of senses, demands that she knew her husband was the greatest financial criminal mastermind in history. 'Ruth Madoff did not know of or participate in any of her husband's wrong-doing,' says her lawyer Peter Chavkin.[5] Others point to the Madoffs' luxury lifestyle as proof that the family must have known Bernie was up to no good. Yet Madoff was one of the best-known market-makers on Wall Street and had been for decades. He was very wealthy, certainly, but there were many wealthier. He and Ruth lived on East Sixty-forth Street, not Park Avenue or Central Park West. Unlike Ezra Merkin, he did not have a world-renowned collection of modern art, or a property portfolio to outclass Walter Noel's collection of holiday homes. By Manhattan standards the market-making business would have seemed sufficiently profitable to finance the Madoffs' lifestyle.

After her husband's arrest the mob descended on Ruth. She was ostracised and pursued by paparazzi whenever she stepped outside her front door. The New York tabloids and gossip blog sites like Gawker delighted in taunting her. She was attacked for her hair colour, her clothes, her facial expression. The *New York Post*'s Page Six gossip column gleefully reported Ruth's visit to a pizzeria: 'Slinking into the East Side eatery with a young female friend, she ordered a salad and white wine, but quickly got flustered. "The waiter said she was upset because she had coupons and they expired before she could use them," a witness told us, adding that several diners told the waiters they shouldn't serve her.'[6]

This was trial by media mob, with more than a hint of misogyny. Ruth's refusal to comment while her husband's legal process continued sparked particular fury: she was cold, heartless, had no feelings for her victims, the tabloids shrieked. There was fury that she had tried to keep some of the family's assets and had been left $2.5 million after everything else was seized. After her husband was sentenced Ruth issued a statement. From the day of her husband's arrest, she said, she had had two thoughts: for the ruined lives of her husband's victims, and that her life with the man she had known for over fifty years was over. 'I am embarrassed and ashamed. Like everyone else I feel betrayed and confused. The man who committed this horrible fraud is not the man whom I have known for all these years ... Nothing I can say seems sufficient regarding the daily suffering that all these innocent people are enduring because of my husband. But if it matters to them, please know that not a day goes by when I don't ache over the stories that I have heard and read.'[7]

In July 2009 the *Wall Street Journal* reported that criminal charges against Ruth were unlikely as federal investigators had failed to find any evidence that she participated in or knew of her husband's fraud.[8] But later that month, Irving Picard, the Madoff Trustee, filed a lawsuit against Ruth for $44 million, apparently also including the $2.5 million she had been allowed to keep. The suit alleged: 'For decades, Mrs Madoff lived a life of splendour using the money of BLMIS's customers. Regardless of whether or not Mrs Madoff knew of the fraud her husband perpetrated at BLMIS, during the past two- and six-year statutory periods, she received tens of millions of dollars from BLMIS for which BLMIS received no corresponding benefit or value and to which Mrs Madoff had no good faith basis to believe she was entitled.'[9]

Peter Chavkin, Ruth's lawyer, said that Picard's complaint against Ruth was 'particularly perplexing', 'totally unjustified' and wrong as 'a matter of law and fairness'. The suit does not allege that Ruth knew of or participated in her husband's wrongdoing. 'To the contrary the Trustee is alleging that she should have to give up her remaining money even if she was completely unaware of her husband's crimes.' She had already forfeited most of the assets named in the complaints, which the US Attorney's Office has publicly committed to distributing to the victims of Madoff's Ponzi scheme. Ruth had been allowed to keep property worth $2.5 million as it was determined that it could not be linked to the fraud, he said.

Bernard Madoff has rendered the family's very name toxic. After Roger Madoff's death his widow Jennifer published his chronicle of his illness, *Leukemia for Chickens*. The book is now used by members of the medical profession as a guide to patient experience of the illness. Jennifer worked with Peter and Marion Madoff to set up an annual $10,000 literary fellowship in Roger's name at the Queens Council on the Arts, which was scheduled to start in December 2008. There was a lot of excitement about the project, says Hoong Yee-Lee Krakauer, the council's executive director. 'It wasn't just the money, but that the family believed in supporting writers in Queens. We developed a series of workshops and community building events to support this very prestigious fellowship.' There were plans for translations and anthologies to showcase the work of Queens writers who come from very diverse cultural backgrounds. There were sixty applicants for the first fellowship. Jennifer Madoff and the other panellists began planning the review process to draw up a shortlist of finalists. The Roger Madoff Literary Fellowship has since been cancelled. In February 2010 Stephanie Madoff, the second wife of Mark Madoff, citing threats made against the Madoff family, filed court papers to legally change her surname, and those of her two children, to Morgan.[10]

Meanwhile, Madoff's victims and their families are left to pick up the pieces and try to rebuild their lives. Two weeks after Madoff's arrest, Thierry Magon de la Villehuchet, a co-founder of Access International Advisers, a Madoff feeder fund, locked himself in his office on Madison Avenue. Tidy and fastidious to the last, the French aristocrat put a rubbish bin by his desk. He opened both his wrists with a box cutter and watched his life blood drain away into it. His body was found the following morning.

In Palm Beach the news of Madoff's arrest hit like a hurricane. There were screams of disbelief, tears and bitter recriminations. For a place that worships money like nowhere else on earth, the news that the money did not exist triggered the greatest collective trauma in the island's history, one from which it has still not recovered. Palm Beach went into a kind of psychological shock, says Richard Rampell, a prominent accountant. 'It was almost like being in Ground Zero New York after 9/11. Of course the two events are not comparable, but for days everyone here was whispering to each other, and walking slowly.' Lord Jacobs remains amazed and angry at the SEC's failure to shut down Madoff's Ponzi scheme in 2006. Sometimes he reads through Harry Markopolos's densely typed nineteen-page memo, 'The World's Biggest Hedge Fund is a Fraud'. 'I try to put myself in a regulator's head, but I still don't understand how anyone could read that document and not be persuaded that it could lead to the biggest coup their team could ever pull off. We now know that there were zero transactions taking place, so it would have taken the SEC less than a week to examine the books and expose the fraud.' That winter the shopkeepers on Worth Avenue and its surrounds reported a new phenomenon: returns. Madoff victims started emptying out their wardrobes, trying to cash in the designer gowns that they had paid thousands of dollars for, just a few weeks earlier. They pleaded with the shopkeepers that the clothes had been worn only once or twice, but to no avail.

Those who knew Madoff personally, either as a friend or a business associate are still trying to reconcile the man they knew with the monster of Wall Street. Joe Kavanau, who attended Brooklyn Law School with Madoff, says: 'When I heard the news it was impossible to process. I try to accept the reality of it, but when you knew someone as I knew him, I still can't.' Ezra Merkin, who ran the Ascot, Gabriel, and Ariel feeder funds, resigned as the president of the Fifth Avenue Synagogue, to its congregation's relief. Merkin has also sold his Rothko collection for $310 million. On 13 December 2008, the Saturday after Madoff's arrest, Victor Teicher, Merkin's former business associate, sent him an email in characteristically earthy language. 'Many years back, you told me that I had (via a single criminal conviction) single-handedly ruined a most promising career – mine. By that nature, criminal convictions (especially based on vague acts as in my case) are somewhat random. You however took a brilliant career and wiped your ass with it.' Teicher continued: 'I don't mean to sound harsh; I'm just appreciative and thankful to you for providing another example of how life begins as tragedy and ends as farce.' After two more emails, Merkin told Teicher that such communications were not 'helpful'.[11] Ezra Merkin's legal travails continued in spring 2010. In February a New York state judge denied Merkin's motion to dismiss the civil lawsuit brought against him by Andrew Cuomo, the New York Attorney General. Cuomo's lawsuit, issued in April 2009, had accused Merkin of failing to adequately reveal Madoff's role in Merkin's investment funds. Justice Richard B. Lowe III argued that 'there is a substantial likelihood that disclosure of these facts [ie. Madoff's role] would have been viewed by the reasonable investor as having significantly altered the total mix of information made available'. Andrew Levander, Ezra Merkin's lawyer, said that the ruling was a decision on 'the adequacy of the attorney general's allegations' and that it did not address 'the facts of the case'.[12]

While Ezra Merkin suffered a legal defeat in February 2010, that same month lawyers for Cohmad, the brokerage firm which was co-founded by Bernard Madoff and also housed in the Lipstick Building, won a significant victory. A federal judge in New York City dismissed all of the SEC's fraud complaints against Cohmad. In a ruling that was absorbed with great interest among the parties to the numerous legal battles swirling around the aftermath of the Madoff fraud, especially those concerning feeder funds, Judge Louis L. Stanton said that the SEC had 'failed to allege facts giving rise to a plausible inference' that the owners and managers of Cohmad had intended to defraud anyone or had knowingly aided and abetted Bernard Madoff's fraud. 'One who conducts normal business activities while ignorant that those activities are furthering a fraud is not liable for securities fraud', said Judge Stanton. The judge did not dismiss claims of violations of record-keeping and said that the SEC could amend its complaint and re-submit it in 30 days, the *New York Times* reported.[13] The following month, in a separate case, a federal judge in New York dismissed a case against Union Bancaire Privee, a Swiss bank, which had lost $700 million with Madoff. UBP has offered its investors compensation of 50 per cent of their losses.

Like Ezra Merkin, Walter Noel, Jeffrey Tucker and Andres Piedrahita now spend much time communicating with their lawyers over the various lawsuits against them. The Fairfield Sentry Funds have closed. Andres Piedrahita cancelled plans for a lavish fiftieth birthday party at his hacienda in Majorca. He wrote to his guests: 'What this monster has done to so many people including us is known in the bible as "an abomination". It means an act so alien to our values and our cultures that it cannot be understood or explained.'[14] In September 2009 the State of Massachusetts lawsuit against Fairfield Greenwich was settled, with no admission of wrong-doing. Fraud charges were dropped and Fairfield Greenwich agreed to pay up to $8 million to residents of Massachusetts who lost money through the Fairfield Sentry fund, including $500,000 to cover the cost of the Massachusetts investigation. Lawyers for Fairfield Greenwich have also been engaged in settlement discussions with Irving Picard, the Madoff Trustee.

Charles Gevirtz, the engineer with an MBA to whom Madoff hinted that he might offer a job when he started asking pointed questions, withdrew $20,000 a few weeks before Madoff was arrested and wishes he had added another zero on his withdrawal form. He was laid off from the Ford Motor Company and now counts every dollar. He now works for the US Treasury Department but spends more time hunting for bargains, buys generic products and makes his own meals. There is no money for restaurants or cinema trips, or other entertainment, which makes dating difficult, he says. Bennet Goldworth, who brought another fourteen accounts to Madoff, moved back in with his octogenarian father. Goldworth received a 'significant' amount of compensation from the SIPC, and the Internal Revenue Service. Looking back over the last year or so, Goldworth describes his involvement in the Madoff fraud as 'traumatic'. His whole life has been up-ended. 'It's all about the money, but it's also not about the money. You cannot socialise like you used to, so you find new friends. I had stopped working when this happened, and now I have to start again. It feels like when I was in my twenties, thirty years ago, except then all of my friends were young and in the same place.' Goldworth, like many of those who lost almost everything with Madoff, is adamant that he is not a victim. Now rebuilding his life, he says he is a 'survivor'. Jeffry Picower, the philanthropist and Madoff investor, did not survive. Picower's charitable foundation had more than $1 billion invested with Madoff. In May 2009 Irving Picard, the Madoff Trustee, launched a lawsuit against Jeffry Picower and others, seeking the return of $5.1 billion. Picower's body was found at the bottom of the swimming pool at his home in Palm Beach in October 2009 by his wife and a housekeeper. The autopsy report blamed his death on accidental drowning, listing heart disease as an aggravating condition.[15]

Few of those who know Madoff feel more betrayed than Elaine Squillari, who worked with him for twenty-five years. Fuelled by anger, Squillari has told the FBI everything she knows about how the family members, employees, clients, and executives were connected. Julia Fenwick, who ran Madoff's London office for more than seven years, has never been contacted by any of the Madoff family. She last spoke to her friend Shana on her birthday on 8 December 2008, three days before Madoff's arrest. In spring 2010 the Serious Fraud Office stated that it had dropped its investigation into the officers of Madoff's London firm, although the SFO continued to investigate the role of Madoff's feeder funds. Elie Wiesel believes the best punishment for Madoff would be a form of psychological torture, eerily reminiscent of the continual flow of faces of Holocaust victims at the Yad Vashem Holocaust Memorial in Jerusalem: 'I would like him to be in a solitary cell with a screen, and on that screen, for at least five years of his life, every day and every night there should be pictures of his victims, one after the other after the other, always saying, "Look, look what you have done to this poor lady, look what you have done to this child, look what you have done." But nothing else – he should not be able to avoid those faces, for years to come. This is only a minimum punishment.'[16] Others are trying to wipe Madoff's face from their history – the page on Yeshiva University's website where Madoff welcomed guests to the 2008 Sy Syms School of Business gala dinner has been removed.

In August 2009 Frank DiPascali, Madoff's right hand man,

who has been cooperating with investigators, pleaded guilty to ten felony counts including conspiracy and tax evasion, which could result in up to 125 years imprisonment. The charges against him reveal a wealth of extraordinary detail of the inner workings of the Ponzi scheme, and how, under Madoff's guidance, DiPascali and his co-conspirators, as yet unnamed, engineered the elaborate fraud. 'By the early 1990s DiPascali was one of the BLMIS employees responsible for managing the vast majority of BLMIS's IA [Investment Advisory] accounts into which thousands of BLMIS clients invested, and eventually lost, billions of dollars.' DiPascali, Madoff and other co-conspirators were responsible for: receiving funds sent by investment clients, transferring clients' monies between various BLMIS bank accounts, handling requests for redemptions, answering clients' enquiries about their investments and developing the BLMIS computer system that generated the fake statements. The charges detail how DiPascali helped develop the famed 'split-strike conversion strategy' which was used to market the investment fund – even though the purported trades never took place. Madoff provided guidance to DiPascali and his co-conspirators about the gains or losses that he wanted reflected in the client statements. 'Based on that guidance, DiPascali and other co-conspirators prepared model baskets of S&P 100 stocks based on historical market prices and tracked how those hypothetical baskets would have performed in the actual market place to determine whether and when to "enter the market".'

When Madoff decided to enter the market, DiPascali and his co-conspirators instructed BLMIS staff to enter the data into the ancient IBM AS/400 computer on the 17th floor, which then produced tens of thousands of fake trading slips to record the purchase of securities which had not been purchased. A similar process took place when Madoff decided it was time to exit the market and sell the non-existent shares and options positions. Madoff and DiPascali used hindsight to determine when to sell. They instructed BLMIS staff to input the data to the IMB AS/400 which then printed tens of thousands of confirmation slips of sales, which like the fictional purchases, had never taken place. The non-existent proceeds of the non-existent trading were then supposedly used to buy (non-existent) US Treasury Bills. Under Madoff's direction, DiPascali and others also created 'false and fraudulent' books and records for 'the express purpose of misleading the SEC and others about the nature, scale and operations' of the investment business.[17]

DiPascali told the court: 'No purchases or sales of securities were actually taking place in their accounts. It was all fake. It was fictitious. It was wrong and I knew it was wrong at the time.' DiPascali had regarded Madoff as his mentor, he said. 'I was loyal to him. I ended up being loyal to a terrible, terrible, fault.' He told the court that he wanted to apologise to every victim, and that he was 'very, very, very sorry'.[18] DiPascali was eventually released on $10 million bail in February 2010, under strict conditions, including being confined to his home with an electronic monitoring device and being placed under surveillance by federal agents. Madoff's former lieutenant has provided the government investigation into the fraud with 'substantial assistance', prosecutors said, arguing in court that they expect to recommend 'extra-ordinary leniency' for DiPascali.[19] That same month, Daniel Bonventre, Madoff's former director of operations, was arrested on fraud and conspiracy charges. The SEC also filed a civil lawsuit against Bonventre, on similar grounds. Andrew Frisch, Bonventre's lawyer, said: 'I'm not just saying he is not guilty or that they can't prove it. I'm saying Dan Bonventre is absolutely innocent.' Bonventre was released on bail of $5 million.[20] He pleaded not guilty in April 2010. Meanwhile, David Friehling, Madoff's accountant and auditor, plead guilty in November 2009 to nine charges including securities fraud, making false filings to the SEC and obstructing federal tax laws. But he insisted that he had simply trusted Madoff and accepted the figures he was given, and that he had known nothing about the Ponzi scheme.[21] He faces a maximum sentence of 114 years and was released on $2.5 million bail.

As Madoff discusses investment options with his fellow felons, his investors are fighting to recover their assets. By March 2010 Irving Picard, the Madoff Trustee, had recovered about $1.5 billion. Fourteen lawsuits had been launched to recover a further $14.8 billion. Picard also expected to bring further actions. The Trustee's investigations also revealed new information about the international scope and scale of Madoff's fraud and the myriad of actors involved. The Trustee is seeking to recover assets in eleven jurisdictions including England, Bermuda, Gibraltar, the British Virgin Islands, the Cayman Islands, France, Switzerland and Spain. Those who invested directly with Madoff may receive government compensation of up to $500,000 for each account. But those who went through feeder funds, known as 'indirects' are not eligible, and have to file their own lawsuit against whoever sent them to Madoff. Of 12,187 determined claims, 1,974 have been allowed, with a value of $5.2 billion, and 10,213 denied. Numerous claims were rejected as the accounts were not in the account-holders' names but had been invested through feeder funds. Investors receive compensation based on their actual equity, minus any withdrawals, not the amount of their account statements. This rule, known as the 'cash in, cash out' method, was fiercely opposed by many Madoff investors who demanded compensation for the full value of their account statements. But in March 2010 a federal judge ruled in its favour.

A short walk from the Madoffs' apartment, at Temple Israel on East Seventy-fifth Street, Rabbi David Gelfand and his congregation are still trying to come to terms with Madoff's impact. 'It made the unbelievable and the surrealistic real, and took us into the realm of our community's deepest fears and darkest night. One of our own was preying on us.' After Madoff's arrest much press coverage focused on his Jewishness and connections to Jewish organisations. There were fears of a new wave of anti-Semitism, which apart from some sour media coverage never materialised. But many community leaders such as Rabbi Gelfand thought it vital to make it clear that Madoff had violated several key tenets of Judaism: the duty to care for the widow and the stranger, to be honest in business dealings and to care for one's family. He organised a discussion group around a set of Jewish texts to try to understand what had happened. 'There is a fascination, an endless searching about this within the Jewish community, and a desire to understand. Where did we go wrong, why did we trust him?' Once again Maimonides, the twelfth-century sage who had ruled that the best charity is given anonymously, proved most apposite. 'A person is forbidden to act in a smooth-tongued and alluring manner. He should not speak one thing outwardly and think otherwise in his heart. Rather, his inner self should be like the self which he shows to the world.'

But as the shock wore off, Rabbi Gelfand, like many in New York, began to think about the wider issues. Madoff had not arrived from outer space. He was part of a society that too often revered not human or spiritual values, but money and acquisition. 'There is an almost religious aura that has grown up around this, a belief that in American culture you can trust successful financial advisers. Clearly, there is an element of obsession that we have had in the United States prior to this recession that is very self-absorbing with a tremendous sense of entitlement that has gone with it. It is a culture that has nurtured both narcissism and the desire for acquisition. It seems there are no legitimate parameters here. Many people have allowed themselves to be absorbed in this and not ask the hard question: is this right?'[22]

Now, thanks to the information age, investors are panicking about the value of their assets, says Spencer Sherman, a wealth adviser. The Internet and television bring real-time news of market fluctuations, which triggers information overload. 'We want instant gratification. People keep asking themselves when will the market turn around, when will prices go up? But investing is a long-term endeavour. We have access to all this moment-to-moment information but it is irrelevant to our financial future. It doesn't matter what your portfolio is worth at 10 a.m. and 3 p.m. The extra information is not beneficial, it's destructive to your wallet and your health.' The appeal of Uncle Bernie, the avuncular investment guru, says Sherman, was that he offered immunity from uncertainty. 'People cannot stand these short-term fluctuations. Imagine if you had a ticker tape in front of your house, telling you what it was worth hour by hour. It would drive you crazy. It's like me asking my wife every few minutes how our marriage is doing. I would be divorced by now.'[23]

When I began researching and writing this book, I was a newcomer to high finance and Wall Street. What interested me was the psychology of Madoff's fraud and why so many intelligent investors, including some of the most renowned financial institutions, believed that Bernard Madoff, and he alone, could beat the markets, year in, year out. Writing *The Believers* was a fascinating odyssey into a world where billions of dollars flow back and forth with the same insouciance with which we pay our grocery bills. But the lasting legacy of my journey is amazement and profound unease at the immeasurable quantities of intellectual energy and human capital consumed by Wall Street. And for what? No homes are built there, no crops grown, no portraits painted. No cures for disease are discovered, no plays staged, no children or students taught the wonder of the world.

Wall Street's defenders argue that it is finance and capitalism's raw energy that make all these things happen. Entrepreneurs raise money to form companies. The companies' shares are traded, so that the bricks can be baked, the roads built and new homes arise. The exchange of goods and services is as old as humanity itself. But now technology has honed the pursuit of profit to such levels that it is draining society of some of its brightest minds. Renowned physicists and scientists are deserting university laboratories to work on Quant Theory, the study of quantative finance. The most talented software writers devote themselves to high-frequency trading, the new buzzword on Wall Street, designing systems of unprecedented speed and power that transmit millions of orders simultaneously.

Even now, with all that we know of the cult of Bernard Madoff, the madness of crowds still flourishes. Numerous investors are demanding not just the return of the monies that they invested, but the sum total of the profits detailed on their fictional monthly statements. The alchemists of high finance stare entranced at their computer screens, hunting the magic algorithm that will turn binary code into gold. The believers still await the next Shabbetai Zvi, who will marry not the Torah, but an investment prospectus, and lead them dancing into a bright new world.

Notes

Notes to Prologue

1. Declaration of Ira Lee Sorkin (Bernard Madoff's lawyer) in support of Bernard Madoff's application for bail pending sentencing to State of New York, 31 December 2008. Available at: http://online.wsj.com/public/resources/documents/031309madofffinance.pdf.
2. US SEC, 'Ponzi Schemes'. http://www.sec.gov/answers/ponzi.htm.
3. Simon Levy is a pseudonym.
4. US SEC, 'Ponzi Schemes'. http://www.sec.gov/answers/ponzi.htm.
5. SEC vs. Cohmad and others, 22 June 2009, New York, p. 10.
6. Erin E. Arvedlund, 'Don't Ask, Don't Tell', *Barron's*, 7 May 2001.
7. Adam Geller, 'Ripples of Madoff scandal spread everywhere', *Associated Press*, 19 December 2008.
8. Philoctetes Center, 'The Future of the Stock Market, 20 October 2007. http://philoctetes.org/Past_Programs/The_Future_of_the_Stock_Market

Notes to Chapter 1: *Yekkes* vs. *shtarkers*

1. James Bandler and Nicholas Varchaver with Doris Burke, 'How Bernie did it', *Fortune* magazine, 11 May 2009.
2. Chaim Waxman, 'The Sociohistorical Background and Development of America's Jews', in *Jews in America: A Contemporary Reader* (Hanover, NH, and London: 1999), p. 7.
3. Waxman, op. cit., p. 9.
4. Stephen Birmingham, *Our Crowd: The Great Jewish Families of New York* (Syracuse: 1996), p. 5.

[5] Marie Brenner, 'Madoff in Manhattan', *Vanity Fair* web exclusive, 27 January 2009.

[6] Rich Cohen, *Tough Jews: Fathers, Sons and Gangster Dreams* (London: 1998), p. 53.

[7] Neil Sheehan, 'Crooked Deal in Swiss Accounts Aided by Inaction of Banks: Brokers Decline to Query Clients', *New York Times*, 1 December 1969.

Notes to Chapter 2: Happy days

[1] James Bandler and Nicholas Varchaver with Doris Burke, 'How Bernie did it', *Fortune* magazine, 11 May 2009.

[2] Author telephone interview, May 2009.

[3] Julie Creswell and Landon Thomas Jr., 'The Talented Mr Madoff', *New York Times*, 25 January 2009.

[4] Bandler, Varchaver and Burke, op. cit.

[5] http://www.farrockaway.com/laurelton.html.

[6] John Maccabee, 'Mum and Dad and Ruth and Bernie', *New York*, 22 February 2009.

[7] *Fortune* magazine, op. cit.

[8] Allen Salkin, 'Bernie Madoff: Frat Brother', *New York Times*, 16 January 2009.

[9] Bandler, Varchaver and Burke, op. cit.

Notes to Chapter 3: Early adopters

[1] David Segal and Alison Leigh Cowan, 'Madoffs Shared Much; Question is How Much?', *New York Times*, 15 January 2009.

[2] Shannon Donnelly, 'Palm Beachers call Bernie Madoff arrest "knife in the heart"', *Palm Beach Post*, 15 December 2008.

[3] Robert Frank and Amir Efrati, 'Madoff Tried to Stave off Firm's Crash Before Arrest', *Wall Street Journal*, 7 January 2009.

[4] Benefit Technology, 'Private Foundations: Preliminary Estimates of Madoff Exposure', p. 5, www.nytimes.com/packages/pdf/opinion/madoff_exposure_6.pdf.

[5] John Maccabee, 'Mum and Dad and Ruth and Bernie', *New York*, 22 February 2009.

[6] PBS, 'The Madoff Affair', 12 May 2009, Michael Bienes interview, http://www.pbs.org/wgbh/pages/frontline/madoff/view/bienes.html.

[7] James Bandler and Nicholas Varchaver with Doris Burke, 'How Bernie did it', *Fortune* magazine, 11 May 2009.

[8] Ibid.

[9] Philoctetes Center, 'The Future of the Stock Market', 20 October 2007, http://philoctetes.org/Past_Programs/The_Future_of_the_Stock_Market.

[10] PBS, 'The Madoff Affair', 12 May 2009, Michael Bienes interview. All quotes from Michael Bienes are taken from this interview unless otherwise stated.

[11] David Arenson, CLL Diary, http://clldiary.blogspot.com/2009/01/bernie-madoff-screws-leukemia-patient.html.

[12] PBS, op. cit.

Notes to Chapter 4: Getting rich in Roslyn

[1] Philoctetes Center, 'The Future of the Stock Market, 20 October 2007, http://philoctetes.org/Past_Programs/The_Future_of_the_Stock_Market.

[2] Author interview, New York City, March 2009.

[3] John Steele Gordon, 'The Country Club', *American Heritage*, September/October 1990.

[4] Florida Resort Discrimination, ADL, *Rights*, April–May 1960.

[5] Evan Thomas, 'A Wasp Madoff', *Newsweek*, 7 January 2009.

[6] Ron Rosenbaum, 'Where Are the Jewish Gangsters of Yesteryear', *Slate*, 18 December 2009.

[7] James Bandler and Nicholas Varchaver with Doris Burke, 'How Bernie did it', *Fortune* magazine, 11 May 2009.

[8] Tom Wolfe, 'The Me Decade and the Third Great Awakening', *New York*, 23 August 1976.

[9] PBS, 'The Madoff Affair', 12 May 2009, Diana Henriques interview.

[10] Philoctetes Center, op. cit.

[11] *Fortune* magazine, op. cit.

[12] Original research by Nick Varchaver of *Fortune* magazine.

[13] Gay Talese, 'Share in a Bull Sold for $187,500', *New York Times*, 17 October 1964.

[14] Lacey Fosburgh, 'Art Collector Indicted in Theft', *New York Times*, 3 September 1971.

[15] With thanks to Nicholas Varchaver of *Fortune* magazine, for his original research.
[16] *Fortune* magazine, op. cit.

Notes to Chapter 5: The first millions
[1] PBS, op. cit.
[2] James Bandler and Nicholas Varchaver with Doris Burke, 'How Bernie did it', *Fortune* magazine, 11 May 2009.
[3] USA vs. Bernard Madoff, Southern District of New York, p. 2.
[4] Peter Chapman, 'Before the Fall', *Traders* magazine, March 2009.
[5] Mark Seal, Elaine Squillari, 'Madoff!', *Vanity Fair*, June 2009.
[6] Sam Jaffa, *Safe as Houses* (London: 1997), p. 144.
[7] Joe Lauria, 'Madoff's Personal Messenger Offers Window into Life at Firm', *Wall Street Journal*, 22 March 2009.
[8] Author telephone interview, June 2009.
[9] Inducements for Order Flow, Report to the NASD Board of Governors, July 1991, p. 32.
[10] Peter Chapman, 'Before the Fall', *Traders* magazine, March 2009.
[11] David A. Vise, 'A Broker and the Angry Exchanges; Bernie Madoff's Stock Buying Rivalry Irks NYSE, Amex', *Washington Post*, 14 April 1993.
[12] Vise, op. cit.

Notes to Chapter 6: When Bernie met Ezra
[1] Ezra Merkin, contribution to *Security Analysis*, by Benjamin Graham and David L. Dodd (Columbus: 2008), p. 266.
[2] Author telephone interview, 30 July 2009.
[3] Author interview, New York, March 2009.
[4] Author interview, New York, March 2009.
[5] Daphne Merkin, *Enchantment* (New York: 1986), p. 119.
[6] The People of the state of New York, op. cit. Exhibit One: Deposition of J. Ezra Merkin, p. 8, http://documents.nytimes.com/andrew-cuomo-civil-suit-ezra-merkin-gabriel-capital/page/670?scp=7&sq=ezra%20merkin&st=cse#p=58.
[7] Author interview, New York, March 2009.
[8] Steve Fishman, 'The Monster Mensch', *New York* magazine, 22 February 2009.

9   The People of the state of New York against J. Ezra Merkin and Gabriel Capital Corporation, 6 April 2009.

10 The People of the state of New York against J. Ezra Merkin and Gabriel Capital Corporation, 6 April 2009.

11 Email to author, 30 July 2009.

12 New York against Ezra Merkin, op. cit., pp. 8 and 9, point 24.

13 Victor Teicher witness deposition, 9 February 2009, New York University vs. Ariel Fund Ltd, Gabriel Capital Corporation, J. Ezra Merkin, and others, http://www.scribd.com/doc/14347258/Teicher-Deposition.

14 Dealbook, 'Judge Restrains Merkin Funds in Madoff Suits', *New York Times*, 7 January 2009.

15 Teicher, op. cit.

16 Lindsay Pollock, 'Merkin's Art Adviser Bought Expensive Rothkos, Lost Millions', *Bloomberg News*, 8 January 2009.

17 Mark Seal, Elaine Squillari, 'Madoff!', *Vanity Fair*, June 2009.

Notes to Chapter 7: Feeling frenzy

1   PBS, 'The Madoff Affair', 12 May 2009, Sherry Shameer Cohen interview.

2   Ibid.

3   Kristina Stewart, 'Golden in Greenwich', *Vanity Fair*, October 2002.

4   Vicky Ward, 'Greenwich Mean Time', *Vanity Fair*, April 2009.

5   Author telephone interview, July 2009.

6   Author telephone interview, June 2009.

7   PBS, 'The Madoff Affair', 12 May 2009, Michael Bienes interview.

8   Randall Smith, 'Wall Street Mystery Features Big Board Rival', *Wall Street Journal*, 16 December 1992.

9   James Bandler and Nicholas Varchaver with Doris Burke, 'How Bernie did it', *Fortune* magazine, 11 May 2009.

10 http://www.sec.gov/news/testimony/2009/ts112709lct.htm.

11 Mark Seal, Elaine Squillari, 'Madoff!', *Vanity Fair*, June 2009.

Notes to Chapter 8: A family affair

1   Joe Lauria, 'Madoff's Personal Messenger Offers Window into Life at Firm', *Wall Street Journal*, 22 March 2009.

2 Thomas Zambito, 'An Inside Look at the Luxury Apartment Bernie and Ruth Will Never See Again', *New York Daily News*, 29 June 2009.

3 Mark Seal, Elaine Squillari, 'Madoff!', *Vanity Fair*, June 2009.

4 Author interview, New York, March 2009.

5 Michael Skakun and Ken Libo, 'Sconces and Scrapbooks: A Visit to the Madoffs', *Forward*, 18 December 2008.

6 Author telephone interview, March 2009.

7 Alison Leigh Cowan, 'A Madoff Cookbook Has Secrets, Too', *New York Times*, 14 January 2009.

8 Anthony Guerra, 'The Madoff Dynasty', *Wall Street & Technology*, 7 July 2000.

9 Ibid.

10 Ibid.

11 Jacob Bernstein, 'Extreme Brand Loyalty', *New York* magazine, 16 August 2004.

12 'Inside the Operation', *Wall Street Journal*, 29 January 2009, http://online.wsj.com/article/SB123320068366227693.html#project%3DMADOFF_BUILDING%26articleTabs%3Dinteractive.

13 Mark Seal, Elaine Squillari, 'Madoff!', *Vanity Fair*, June 2009.

14 Irving H. Picard vs. Cohmad Securities and others, Southern District of New York, 22 June 2009, p. 14.

15 PBS, 'The Madoff Affair', 12 May 2009, Nader Ibrahim interview, http://www.pbs.org/wgbh/pages/frontline/madoff/interviews/ibrahim.html.

16 Joe Lauria, 'Life Inside the Weird World of Bernie Madoff', *Sunday Times*, 22 March 2009.

17 Joe Lauria, 'Madoff's Personal Messenger Offers Window into Life at Firm', *Wall Street Journal*, 22 March 2009.

18 Mark Seal, Elaine Squillari, 'Madoff!', *Vanity Fair*, June 2009.

19 Irving H. Picard vs. Cohmad Securities and others, Southern District of New York, 22 June 2009, p. 40.

20 Email to author, 13 July 2009.

21 David Voreacos, David Glorin and Patricia Hurtado, 'Madoff's, "Street-Smart" Aide DiPascali was Investors' Go-To Guy", *Bloomberg Business News*, 16 January 2009.

Notes to Chapter 9: Red flags flying

1 PBS, 'The Madoff Affair', 12 May 2009, Frank Casey interview.
2 Author telephone interview, May 2009.
3 Author telephone interview, June 2009.
4 PBS, 'The Madoff Affair', 12 May 2009, Frank Casey interview.
5 Testimony of Harry Markopolos before the US House of Representatives Committee on Financial Services, 4 February 2009.
6 Michael Ocrant, 'Madoff Tops Charts: Sceptics Ask How', *MAR/Hedge*, May 2001.
7 Erin Arvedlund, 'Don't Ask, Don't Tell,' *Barron's*, 7 May 2001.
8 Erin Arvedlund interview on NPR *Morning Edition*, 18 December 2008.

Notes to Chapter 10: Impossible returns

1 Ezra Merkin, in Benjamin Graham and David L. Dodd, *Security Analysis* (Columbus: 2008), p. 265.
2 Charles Mackay, *Extraordinary Popular Delusions and the Madness of Crowds* (Ware: 1995), p. xv.
3 Robert J. Shiller, *Irrational Exuberance* (Princeton: 2005), p. 56.
4 Author telephone interview, July 2009.
5 Roger Cohen, 'Mystery Man Pushing the Pawns', *New York Times*, 1 September 1992.
6 Adam LeBor, *Milosevic: A Biography* (London: 2002), p. 213.
7 Jane Perlez, 'Pyramid Scheme: A Trap for Many Romanians', *New York Times*, 13 November 1993.
8 Christopher Jarvis, 'The Rise and Fall of Albania's Pyramid Schemes', *Finance and Development*, March 2000.
9 Mark Seal, Elaine Squillari, 'Madoff!', *Vanity Fair*, June 2009.

Notes to Chapter 11: The *shetl* on the sand

1 David Segal, 'Recession Pain, Even in Palm Beach', *New York Times*, 12 April 2009.
2 Lawrence Leamer, 'Dispatch: Reversal of Fortune', *Boston Magazine*, January 2009.
3 Stefan Zweig, *The World of Yesterday* (Lincoln: 1943), pp. 10–11.
4 Ibid., p. 6.
5 Business News updates, *Boston Globe*, 15 December 2008.

6 Irving Picard vs. Jeffrey Picower and others, Southern District of New York, May 2009, p. 3.

7 Schulte, Roth and Zabel LLP Memorandum of Law in matter of BLMIS and Irving H. Picard, pp. 12–13, 31 July 2009; William Zabel statement, email to author, 3 August 2009.

8 SEC against Cohmad and others, 22 June 2009, p. 10.

9 Email to author from Elliot Sloane, copied to Stanley Arkin, one of Robert Jaffe's lawyers, 6 July 2009.

10 Jenn Abelson, Beth Healy and Casy Ross, 'Access to Bernard Madoff Made Middleman Robert Jaffe a "Superstar"', Boston Globe, 21 December 2008.

11 Henry James, The American Scene, 1907, Florida chapter, etext: http://www2.newpaltz.edu/~hathawar/americanscene2.html.

12 Lawrence Leamer, Madness Under the Royal Palms (New York: 2009), p. 81.

13 Bonnie Reuben, email to author, 30 June 2009.

14 Author interview, Palm Beach, March 2009.

Notes to Chapter 12: Going global

1 Vicky Ward, 'Greenwich Mean Time', Vanity Fair, April 2009.

2 Kristina Stewart, 'Golden in Greenwich', Vanity Fair, October 2002.

3 Vicky Ward, op. cit.

4 Telephone interview with author, July 2009.

5 Jose de Cordoba and Thomas Catan, 'The Charming Mr Piedrahita Finds Himself Caught in the Madoff Storm', Wall Street Journal, 31 March 2009.

6 Irving H. Picard vs. Fairfield Greenwich Group, New York Southern District, 18 May 2009, p. 21.

7 Diana Henriques, 'Trustee Sues Hedge Fund Over Losses to Madoff', New York Times, 18 May 2009.

8 Picard vs. Fairfield Greenwich, op. cit., pp. 2–3.

9 State of Massachusetts against Fairfield Greenwich, 1 April 2009, pp. 4, 5, 8 and 9.

10 Fairfield Greenwich response to state of Massachusetts, 29 April 2009 and statement.

11 Saijel Kishan and Katherine Burton, 'L'Oreal Heiress Bettencourt

Invested With Madoff', *Bloomberg Business News*, 24 December 2008.

12 Alex Berenson and Matthew Saltmarsh, 'Madoff Investor's Suicide Leaves Questions', *New York Times*, 2 January 2009.

13 Adam Shapiro, 'Widow of Madoff Investor Speaks Out' *Fox Business News*, 22 June 2009.

14 Alan Katz, 'Madoff's Three Bedroom Riviera Retreat Belied Ponzi Scheme Role,' *Bloomberg Business News*, 9 January 2009.

15 Author interview, July 2009.

16 Testimony of Harry Markopolos before the US House of Representatives Committee on Financial Services, 4 February 2009. Available at scribd.com, http://www.scribd.com/doc/11650020/Markopolos-Testimony-on-Madoff, pp. 31–7.

Notes to Chapter 13: Plundering the *shetl*

1 Alex Nussbaum and Miles Weiss, 'Yeshiva Had Losses of $110 Million Linked to Madoff', *Bloomberg News*, 16 December 2009.

2 Benefit Technology, 'Private Foundations: Preliminary Estimates of Madoff Exposure', www.nytimes.com/packages/pdf/opinion/madoff_exposure_6.pdf.

3 The People of the state of New York against J. Ezra Merkin and Gabriel Capital Corporation, 6 April 2009, pp. 48–9.

4 Ibid., p. 48.

5 Memorandum in support of defendants' motion to dismiss amended complaint against J. Ezra Merkin, Gabriel Capital and others, Dechert LLP, 1 July 2009.

6 Janet Frankston Lorin, 'Yeshiva's Losses Based on "Fictitious" Profits', *Bloomberg News*, 30 December 2008.

7 Karen Freifeld, 'Cuomo Said to Subpoena Merkin, 15 Nonprofit Group', *Bloomberg News*, 15 January 2009.

8 Mort Zuckerman, email to author, 11 March 2009.

9 Patricia Hurtado, 'Zuckerman sues Merkin over $40 million Madoff loss', *Bloomberg News*, 6 April 2009.

10 Shabbetai Zvi, *Jewish Virtual Library*: http://www.jewishvirtual library.org/jsource/biography/Zvi.html.

11 Author interview, New York, March 2009.

12 Author interview, New York, March 2009.

[13] The Madoff Panel Transcript, *Portfolio*, 26 February 2009, http://www.portfolio.com/executives/2009/02/26/Wiesel-and-Madoff-Transcript.

[14] J. Ezra Merkin, in Benjamin Graham and David L. Dodd, *Security Analysis* (Columbus: 2008), p. 266.

Notes to Chapter 14: Making merry in Montauk

[1] http: ft.podhoster.com/pop-up.player.php?pid_76

[2] Philip Sherwell and Louise Armistead, 'Nicola Horlick's Anger at £33 Million Swindle', *Daily Telegraph*, 13 December 2009.

[3] Francesco Guerra and Henny Sender, 'HSBC Joins Victims of Madoff's Alleged Fraud', *Financial Times*, 14 December 2008.

[4] Jerome Koechlin, UBS Head of Corporate Communications, email to author, 23 July 2009.

[5] Nelson D. Schwartz, 'European Banks Tally Losses Linked to Fraud', *New York Times*, 17 December 2008.

[6] 'Sonja Kohn Wooed Bernard Madoff Billions with Medici "Fantasy"', Matthias Wabl, *Bloomberg Business News*, 18 February 2009.

[7] Yuri Bender, 'Push to Put Vienna on Finance Map', *Financial Times*, 16 June 2009.

[8] Zoe Schneeweiss and Matthias Wable, 'Bank Medici Manages Up to $3.2 Billion of Assets Tied to Madoff', *Bloomberg Business News*, 31 December 2001.

[9] State of Massachusetts against Cohmad Securities, 11 February 2009, p. 4.

[10] Irving H. Picard against Cohmad Securities and others, 22 June 2009, p. 42.

[11] Matthias Wabl, 'Madoff Wasn't Friend, Pain is "Unbearable"', *Bloomberg Business News*, 15 January 2009.

[12] *Jewish Chronicle*, 9 July 2009.

Notes to Chapter 15: A *mensch*, sometimes

[1] Roger Madoff, *Leukemia for Chickens: One Wimp's Tale of Living Through Cancer* (New York: 2007).

[2] Ibid.

3 Mark Seal, Elaine Squillari, 'Madoff!', *Vanity Fair*, June 2009.

4 Eugenia Levenson, 'One Madoff Charity Goes Unscathed', *Fortune* magazine, 17 December 2008.

5 Marie Brenner, 'Madoff in Manhattan', *Vanity Fair* web exclusive, 27 January 2009.

6 Michael Steinhardt, *No Bull: My Life in and Out of Markets* (New York: 2004).

7 State of Massachusetts vs. Fairfield Greenwich, Exhibit 1, p. 41.

8 SEC Division of Enforcement, Case Closing Recommendation, Case NY-07563, 21 November 2007.

9 Professor David Ruder, author telephone interview, June 2009.

10 PBS, 'The Madoff Affair', 12 May 2009, Harvey Pitt interview.

11 State of Massachusetts vs. Fairfield Greenwich, Exhibit 18, p. 23.

12 State of Massachusetts vs. Fairfield Greenwich, p. 69.

13 State of Massachusetts vs. Fairfield Greenwich, p. 69.

14 Answer of Fairfield Greenwich to State of Massachusetts, pp. 40–1.

15 SEC against David Friehling, page 3, 5 March 2009.

Notes to Chapter 16: Countdown

1 State of Massachusetts vs. Fairfield Greenwich, Exhibit 2, pp. 2–3.

2 Author telephone interview, 24 May 2008.

3 David Margolick, 'Did the Sons Know?', *Vanity Fair*, July 2009.

4 Securities Investor Protection Corporation vs. BLMIS, US Bankruptcy Court, Southern District of New York, 5 May 2009.

5 John Wing, email to author, 2 June 2009.

6 David Budworth, 'The Credit Crunch Explained', *The Times*, 11 June 2009.

7 Mark Seal, Elaine Squillari, 'Madoff!', *Vanity Fair*, June 2009.

8 State of Massachusetts against Fairfield Greenwich, 1 April 2009, pp. 27, 28 and 29.

9 State of Massachusetts against Fairfield Greenwich, 1 April 2009, pp. 35–6.

10 Robert Frank and Amir Efrati, 'Madoff Tried to Stave off Firm's Crash Before Arrest', *Wall Street Journal*, 7 January 2009.

11 State of Massachusetts against Fairfield Greenwich, Exhibit 2, pp. 2–3.

[12] USA vs. Bernard Madoff, Southern District of New York, pp. 3–4.

Notes to Afterword to the Paperback Edition

[1] Dionne Searcey and Amir Efrati, 'Madoff Beaten in Prison', *Wall Street Journal*, 18 March 2010.

[2] 'SIPC Trustee Irving Picard Sues Four Madoff Family Members', SIPC Press Release, 2 October 2009.

[3] Memorandum of Law In Support of Defendants Mark and Andrew Madoff's Motion to Dismiss, US Bankruptcy Court, Southern District of New York, 15 March 2010, pp 1–3.

[4] Chad Bray, 'Madoff Sons: We're Victims', *Wall Street Journal*, 17 March 2010.

[5] Peter Chavkin, email to author, 20 July 2009.

[6] Richard Johnson, 'Pizza Predicament for Ruth Madoff', *New York Post*, 11 July 2009.

[7] Ruth Madoff, 'Ruth Madoff Breaks Her Silence', *New York Times*, 29 June 2009.

[8] Amir Efrati, 'Evidence to Charge Ruth Madoff Lacking', *Wall Street Journal*, 2 July 2009.

[9] Irving Picard vs. Ruth Madoff, US Bankruptcy Court, Southern District of New York, 29 July 2009, p. 2.

[10] Patricia Hurtado, 'Madoff Daughter-in-Law Seeks to Change Name', *Bloomberg Business News*, 25 February 2010.

[11] Victor Teicher witness deposition, 9 February 2009, New York University vs. Ariel Fund Ltd, Gabriel Capital Corporation, J. Ezra Merkin, and others, pp. 190–194.

[12] Diana Henriques, 'In Ponzi Case Judge Denies Motion to Dismiss', *New York Times*, 18 February 2010.

[13] Diana Henriques, 'Madoff-related Fraud Complaint is Dismissed', *New York Times*, 2 February 2010.

[14] Vicky Ward, 'Greenwich Mean Time', *Vanity Fair*, April 2009.

[15] Margie Kacoha, 'Autopsy: Picower Died by Accidental Drowning', *Palm Beach Daily News*, 12 January 2010.

[16] The Madoff Panel Transcript, *Portfolio*, 26 February 2009. http://www.portfolio.com/executives/2009/02/26/Wiesel-and-Madoff-Transcript.

[17] United States of America vs. Frank DiPascali, US District Court, Southern District of New York.

[18] Jack Healy and Diana Henriques, 'Madoff Aide Reveals Details of Ponzi Scheme', *New York Times*, 12 August 2009.

[19] Diana Henriques, 'US Strongly Favours Leniency for a Madoff Aide', *New York Times*, 20 February 2010.

[20] Diana Henriques, 'Another Madoff Aide Faces Fraud Charges', *New York Times*, 26 February 2010.

[21] Diana Henriques, 'Madoff's Accountant Pleads Guilty in Scheme', *New York Times*, 4 November 2009.

[22] Author interview, New York, March 2009.

[23] Author interview, New York, March 2009.

Bibliography

Birmingham, Stephen, *Our Crowd: Great Jewish Families of New York* (Syracuse: Syracuse University Press, 1996).

Bursten, Ben, *The Manipulator: A Psychoanalytic View* (New Haven: Yale University Press, 1973).

Cohen, Rich, *Tough Jews: Fathers, Sons and Gangster Dreams* (London: Jonathan Cape, 1998).

Freedman, Samuel, G, *Jew vs Jew: The Struggle for the Soul of American Jewry* (New York: Simon & Schuster, 2000).

Freely, John, *The Lost Messiah: The Astonishing Story of Sabbatai Sevi* (London: Penguin, 2002).

Gladwell, Malcolm, *Outliers: The Story of Success* (London: Penguin, 2009).

Greenspan, Stephen, *Annals of Gullibility: Why We Get Duped and How to Avoid It* (Westport: Praeger, 2009).

Gross, Michael, *740 Park: The Story of the World's Richest Apartment Building* (New York: Broadway Books, 2006).

Jaffa, Sam, *Safe As Houses: The Schemers and Scams Behind Some of the World's Greatest Financial Scandals* (London: Robson, 1997).

James, Henry, *The American Scene* (etext: http://www2.newpaltz.edu/%7Ehathawar/americanscene2.html)

Leamer, Lawrence, *Madness Under the Royal Palms* (New York: Hyperion, 2009).

LeBor, Adam, *Milosevic: A Biography* (London: Bloomsbury, 2002).

Lewis, Michael, *Liar's Poker* (London: Hodder, 2006).

Mackay, Charles, *Extraordinary Popular Delusions and the Madness of Crowds* (Ware: Wordsworth Editions, 1995).

McInerney, Jay, *Brightness Falls* (London: Bloomsbury, 1992).

McInerney, Jay, *The Good Life* (London: Bloomsbury, 2006).

Merkin, Daphne, *Enchantment* (New York: Harcourt, Brace, Jovanovich, 1986).

Merkin, Daphne, *Dreaming of Hitler* (New York: Harcourt Brace and Company, 1997).

Merkin, Ezra, *Blood and Judgement*, included in Graham, Benjamin and Dodd, David, *Security Analysis, Sixth Edition* (Columbus: McGraw-Hill, 2008).

Partnoy, Frank, *The Match King: Ivar Kreuger and the Financial Scandal of the Century* (London: Profile, 2009).

Rolfe, John and Troob, Peter, *Monkey Business: Swinging Through the Wall Street Jungle* (New York: Business Plus, 2001).

Rosenberg Farber, Roberta and Waxman, Chaim, *Jews in America: A Contemporary Reader* (Hanover, NH and London: Brandeis, 1999).

Sherman, Spencer, *The Cure for Money Madness* (New York: Broadway Books, 2009).

Shiller, Robert J., *Irrational Exuberance* (Princeton: Princeton University Press, 2005).

Surowiecki, James, *The Wisdom of Crowds: Why the Many are Smarter than the Few* (London: Abacus, 2005).

Wolfe, Tom, *The Bonfire of the Vanities* (London: Picador, 1991).

Zweig, Stefan, *The World of Yesterday* (Lincoln: University of Nebraska Press, 1964).

Index